navigation
in the **mountains**

Design and production

VERTEBRATE **GRAPHICS**

info@v-graphics.co.uk

navigation
in the **mountains**

THE DEFINITIVE GUIDE FOR HILL WALKERS, MOUNTAINEERS & LEADERS
The official navigation book for all Mountain Training schemes

By Carlo Forte

Navigation in the Mountains –
The definitive guide for Hill Walkers, Mountaineers & Leaders
The official navigation book for all Mountain Training schemes

Published by Mountain Training UK
www.mltuk.org

ISBN 978 0 9541511 5 7

Cover photo: Dave Cheetham

All photography by Carlo Forte unless otherwise credited

Designed, typeset and illustrated
by **Vertebrate Graphics**, Sheffield
www.v-graphics.co.uk

MIX
Paper from
responsible sources
FSC® C010256
FSC
www.fsc.org

Printed in China

While every attempt has been made to ensure that the instructions in this book cover the subject safely and in full detail, the authors and publishers cannot accept any responsibility for any accident, injury, loss or damage sustained while following any of the techniques described.

Contents

Our other titles are:

Hillwalking – by Steve Long, 2011, ISBN 978-0-95415-110-2
Rock Climbing – by Libby Peter 2011, ISBN 978-0-95415-116-4
Winter Skills – by Andy Cunningham and Allen Fyffe, 2011, ISBN 978-0-95415-113-3
International Mountain Trekking – by Plas y Brenin Instructional Team *(due out October 2012)*

Author's acknowledgements

To produce such a book without the assistance of many others who have contributed their ideas, time and experience would have been impossible for me. I would like to take this opportunity to say thank you to everyone who has offered their advice, feedback and help so willingly.

It was a daunting prospect taking on writing the fourth book in an already successful series of publications, whilst trying to maintain the high standards set by the previous authors. Starting this project was made much easier by having the high quality navigation sections from Hill Walking and Winter Skills to work with. I would like to thank Steve Long, Allen Fyffe and Andy Cunningham who wrote these sections, for allowing them to be used within this book and for providing me with their advice and support throughout. I only hope that the others sections added to these compliment the high standards they have set.

I would like to thank Iain Peter and John Cousins for offering me the opportunity and for their support and at times great patience and equally to the team at Vertebrate Graphics who have done an unbelievable job of turning my scribbles and sketches into a book.

I am indebted to Karl Midlane and Keith Ball who spent many hours reading the text on numerous occasions to provide me with some invaluable feedback and ideas. I would also like to thank Martin Chester and Malcolm Campbell who also gave their time to review and provide advice on various sections. Rick Shearer has an amazing knowledge of digital mapping and GPS and without his help these chapters would have been sadly lacking. Thanks also to Steve Wood from Mapyx Quo and Matt Palmer from Garmin for their contribution to this section. Thank you also to Andy Teasdale and Neil Johnson who provided their time to help with the alpine navigation section. Thanks also to Karl Midlane, Keith Ball, Andy Teasdale, Ben Lawes, Tom Hecht and Mo Laurie who searched their photo libraries for images to help compliment the text and helped with some of the technical photography. My thanks are also extended to all my colleagues at Plas y Brenin for their help with ideas and suggestions.

Very special thanks must go to Liz Campbell who originally inspired me into looking more closely at maps when I first started working in the mountains and provided a wealth of experience and advice to help with all sections of the book. Most importantly Liz wrote the material for the *improving your navigation through practice* section and should rightly be credited with developing the table for describing levels of navigation difficulty.

Finally I would like to thank my friends and family, Liz, Issy and Millie for their support, patience and tolerance of the many hours and late nights spent working on this project. I hope this book provides them with the skills to safely enjoy and explore some of the most beautiful places on earth in the future.

Carlo Forte
April 2012

Editor's note

I am very proud to be writing the final words to this fantastic book. Carlo Forte has done an excellent job of editing the first two chapters which appeared in our *Hill Walking* and *Winter Skills* books and then making the book his own by adding chapters on overseas navigation, GPS, Digital Mapping and finally the subject of teaching navigation. Steve Long and Allen Fyffe deserve great thanks for these first two chapters.

In editing the book I've had invaluable assistance from Mal Creasey, Mary Matthews, Nigel Williams, Ros Morley, Jonny Garside and Allen Fyffe. Iain Peter, Brian Griffiths, Anne Newcombe, Mary Matthews, Sue Doyle, Andy Boorman and Pete Stacey have all assisted with the planning and production of this book while Jane Beagley, Simon Norris and Jon Barton at Vertebrate Graphics have performed their usual magic in illustrating, compiling and producing it. The final link in the chain is our distributors Cordee and the regular help and advice that we receive in particular from Richard Robinson.

The books produced by Mountain Training Publications make a significant contribution towards the work carried out by Mountain Training. MTUK's purpose is the advancement for the public benefit of education and training (in conjunction where appropriate with other bodies or persons) in the skills required for the leadership and instruction of safe hill, mountain and moorland walking, mountaineering, rock and ice climbing and other associated activities practised in cliff and mountain environments and to offer advice on matters of training and safety. MTUK achieves its aims, in conjunction with the home nation boards by agreeing a range of nationally-recognised mountain leadership, instruction and coaching awards. MTUK also supports the existing workforce through a dedicated membership association for leaders (MTA) as well as by providing services for the other three relevant membership organisations.

John Cousins

This book is published by Mountain Training UK, which is a registered charity. Revenue from the sale of books published by MTUK is used for the continuation of its publishing programme and for charitable purposes associated with training leaders.

Introduction

For many people, walking in the hills and mountains is one of life's great pleasures, and for good reason. Fresh air, exercise, open vistas and adventurous exploration all combine to provide the perfect antidote to the hustle and bustle of everyday life. The beauty and challenges presented by the mountains can provide many memorable experiences, especially when shared with others. Many of the most vivid memories come from finding ourselves in testing situations requiring the careful selection of skills and judgement to keep us safe.

Navigation is the fundamental skill required by anyone wishing to travel safely through the mountains and hills in all the conditions they present. On clear sunny days this can be simply nothing more than making sure you are on the correct path at the start of the day, leaving you more time to appreciate the environment. On days when the conditions are less favourable, navigation can be more testing, requiring skill, judgement, concentration and confidence.

Efficient navigation is not about knowing where you are every minute of the day; indeed some would argue that if you spend your whole time in the mountains with your head buried in the map you might as well stay at home. Efficient navigation is about knowing how to find out where you are and how to get to where you want to go. It is about having a good range of skills, knowledge and experience; the real art of efficient navigation relies on being able to exercise good judgement in selecting the most appropriate 'tools' for the job. However, there is one other essential ingredient: confidence. When conditions are very challenging, for example in darkness or winter, a good navigator will need confidence in their ability to use their skills. Confidence and self-belief in these situations becomes important and can only be acquired through experience. Books and teaching may help to short cut this experience but it is important to practise in order to keep skills finely tuned. Structured practice will provide valuable feedback and help to develop judgement and confidence in your ability. Choosing the terrain and conditions in which you

⏱ NOTES FOR INSTRUCTORS Notes for Instructors

Throughout this book these coloured boxes contain useful exercises and methods for teaching certain aspects of navigation. The exercises shown are appropriate for anyone wishing to improve their understanding and practical experience of navigation. These are merely starting points and with a little innovation many can be developed further to suit the environment and the needs of anyone involved.

practice carefully can allow skills to be learned in safety. As your skills and knowledge build you will develop the confidence with which to be able to venture further afield or into more challenging environments.

Commissioned by Mountain Leader Training this volume is intended as a resource for anyone wishing to learn how to navigate and for those who wish to improve their skills, and provides useful information for the many people involved with teaching navigation skills. Thus many of the exercises shown throughout the text are useful to both those who teach and also those who are learning. The exercises are designed to help practise certain skills and to build confidence and an understanding of the techniques. Beginning with the fundamentals, these are the skills that underpin navigation regardless of the conditions. Relating the ground to the map, interpreting contour lines and using a compass are all necessary skills to help you navigate in summer, winter or in darkness. Further chapters show how these skills can be adapted for use in different environments. Navigating in winter brings the added challenge of snow covered terrain, the risk of avalanches and the ferocity of the weather, all of which need to be considered when planning a day out. Chapters on navigating in other countries and in an alpine environment illustrate how navigation skills can be used in different settings. With technology becoming more accessible, no navigation book would be complete without reference to GPS and digital mapping software.

These are extremely powerful tools when used well and both chapters on these topics show how this technology may be integrated with the more traditional navigational techniques.

Teaching people to navigate can be very rewarding; watching them develop their skills and confidence as navigators on the strength of your instruction is extremely satisfying. Teaching navigation requires a great deal of personal knowledge and skill but above all it needs careful planning and consideration. The final chapter, Teaching Navigation, is designed to help with the planning process and makes some suggestions as how best to deliver sessions.

The material in this book is in no way intended as a substitute for personal experience. It is hoped readers will find many practical suggestions to help improve skills, judgment and confidence when navigating on the hills and mountains. Learning can be accelerated further by taking time at the end of a day to reflect on performance. This can help to develop skills and understanding and provide an opportunity to learn from any mistakes. Every day spent in the mountains and hills teaches us something and even when errors have occurred there is always something to be learnt. Enjoy your days in the hills and remember getting lost is a good learning opportunity!

Photo: BMC

Part I

The Fundamentals

Navigation aids

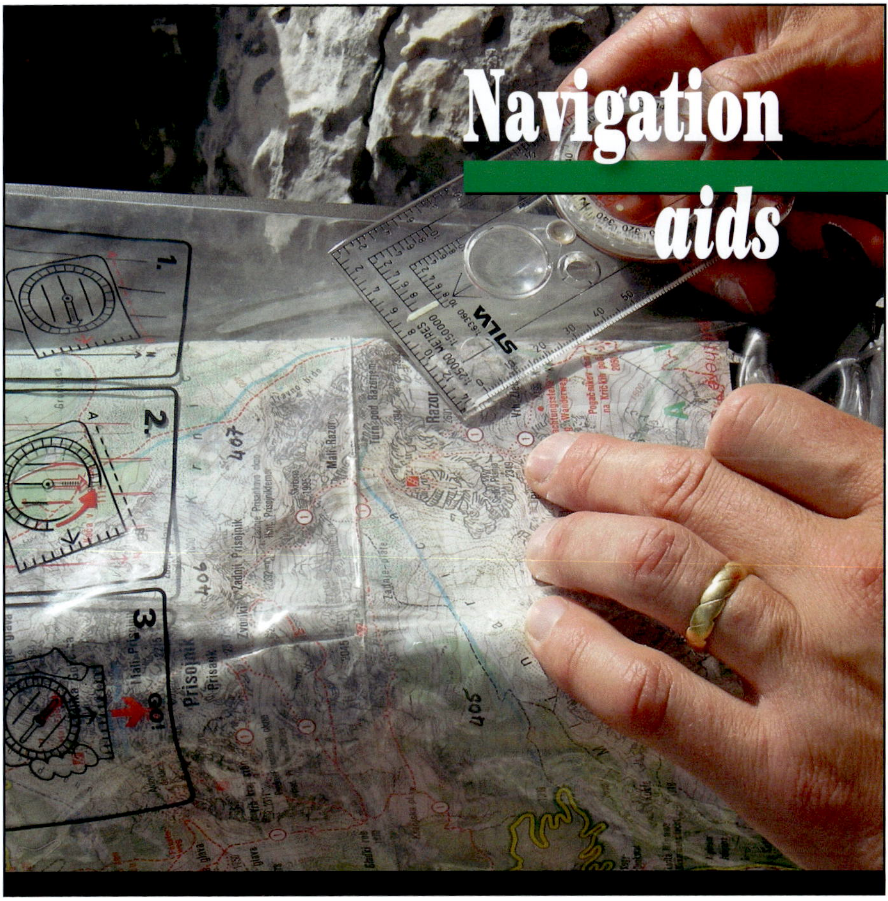

Photo: Keith Ball

Navigation is the ability to get consistently and efficiently from one place to another. On a clear day with distant horizons, this can be deceptively simple. However, complex terrain in difficult conditions can demand total concentration from even the most skilled practitioner and can become impossible without the competent use of a map and compass.

1.1 The senses

Probably the most important navigational aid we have is our body. Using our various senses it is possible to gain a wealth of information that can help with any navigation process. The obvious starting point would be to consider sight; many of the navigation strategies covered in later chapters require the use of good observation skills. Picking out detail from the landscape can allow us to transfer more information to the map and vice versa.

However it is more than just using our eyes to observe; it involves tuning our whole body into the environment so we also pick up on the sounds, smells and feelings. While our senses gather and process information all the time on a subconscious level, in some situations we may have to trigger them into action consciously, or at least focus on the essential detail we need. This could be looking for something specific, feeling for a change in the angle of slope or listening for the sound of a stream.

Sensations in our muscles and throughout our body can help us determine the type of terrain we are walking over, all very well when we can see clearly. However tuning into these feelings when the visibility is poor can provide essential information. For example, when navigating through a 'white out' in winter, sensing that we are walking up, down or across a slope can provide vital clues as to our route or location. In these conditions sensing how the ground is changing beneath our feet is sometimes the only information we may have to work with.

Sensing a change in wind direction should signal a need to check that the intended route is still being followed. The same could be said for where our shadow is cast, or the direction of the sun compared to our line of travel. If our route travels towards the sun and we find ourselves walking with the sun warming the right side of our body, a close look at the map may reveal a deviation from our intended route.

Using our senses in this way allows us a more intimate involvement with our environment, greatly benefiting our ability to navigate effectively and also enhancing the experience of being in the mountains.

1.2 Nature

Animals have navigated by nature since the dawn of time, this need being borne out of necessity to survive and succeed. Humans would have developed these skills from an early age to help find such things as food, shelter, a mate or better weather. Many would argue that even today we *navigate* in similar ways for similar reasons. Early humans developed their navigation skills by learning how to use the sky, stars, sun, wind, vegetation and animals to find direction. Nowadays many of these ancient skills have fallen from favour with preference for the use of more modern tools. By spending time out in the hills and mountains we automatically develop a certain amount of experience and skill as a *'natural navigator'*. Knowledge of plants and vegetation cover is particularly useful when considering a route through terrain. As examples, the nodding heads of cotton grass and the red tinge of rushes

FIGURE 1.01   NAVIGATION IN DIFFICULT WINTER WHITE OUT CONDITIONS   Photo: Keith Ball

FIGURE 1.02   VISUAL CLUES – **A** AND **B** WET GROUND VEGETATION   **C** A MINOR PATH THROUGH DRY TERRAIN
D WALKING THROUGH AWKWARD TUSSOCK GROUND HEADING TOWARD DRYER MORE FAVOURABLE TERRAIN BEYOND

indicate wet boggy areas which can then be avoided (*see Figure 1.02*). A dense cover of heather can make terrain difficult to walk through, also provoking a change of route. Other aspects of the natural environment can provide good information. Habitual tracks created by sheep usually go round a hill rather than directly up or down and often contour into cols or flat areas, making them useful paths in certain situations.

Nature can also provide us with clues to our direction. A simple knowledge of the stars can help to find North. Similarly, improvised methods of using the sun and moon can help to establish the cardinal points. Certain lichens and mosses prefer sunnier aspects and will therefore be commonly found on more south-facing surfaces in the northern hemisphere.

Learning more about these skills and the natural environment will help inform our navigation and add a new dimension to the interaction we have with our surroundings.

For leaders and teachers the skills of using nature can be a fun way of engaging students in navigation as well as the natural environment (*see **Section…improvised methods of finding North*** on page 92-93).

FIGURE 1.03   MOST COMMON AND WIDELY AVAILABLE MAPS FOR NAVIGATING IN THE MOUNTAINS FROM HARVEY AND ORDNANCE SURVEY

1.3 The map

A good quality map is an essential tool for navigation. Maps used by walkers are an accurate pictorial representation of the land in two dimensions with sufficient detail to allow route finding in all conditions. Choosing the right map is a question of balancing the need for a convenient size against the requirement for a certain level of detail.

Map scales

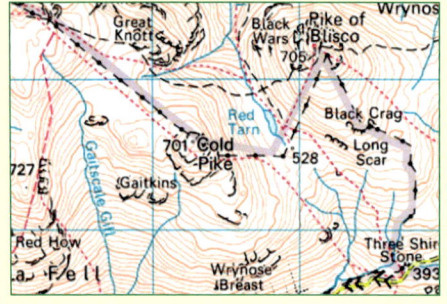

OS 1:50,000 Landranger Maps
1cm = 50, 000cm
1cm = 500m
1mm = 50m
2cm = 1km *(Grid square)*

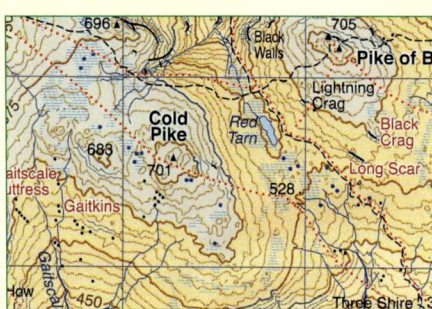

Harvey 1:40,000 Maps
1cm = 40,000cm
1cm = 400m
1mm = 40m
2.5cm = 1km *(Grid square)*

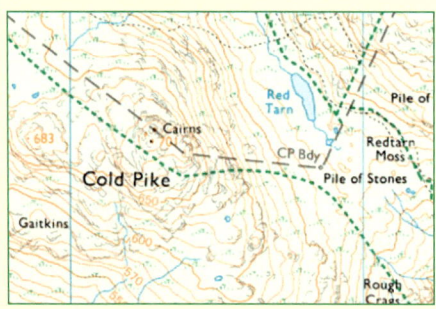

OS 1:25,000 Explorer Maps
1cm = 25, 000cm
1cm = 250m
1mm = 25m
4cm = 1km *(Grid square)*

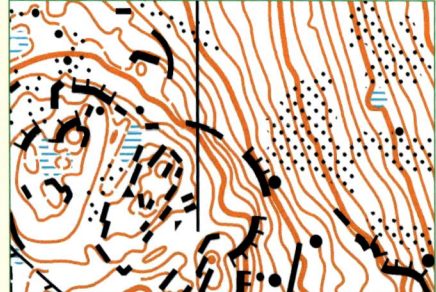

Orienteering Map 1:10,000
1cm = 10,000cm
1cm = 100m
1mm = 10m
10cm = 1km

Small scale maps = **smaller** amount of detail (cover a large area eg: 1:50,000)
Large scale maps = **larger** amount of detail (cover a small area eg: 1:10,000)

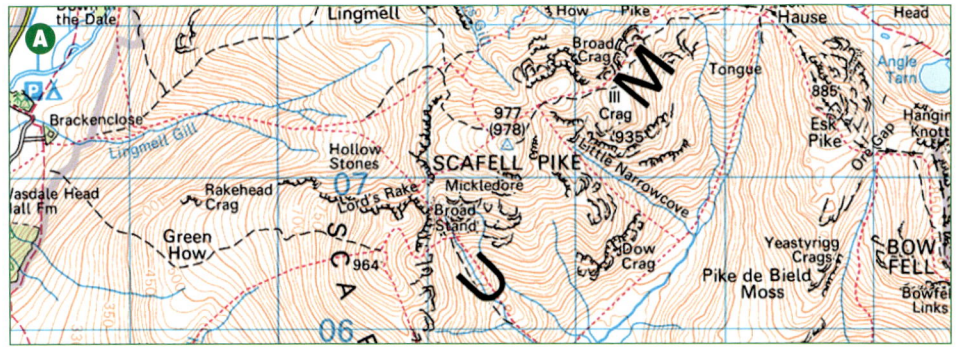

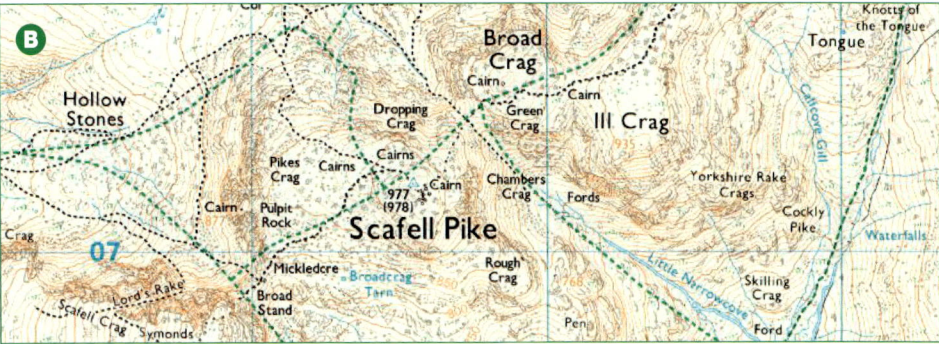

FIGURE 1.04 **A** DETAIL SHOWN ON OS 1:50 000 SCALE MAPS (SMALL SCALE) **B** DETAIL SHOWN ON OS 1:25 000 SCALE MAPS (LARGE SCALE)

In the British Isles the main providers of suitable maps for walkers are the Ordnance Survey (OS) and Harvey. In some more technically demanding upland areas (or even some easily accessible areas) it is possible to obtain specialist orienteering maps. The Ordnance Survey produces maps at a range of scales, surveyed using aerial and ground survey and designed to address the needs of a wide range of users. The information provided by their maps therefore varies in its relevance for hill walkers. The OS maps of the UK are now fully digitised and updated (mainly urban areas) on a daily basis. A recent innovation is to develop a number of interactive layers to these maps where members of the public can update certain types of information such as access information and leisure facilities.

Harvey maps are designed specifically with the needs of walkers in mind and use a sophisticated range of symbols to provide the walker with additional information about the terrain. The base map for a Harvey's map is created by plotting from aerial photos and the consequent map is then field checked on foot to ensure that the significant detail for walkers is included.

Ordnance Survey (OS) is the national mapping agency for the UK, and one of the world's largest producers of maps. The name reflects the original military purpose of the organisation in mapping Britain during the Napoleonic Wars when there was a threat of invasion from France. OS is widely regarded as the most systematic and thorough mapping institution in the world, detailing every corner of the UK long before satellite technology made quality maps of the same standard available elsewhere in the world. Today Ordnance Survey is a self-financing civilian organisation at the forefront of the digital economy, producing digital mapping products and paper maps for a wide range of purposes. For mountain navigators the Landranger and Explorer series of maps has for many years helped to define when and where we can go in to the hills.

Only limited areas of the country are available at the time of writing, but the majority of popular walking destinations are covered by waterproof (laminated) British Mountains Maps, which use Harvey mapping. Orienteering ('O') maps, although of limited availability, provide a great deal of accurate detail which makes them good for practice and teaching. The base map for an 'O' map is also plotted from aerial photos. A detailed field survey is then conducted before the actual map is drawn. Each 'mapper' has their own style but uses standard scales (normally 1:10,000 or 1:15,000) and conventional symbols similar to those used on Harvey's and OS maps.

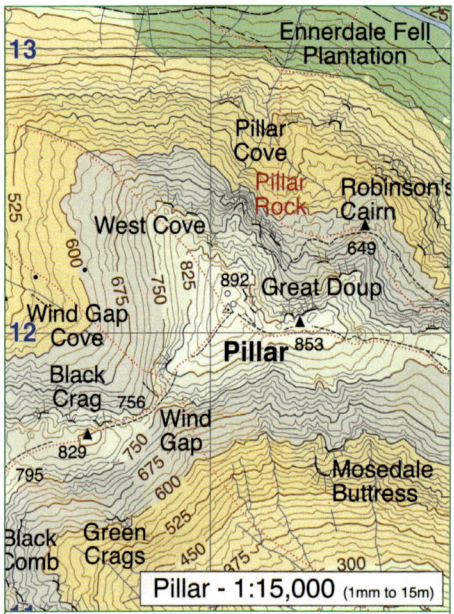

FIGURE 1.05 HARVEY ALSO PRODUCE A RANGE OF ADDITIONAL SCALE MAPS FOR SPECIFIC AREAS. HAVING ACCESS TO THIS LEVEL OF DETAIL FOR COMPLEX AREAS CAN MAKE NAVIGATION MUCH EASIER PARTI-CULARLY IN POOR WEATHER. (MAP NOT TO SCALE)

FIGURE 1.06 EXAMPLE OF MAP CASE/PROTECTION

1.3.1 Choosing the right map

In the UK both OS and Harvey maps provide similar levels of detail although this may be expressed in different ways. Harvey maps are good on complex rocky ground because these areas are shown by grey contours and the major crags are clearly marked. Other rock detail, commonly shown on OS 1:25,000 maps, that is not relevant for navigation or safe passage is not mapped. However in more featureless terrain OS maps show a greater degree of detail due to the difference in contour interval. Harvey maps use a 15 metre contour interval as opposed to OS who use an interval of 10 or 5 metres. This smaller contour interval allows for a more accurate portrayal of the topography. Scale is often a deciding factor when choosing a suitable map. There are advantages and disadvantages to using any scale of map and some are more suited to certain conditions compared to others. In complex ground a 1:25,000 scale map provides a greater amount of detail whereas in featureless terrain (i.e. moorland or snow covered) all this detail can detract from important contour information. In these situations a 1:50,000 map provides a less cluttered impression of the landscape. When out in the mountains it is always worth carrying a spare map and by taking two different scale maps it will allow you to choose the most appropriate map for the terrain and the task ahead as well as having a spare if one should be blown away!

Maps can be rather unwieldy to use, particularly on windy and wet days. A simple improvement is to remove the map's stiff cover. Protecting the map in a plastic map case is popular but these can then be too bulky to slip into a pocket and if worn around the neck tend to flap about in the wind, sometimes even threatening to garrotte the wearer! A good quality rubberised map case will protect the map and allow it to be folded small enough to fit into most map pockets (a strong plastic bag is a cheap and simple alternative). One recurring problem with constantly re-folding the map is the damage that can occur: more often than not the damaged fold is the exact point on the map where you need every shred of information. A more sustainable solution is to cut maps into smaller sections. This needs some thought to make sure the sections include as many access and exit points as possible, as well as grid numbers and reference letters, plus a record of magnetic variation. If this smaller

Access to the mountains

The law regarding access to the uplands of the UK and Ireland is complicated and varies throughout. To cover all the intricacies of legislation for each country greatly exceeds the scope of this book and is better left to respective government bodies to provide up to date information. **Appendix 4** on page 152 provides details on where this information can be found. Various Acts now give us rights of access on foot to some of the wildest landscapes in the UK and Ireland. With legal rights to walk freely there are responsibilities to consider to help insure these rights are maintained and the environment is protected.

Photo: Tom Hecht

The Country Code (England & Wales) and Scottish Outdoor Access Code are examples of good practice guidance given to help people exercise these responsibilities. Maps provide an

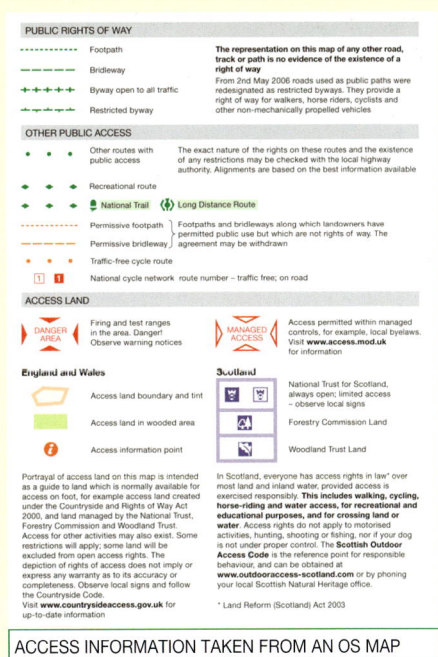

ACCESS INFORMATION TAKEN FROM AN OS MAP

important source of information regarding access. Access land and public rights of way can be easily identified by matching the symbols with the map key. Some maps will give further information regarding access to a particular area.

---

map is laminated, its life expectancy will be dramatically improved, outweighing the preparation costs. This solution is likely to be of more use for the maps to your local area and places you visit on a regular basis. However for the areas you might only visit once a good map case will more than suffice. Some offices have small laminators that can produce adequate results, but check that a flexible plastic is used. Many maps can now be purchased already laminated and some outlets offer the facility to laminate full map sheets.

Digital mapping software is now available and can be readily found via the Internet or through outdoor equipment retailers. Most software is produced under licence and allows an A4 sized map to be printed for personal use only. Use of this technology requires a reliable colour printer with good quality paper, and it is the navigator's responsibility to check that the lines and the scale are not distorted. A poor-quality reproduc-

tion is of little use for navigation. The accuracy of a particular scale can be confirmed by measuring the grid squares and comparing them with the appropriate scale, for example 1:50,000 printouts must show the length of each grid square as 2 centimetres (*refer to Map scales on page 6 for more information*).

1.3.2 Map scales

The *scale* of a map is defined as the ratio of a distance on the map to the corresponding distance on the ground. In the case of a 1:50,000 map, 1 centimetre (or 1 inch or one 'anything') on the map represents 50,000 centimetres (inches or 'anythings') on the ground. For many activities, such as navigating in a car, a small scale map that covers a relatively large area gives adequate information as the route is physically channelled along roads. For walking, a larger scale map with

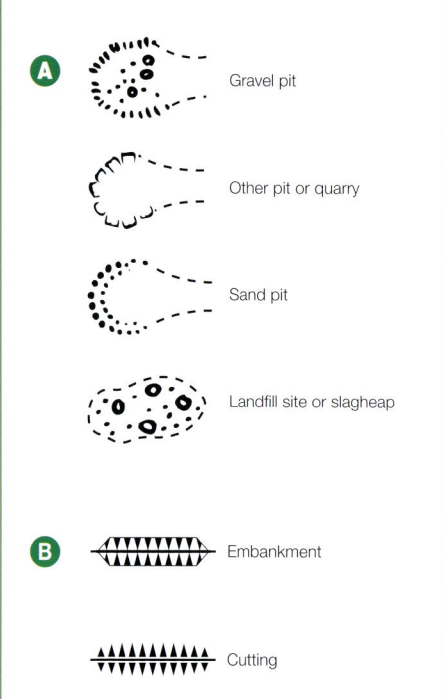

FIGURE 1.07 **A** SYMBOLS FOR DIFFERENT TYPES OF PIT AND QUARRY **B** HACHURES USED TO SHOW EMBANKMENTS AND CUTTINGS

walls and fences which are omitted from smaller scales such as 1:50,000. On the other hand, the wealth of detail at 1:25,000 can make it harder to get an overall picture of the shape of the land. Lying between these scales, 1:40,000 maps cover large enough areas for route planning and yet display enough detail when precise navigation is required. Other scales may well be encountered for specific areas. For example, maps of complex summits such as Ben Nevis are often available in a 1:10,000 scale in order to show the complex ridges and gullies more clearly.

1.3.3 Signs and symbols

Features on the ground are represented on maps using symbols. These show the position of a feature but are not always drawn to scale; most houses would be virtually invisible if drawn to the correct scale on a 1:50,000 map. In general, water features and their names are coloured blue, woodland is shaded green and man-made features have a black outline and are named in black ink. Orienteering maps use a different convention for symbols. White and green are used to depict the density of woodland and the extent to which it impedes progress. Open 'runnable' woodland is left white with progressively darker shades of green meaning increased density, ranging from 'slow run' to 'difficult' (or walk) through to 'impenetrable'(or fight). Yellow is used for non-wooded areas with a solid yellow for grassy spaces such as playing fields and a paler yellow for rougher terrain (rough open) such as heather.

Rights of way are also colour-coded but this varies for different scales and publications. Occasionally paths marked on the map may not

comprehensive representation of the landscape is required.

Since 1:25,000 scale maps are using four times more paper than 1:50,000 maps to represent the same area of land they are able to show a lot more detail. Of particular significance to the walker is their depiction of field boundaries,

1 NOTES FOR INSTRUCTORS Symbols

While the key provides a reference to the map, becoming familiar with the common symbols likely to be encountered can save time. Comparing the key to features on the ground from an early stage will help students to lodge symbols in their memory.

Exercises

Flash cards: use flash cards matching the symbol to the definition (flash cards and games can be downloaded from the Ordnance Survey website).

Symbol search: give people a copy of the key and walk through an area with plenty of features. As they pass a feature they should tick the corresponding symbol on the key. At the end of the leg this information could be transferred to the map to help relocate. By introducing this early it will start to develop the ability to relate the ground to the map: a vital skill required for other aspects of navigation.

appear on the ground and vice versa. There may be any number of reasons why this is the case and it highlights the need to check for other features as you travel.

Before departing for the hills and moors and to avoid regularly unfolding the map, it is worth spending a little time examining the map's key in order to recognise the symbols, which are usually easy to memorise icons. There are also subtle aspects to the shorthand that are only revealed by careful examination of the key. For example, there are different symbols for gravel pits, sand pits, chalk pits and disused pits!

1.3.4 Contours

One of the most important representations on a map is the topography – the shape of the land. Landforms are shown in several ways. At a fundamental level, the form of the land is represented by contour lines. These are generally coloured brown (Harvey maps also use a grey contour line to denote rocky terrain) and connect points that are an equal height above sea level. The interval between contours varies between maps and should always be checked before using a new map.

In the UK, Ordnance Survey maps generally use a 10 metre interval, although lowland regions

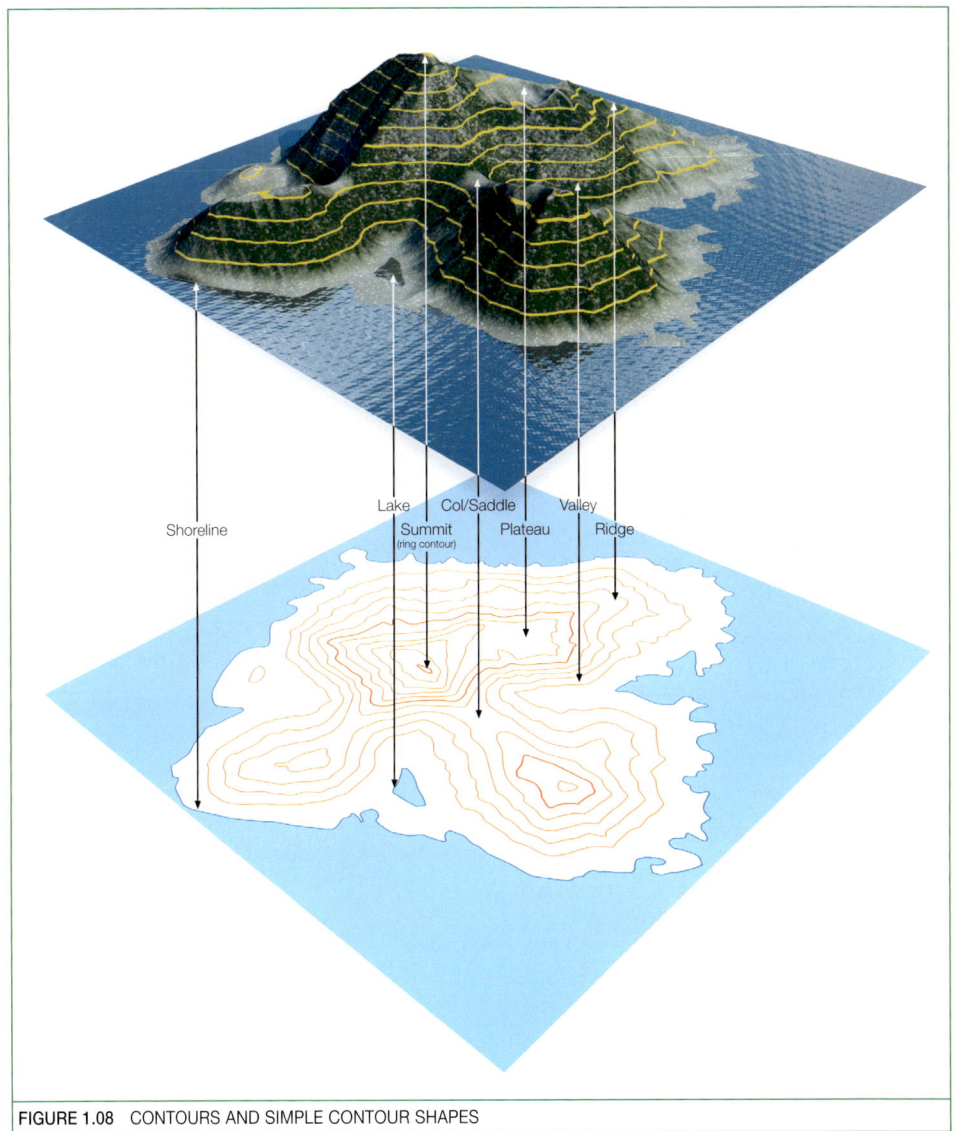

Shoreline   Lake   Col/Saddle   Valley
             Summit   Plateau   Ridge
             (ring contour)

FIGURE 1.08   CONTOURS AND SIMPLE CONTOUR SHAPES

have 5 metre contour intervals on 1:25,000 maps, Harvey's UK maps use 15 metre contour intervals and orienteering maps typically use a 5 metre contour interval in upland areas. Maps with the same horizontal scale but with different contour intervals give a very different impression of the terrain. Contours spaced 1mm apart may represent a 20° slope on one map but a 40° slope on another. French maps use a 10 metre interval, but on the Swiss side of the border, contours are 20 metres apart – this can be very confusing for maps which include both sides of the border, such as when in the Mont Blanc Massif!

Most maps show every fifth (index) contour with a thicker line, which means that counting index contours is a quick way to calculate the height difference between two points. Often on ground steeper than 30° only these thicker lines are shown because the contours are too close to be drawn individually. On orienteering and

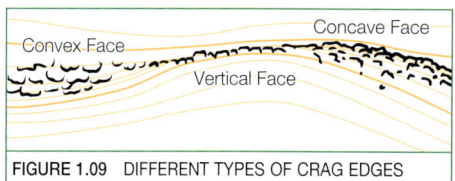

FIGURE 1.09   DIFFERENT TYPES OF CRAG EDGES

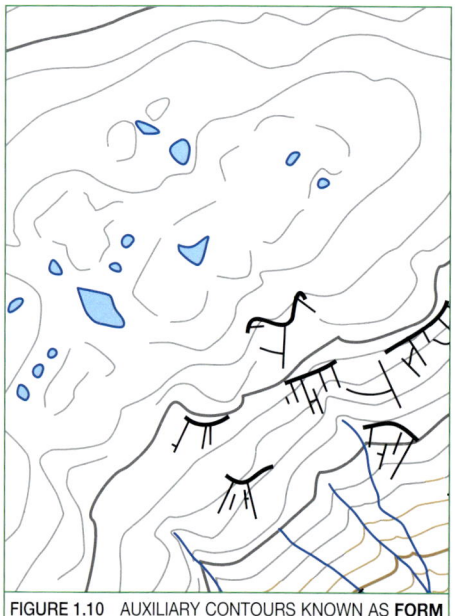

FIGURE 1.10   AUXILIARY CONTOURS KNOWN AS **FORM LINES** (BROKEN CONTOURS) ARE ADDED TO SHOW FEATURES MISSED BY THE STANDARD CONTOURS. THEY ARE APPROXIMATELY HALF WAY IN HEIGHT BETWEEN THE CONTOUR LINES.

Harvey maps significant features that fall between contour lines are marked with 'broken' contour known as a form line (*see Figure 1.10*). Index contours often have a number at some point showing the height above sea level. This number is always drawn so that it is the right way up for someone to read it as they are looking up the hill. In the case of some Harvey maps, colour shading helps the map reader visualise a 3D picture of the terrain.

1.3.5 Other topographical symbols

Symbols are used to show other topographical features; rocky ground is shown with black lines, differentiating between boulders, loose rocks, outcrops and scree. Different sized symbols will be used to mark scree, with larger symbols at the bottom of the slope, and a varying design to show prominent scree runs, vegetation patches and interspersed boulders.

On OS maps crag edges are shown by a representation of the exposed surfaces at the top of the cliff. Concave crags are shown with firm black lines along the top with strata drawn using lighter and more spaced line-work as the angle eases, while convex faces are shown with the thicker black lines at the bottom. It is important to recognise the subtle differences before attempting to negotiate craggy terrain in poor conditions.

1.4 The grid system

A distinctive feature of British maps is the grid structure of blue lines superimposed over the whole country. These grid lines are the basis of a numerical reference system which allows any position to be pinpointed and communicated. The grid reference is prefixed by two letters that identify each specific 100 x 100km square (e.g. NY for northern Lake District, NG for Skye – *see Figure 1.11*). Grid lines are oriented along the cardinal points of the compass, North, South, East and West and can also be used to set the map and to take bearings using a compass. Grid bearings can then be converted to magnetic bearings or vice versa. All these techniques are covered in detail later.

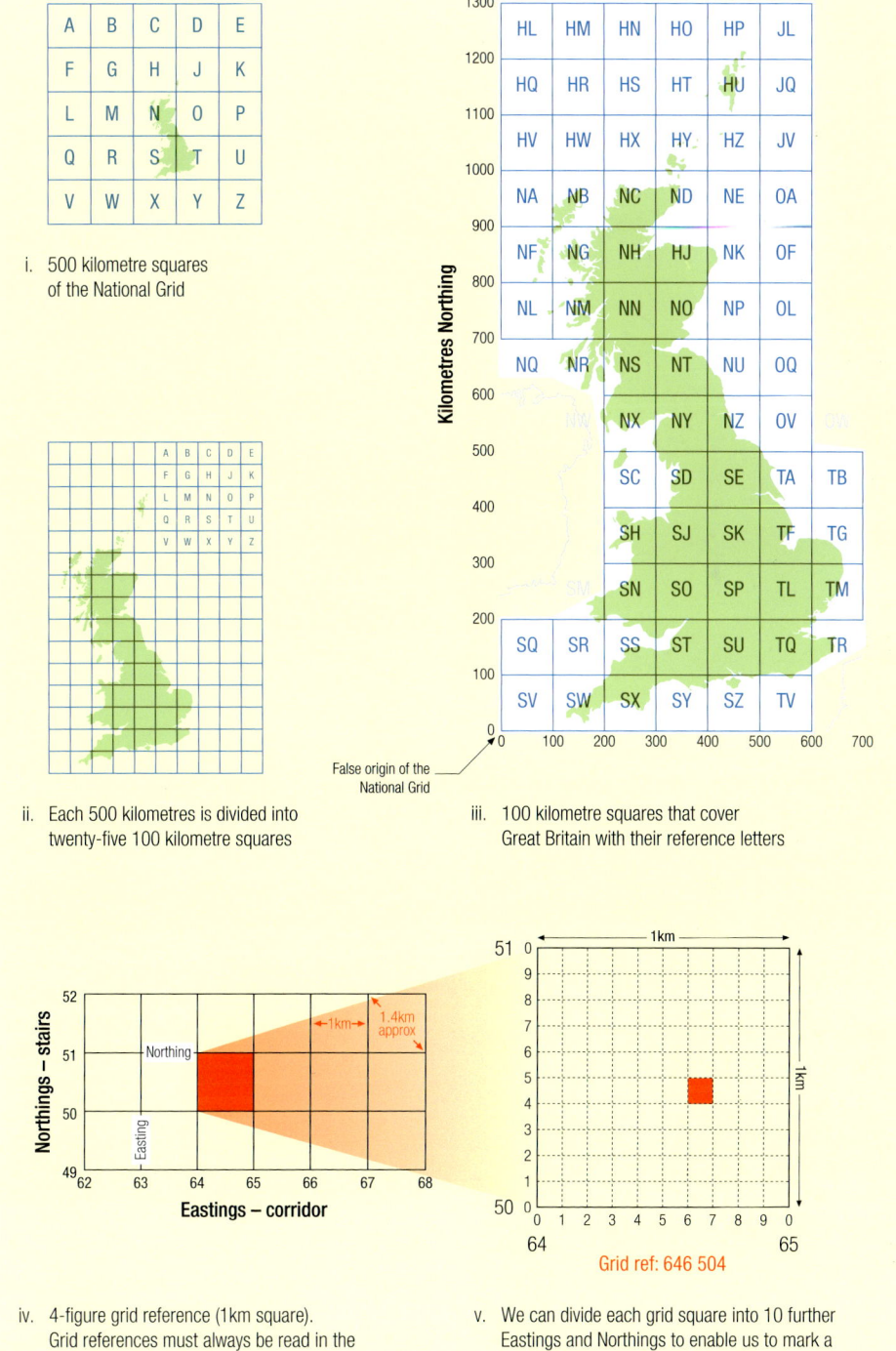

i. 500 kilometre squares of the National Grid

ii. Each 500 kilometres is divided into twenty-five 100 kilometre squares

iii. 100 kilometre squares that cover Great Britain with their reference letters

False origin of the National Grid

iv. 4-figure grid reference (1km square).
Grid references must always be read in the following order:
Eastings – "Along the corridor…" (63, 64, 65 etc.)
Northings– "… and up the stairs" (49, 50, 51 etc.)

v. We can divide each grid square into 10 further Eastings and Northings to enable us to mark a feature to an accuracy of 100 metres. If we take this diagram as grid square 6450 we can plot a specific location within the one square kilometre.

Grid ref: 646 504

FIGURE 1.11   THE NATIONAL GRID

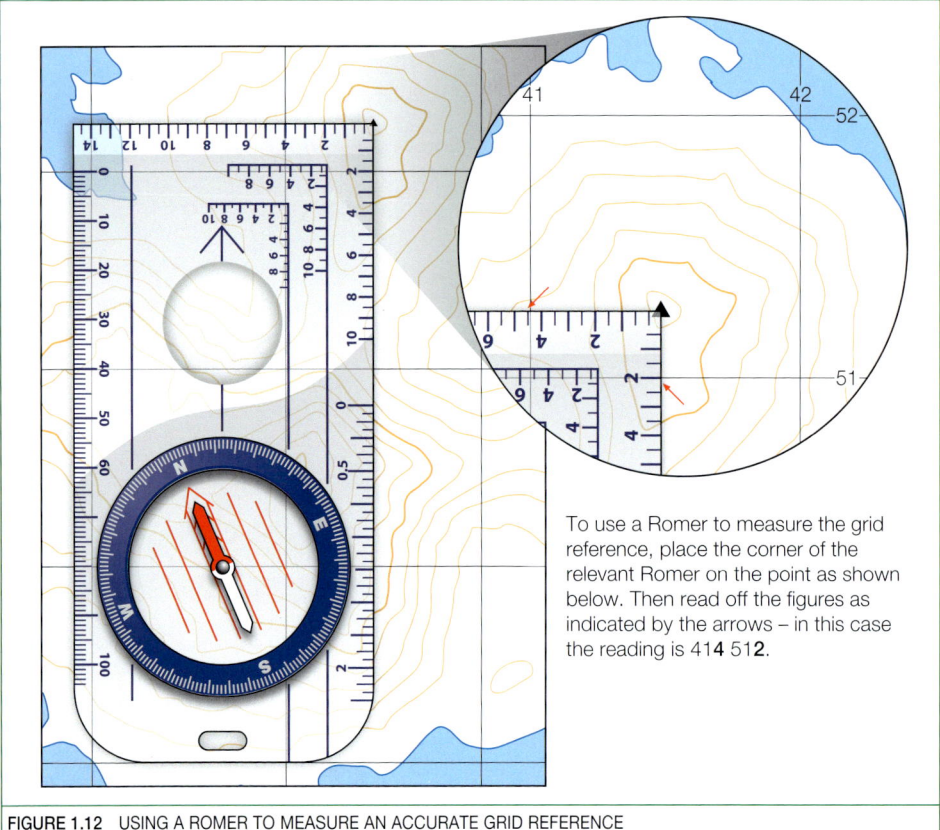

To use a Romer to measure the grid reference, place the corner of the relevant Romer on the point as shown below. Then read off the figures as indicated by the arrows – in this case the reading is 414 512.

FIGURE 1.12   USING A ROMER TO MEASURE AN ACCURATE GRID REFERENCE

1.4.1 Grid references

The main reason for printing a grid system on maps is to create a numerical system for defining a specific location. A grid reference is a descriptive rather than a navigational tool.

The Ordnance Survey National Grid was developed after the First World War. It consists of a grid across the country that is systematically broken down into progressively smaller squares. The larger squares, which have sides of 100 kilometres, are identified by a two-letter suffix, which starts in the South West on the Scilly Isles. Each area is then subdivided into squares with sides of one kilometre and these are superimposed over the map. Each of these grid squares is assigned a specific four-figure reference.

The convention is to define the sideways location (eastings) first, followed by the vertical location (northings). The numbers marked on the map describe the square located diagonally to their right and upwards. While a four-figure grid reference is useful for identifying the location of large features it is too vague for pin-pointing smaller ones. For a more precise location, 100m x 100m it is normal to use a six-figure reference. These can be estimated by eye, measured with the compass ruler, or more simply with a *romer* (a portable co-ordinate measuring device). The latter can either be incorporated into the base plate of a compass or less conveniently as a separate measurer (*see Figure 1.12*).

The ability to calculate grid references is a skill that could be crucial in an emergency. It is also an integral aspect of position plotting with a Global Positioning System (GPS). Teaching and learning about the use of grid references is ideally suited to an indoor session. The use of a romer facilitates understanding of the process as well as being relatively simple and accurate to use.

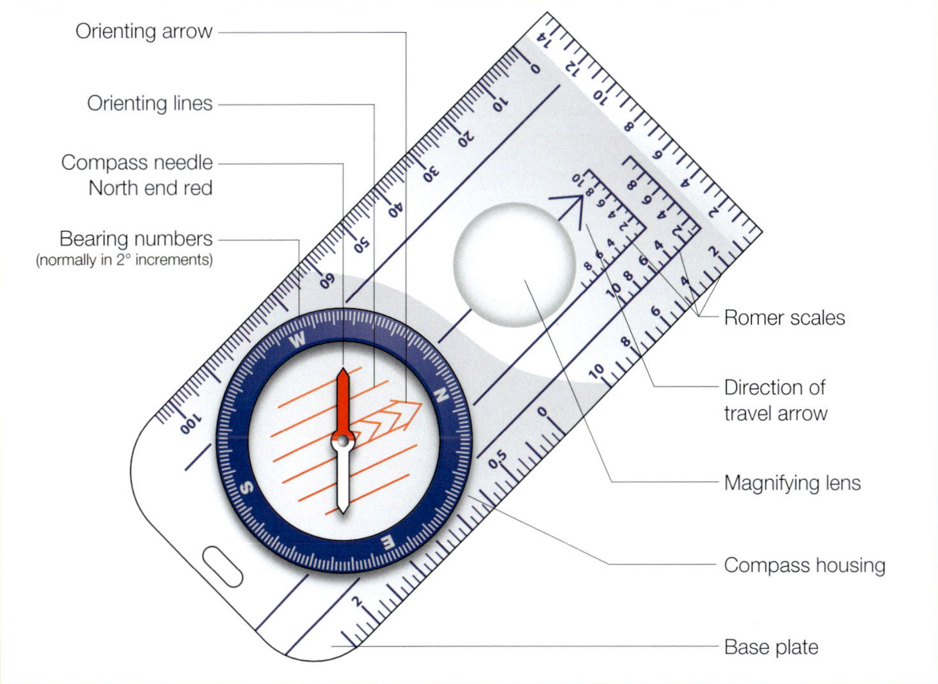

Orienting arrow

Orienting lines

Compass needle
North end red

Bearing numbers
(normally in 2° increments)

Romer scales

Direction of
travel arrow

Magnifying lens

Compass housing

Base plate

FIGURE 1.13   THE BASE-PLATE STYLE COMPASS (EG: TYPE 4 SILVA)

1.5 The compass

For centuries, the magnetic compass has remained the most reliable device for finding direction, requiring almost no maintenance and needing no power supply. In good weather the compass may never leave your pocket. However as the route becomes more complex or as the weather worsens the compass becomes an essential tool for finding direction and navigation. While manufacturers have continued to develop compass design over the years, stripped back to the core it is nothing more than a magnetised needle that responds to the earth's magnetic field. As well as showing direction they are very versatile tools, which can provide assistance with other navigational tasks:

- taking a bearing from the map;
- walking on a bearing;
- measuring distances from the map;
- setting the map in the right direction (see *Section 2.1.1 on page 24*);
- taking an aspect of slope or finding the direction of a linear feature (see *Section 2.9.5 on page 49*).

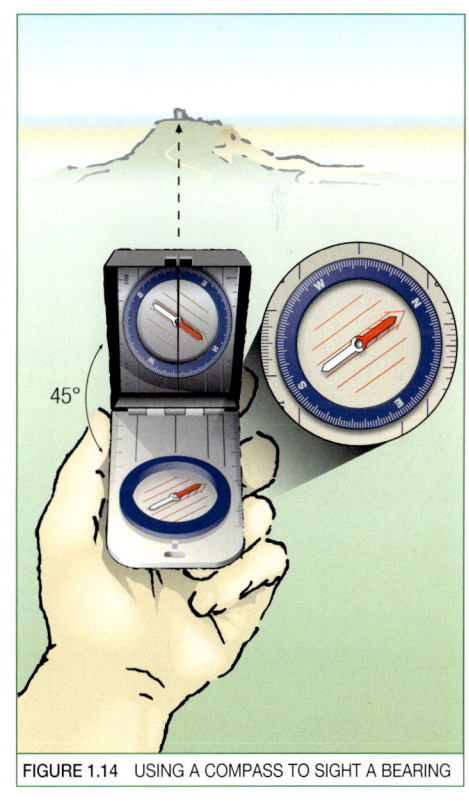

FIGURE 1.14   USING A COMPASS TO SIGHT A BEARING

FIGURE 1.15 **A VARIETY OF DIFFERENT COMPASSES: A** A SIMPLE BASE PLATE COMPASS **B** A GENERAL PURPOSE BASE PLATE COMPASS **C** A SIGHTING COMPASS **D** ELECTRONIC COMPASSES

1.5.1 Choosing a compass

Types of compass

Compasses that can be used in the mountain environment fall into three basic categories.

1 Base plate

This is the most commonly used type of compass for mountain and moorland navigation. Lightweight, robust and reasonably priced they are sometimes referred to as protractor compasses. They consist of two parts, a compass housing containing the needle and a base plate made from transparent plastic.

2 Sighting

There are various types of sighting compass; two of the most common being a mirror compass and the prismatic compass. In practice they are good for sighting on objects and walking on bearing accurately. However, they often have small base plates making it difficult to take bearings from the map or measure distances and grid references. While they can still be a useful tool to the mountain navigator they do require familiarity and practice to achieve accuracy. As a result they are not as versatile as the base plate type (*see Figure 1.14*).

3 Electronic

These are increasingly popular and becoming more reliable with developments in technology. They differ from a GPS compass because they do not require the use of satellites to work out position and direction. However they are often incorporated into watches and GPS units and while they may be good for direction finding the biggest disadvantage is they have no facility for taking a bearing from the map. It also worth remembering that batteries may run down and software might fail so having the backup of a mechanical device such as those highlighted above becomes important.

Compasses are available in a huge variety of shapes and sizes and while they all do the same basic job of indicating direction many are designed for specific applications and are not necessarily suited for use in the mountains. For mountain use a compass will need to be light but tough and consist of all the basic features that would allow it to assist with the tasks outlined previously.

- A freely rotating *magnetic needle* (one end should be a different colour to the other so as to distinguish between north and south).
- A rotating *compass housing* for the needle, filled with fluid to dampen and reduce any vibration, allowing more accurate readings.
- A *graduated scale* around the circumference of the housing – degrees or mils.

FIGURE 1.16   THE MAGNETIC NATURE OF THE ROCK ON CERTAIN PARTS OF THE COUNTRY SUCH AS THE CULLIN RIDGE ON SKYE CAN AFFECT THE COMPASS NEEDLES' ABILITY TO POINT NORTH

- An *orienting arrow* and set of *parallel lines* located below the needle.
- An *index line* marked on the rotating housing, allowing for a grid or magnetic bearing to be read accurately.
- A transparent **base plate** with straight edges and lines for easily measuring bearings from a map.
- A *direction of travel arrow* that can be used to point toward an objective.
- A *romer* scale for measuring grid references or distances.
- A centimetre **ruler** for measuring distances with more accuracy.

Optional extras that are advantageous when having to use a compass in testing conditions include the following.
- Rubber pads on the base plate – allow for better purchase on map covers when taking bearings or measuring distances.
- Option for attaching a lanyard which can then be clipped to a pocket zipper to prevent loss or damage if dropped.
- Magnifying glass for seeing the detail on the map – good for looking beyond other symbols to see the contour information and other minute details.
- Luminous markings make it easier to use at night.

Good clear markings are essential for measuring distances and bearings. As well as the cardinal points of North, East, South and West, the needle housing should be marked around the edge with the 360° of a full circle, most often in 2° intervals.

Other forms of graduation do exist, in particular the 'mils' system used on military compasses. This is more accurate compared to using degrees as there are more mils to a circle than degrees; 360° compared to 6400 mils. For the purposes of recreational mountain walking in all conditions it is universally accepted that a compass graduated in degrees is sufficiently accurate. As some retailers stock both types of compass it is important to check before purchasing; if possible try before you buy. Make sure the needle rotates freely and settles quickly. Good quality compasses use an oily fluid to dampen the needle. This reduces vibration and ensures the compass needle settles to the correct alignment quickly. Moving the compass about will allow you to assess this. Make sure the compass housing rotates freely and can be operated easily with gloves on.

1.5.2 Care and maintenance

Although most products designed for outdoor use are tough and robust there are some steps that can be taken to help increase their lifespan and to ensure they are kept in working order. A protective cover is a worthwhile investment for use on the days when the compass is not needed but carried in your rucksack. In this situation try to ensure it is stored in an accessible pocket and not buried amongst other items of equipment that may cause it damage. Avoid storing a compass next to metallic objects as this can cause reverse polarity leaving the needle pointing South rather than North. Dry compasses carefully when they have been exposed to rain or snow and avoid placing them in direct contact with heat. Periodically clean the compass housing to ensure it is able to rotate freely as this will allow bearings to be taken more easily. When in use try to attach the compass about your person using a lanyard. Attaching to the zipper cord of a pocket allows for easy use and storage.

Occasionally your compass may produce a bubble in the housing around the needle. This should not affect its operation, however it can be annoying. Bubbles develop due to changes in temperature and atmospheric pressure, usually getting larger with increasing elevation and decreasing temperature. Often, when returned to neutral pressure (or temperature), the bubble will disappear. If not, try placing it in a warm environment and if this fails it may have a small leak in the casing allowing air to creep in. A quick check would be to hold it close (but not too close!) to another compass to ensure both needles point in the same direction. If the fluid is missing the needle will be slow to settle and may drag against the compass housing causing it to stick and give an incorrect reading. While it may still be serviceable it may be worth considering a replacement.

1.5.3 Using a compass in other parts of the world

For a compass to work properly, the needle must be free to rotate and align with the earth's magnetic field. There are considerations when using a compass farther afield, especially in the southern hemisphere. The difference between compasses designed to work in the northern and southern hemispheres is the location of the 'balance', a weight placed on the needle to ensure it remains in a horizontal plane and hence free to rotate.

A typical compass can only function effectively within a set range of longitudes because the changes in the earth's magnetic field pulls on the needle, thereby causing it to scrape and press against the compass housing, as a result affecting the accuracy. In the northern hemisphere, the magnetic field dips down into the earth so the

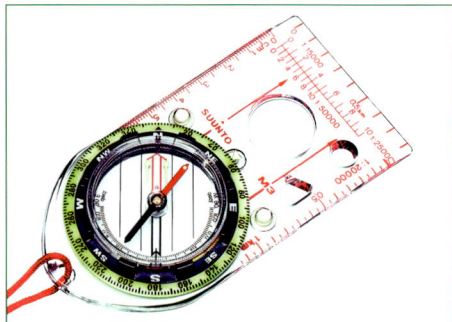

FIGURE 1.17 WORLD COMPASS: THEY LOOK SIMILAR TO OTHER COMPASSES HOWEVER THE NEEDLE IS BALANCED TO WORK IN BOTH NORTHERN AND SOUTHERN HEMISPHERES

compass needle is weighted on the south end to keep it horizontal. In the southern hemisphere, the weight needs to be on the north end of the needle. Compasses are available that allow the user to adjust this weight so that the needle remains balanced throughout the world. Various manufacturers have innovated a solution to this problem and as a result have produced a ***global compass*** suitable for use throughout the world. The compass needle is made of a non-magnetic material that pivots freely and independently of a magnetic disk. The magnetic disk is the part which points to earth's Magnetic North and because the needle is unaffected by the inclination pull of the earth's Magnetic Field, it remains balanced anywhere in the world.

1.5.4 Considerations when using a compass

As already stated a compass relies on a magnetic needle to show direction. Many objects can affect a compass needle's ability to align with the earth's magnetic field causing an inaccurate reading. Metallic zips, cameras, mobile phones, GPS units can all affect a compass needle if held close by. Try to move away from metal gates or fences before using a bearing to avoid setting off in the wrong direction, and in winter be mindful of carrying both your compass and ice axe in the same hand as this will also affect the needle. Certain types of rock that have magnetic properties will also cause the needle to deviate from its normal alignment. The gabbro found on the Isle of Skye is renowned for this. Finally a compass is a precision instrument; to obtain accurate bearings it needs to be held flat and the needle allowed to settle.

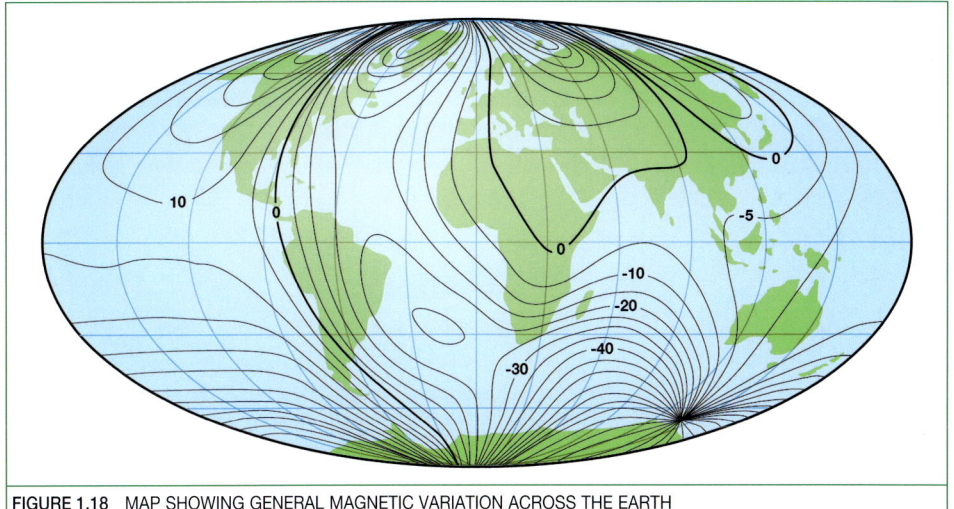

FIGURE 1.18 MAP SHOWING GENERAL MAGNETIC VARIATION ACROSS THE EARTH

1.5.5 Grid North, Magnetic North and True North

Before learning to take and use accurate compass bearings it is essential to understand the relationship between Grid North, Magnetic North, and True North:

- **Grid North** is the direction indicated by the parallel vertical grid-lines on a map and varies very slightly (*see Figure 1.19*) from True North.
- **Magnetic North/South** is the axis along which a compass needle will align itself in the earth's magnetic field. Magnetic North, which is in a different position to True North, is located to the north of Hudson Bay in Canada and is moving very slowly eastward at a

constant rate. In order to use a compass in conjunction with a map, any bearings have to be translated between Magnetic North and Grid North (or True North for continental maps that do not use a grid system). The difference between these two North points is known as **Magnetic Variation** and will vary depending on where you are on the globe (*see Figure 1.18*).

- **True North** (and South) are the geographic poles where the earth's axis meet the surface. For the purposes of land navigation using UK maps True North can be ignored.

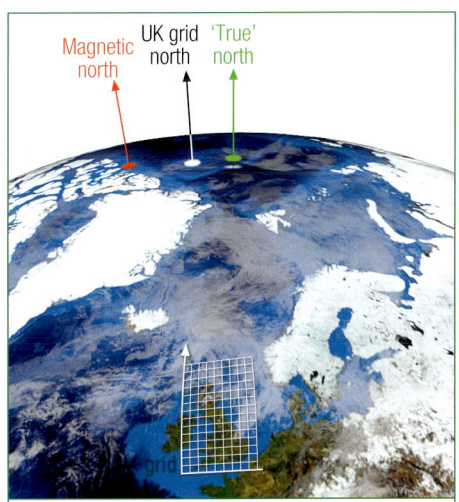

FIGURE 1.19 GLOBE SHOWING THE RELATIONSHIP BETWEEN THE THREE NORTHS

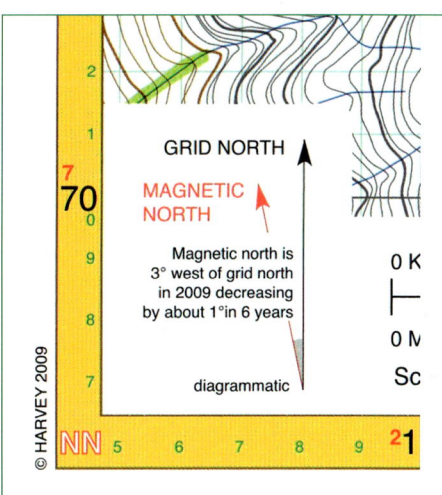

FIGURE 1.20 MAP MARGIN INFORMATION DETAILING THE RELATIONSHIP BETWEEN MAGNETIC & GRID NORTH

1.5.6 Magnetic variation

Magnetic variation sometimes known as magnetic declination varies both from place to place and with the passage of time. In 2011 as a traveller moves eastwards across Europe towards Russia, for example, the magnetic variation differs from 3° West in Lisbon, Portugal (western seaboard) to 10° East in Moscow meaning if bearings are adjusted with the same variation (3° West) throughout the trip the error will increase as they move further East.

Complex fluid motion in the outer core of the earth (the molten metallic region that lies from 2800 to 5000km below the earth's surface) causes the magnetic field to change slowly with time. This change is known as secular variation. Because secular variation is unpredictable corrections given on most maps cannot be applied reliably, particularly if the map is outdated. Therefore, if time is to be spent using bearings en route the magnetic variation for the region will need to be investigated. While information regarding magnetic variation can be found on the Internet (*www.magnetic-declination.com*), a GPS unit can automatically calculate this for your current position.

Information regarding magnetic variation for a particular region is usually found in the margins of the map or written in the key as in the case of OS and Harvey maps. In Britain in 2011 the variation is about one degree greater on the east coast compared to the west. However this will gradually decrease in significance over the next decade. Despite being relatively small in the UK it should still be taken into account when transferring between bearings on the ground and on the map. There are various popular mnemonics which help the navigator to remember how to make this adjustment, although these will probably become redundant in 2015 when magnetic north is predicted to move east of Grid North.

The simplest reminder is to add when getting bigger (from the map to the ground) and subtract when getting smaller. Another popular reminder is to use the following ditty:

Add for Mag, Get rid for Grid

At first glance it would appear that the chore of converting between grid and Magnetic North would be eliminated if maps were drawn in relation to Magnetic rather than Grid North. This is not possible because of the variation as we travel from west to east, which would result in grid lines converging and becoming distorted. In addition, maps would become redundant after a year or two because of the movement of Magnetic North. However orienteering maps are drawn in relation to Magnetic North based on the assumption that they will be redrawn and reprinted on a regular basis.

1.6 GPS and altimeters

It is worth mentioning these two items of equipment at this point even though they are dealt with in greater detail in the coming chapters. Used correctly both GPS and altimeters can provide a wealth of additional information to the navigator. It should be remembered that these items are not a substitute for good map and compass skills. Used well and integrated with these skills GPS devices and altimeters can be a great aid to navigation. *Refer to **Section 4.9 Using Altimeters** on page 97 and **Part V GPS** on page 103 for more detailed information on their use.*

1.7 Torches

In darkness, the map is useless if it cannot be seen. A reliable torch should therefore be regarded as indispensable for night navigation and carried as a contingency whenever there is a possibility of unexpected delay. When navigating with map and compass in the hand, a head torch is particularly useful as it allows one hand to be kept free. For a walking leader a head-torch is really the only practical choice. Selecting a particular model is a compromise between weight and practicality. Tiny lights featuring LED bulbs weigh next to nothing and are perfectly adequate for map reading. In mountain terrain with rocky bluffs, a more powerful torch will allow safer route-finding when weaving through obstacles. At the other end of the scale, halogen bulbs emit exceptionally bright light but rapidly drain batteries so lots of spares will be needed. It is important that the torch is adequately waterproof to cope with heavy rainfall. A red filter over the torch can help to preserve night vision while navigating in the dark. However in practice, with some maps it can be difficult to pick the contour

Darkness is often used as a way of training people for navigating in poor visibility. Learning to navigate in darkness is more about developing strategies using existing skills as opposed to learning any new information. Having the confidence to use these skills and strategies is fundamental to successful navigation in these conditions. Consider carefully the environment when planning a night exercise; make sure this is suitable for the aims and objectives of the session. In darkness shape and perspective can play tricks on the eye, making features seem bigger and farther away. Edges and drops can seem like gaping abysses and for many people just being out at night can be a learning experience without having to navigate. Plan short sessions that keep the group engaged and focused. Ensure group members are suitably equipped and that they have an appropriate torch, preferably a head torch. As well as carrying spare batteries consider a spare torch. If head torches are being used make sure they are worn in such a way that the beam shines straight ahead. If the beam shines to one

side people may trend in this direction when trying to follow a bearing. If conditions are particularly poor with darkness and mist, the torch beam may struggle to penetrate the cloud. By holding the torch at waist level in these conditions the beam will tend to penetrate further; similar to the dipped beam on car headlights when driving in fog. Initially the teaching will be done in groups; however once confidence and experience builds students should be given the opportunity to work in pairs or independently. Many of the exercises shown for use in daylight can be adapted to work in darkness.

FIGURE 1.21   A WELL PREPARED GROUP ON A NIGHT NAVIGATION EXERCISE   Photo: www.pyb.co.uk

FIGURE 1.22   USING ENLARGED MAP, AND MAGNIFIYING GLASS ON COMPASS

FIGURE 1.23   HAVING THE MAP FOLDED MAKES IT EASIER TO 'THUMB' AND QUICKLY CHECK YOUR LOCATION

detail and any other features marked with brown/red lines. Military maps are often produced using ink that can be seen clearly when using red light. On all but the most clear of nights it is advisable to use a torch to find your way over the terrain in the dark so as to avoid any potential hazards.

1.8 Eyesight and vision considerations

Having eyesight or vision problems is not a barrier to navigation; however it may require the development of a slightly different strategy and some additional items of equipment. Digital mapping software can allow for maps to be printed at a variety of scales meaning a 1:25,000 map could be printed at a scale of 1:10,000, and may be laminated, making it much easier to see the detail. A large magnifying glass can be useful and there are many products available specifically made for map reading that are light and easy to use; some even have built in lights. Glasses can present a problem when the weather is poor, often misting up or requiring constant wiping to remove water. A jacket with a shaped wired hood can help prevent the worst of the conditions effecting vision, as can a peaked cap. Various windscreen products that reduce fogging

and increase water repellence can reduce the amount of wiping required. Many manufacturers of goggles now offer the option of fitting prescription lenses to their products. Although they often need wiping in heavy rain a good pair of goggles will have anti-fogging properties. Goggles designed for mountain biking that can be fitted with appropriate lenses offer a solution that are not too dissimilar to ordinary glasses, indeed some products are intended to be worn over prescription glasses. Bifocal lenses or wearing a contact lens in just one eye can help with transferring information from the map to the ground and vice-versa however they do take some getting used to at first, particularly if wearing them while walking. An alternative to these are glasses used for orienteering that have small shaped lenses designed so that it is possible to see over the top of them when looking at the ground. Marking the map with a pen or pencil will help to avoid losing your place and make it easier to locate the last known point when refocusing on the map. A similar method commonly used by orienteers is 'thumbing the map'. By folding the map and marking your position using a thumb as you move along the ground you should move your thumb to your new position on the map. It is usual to move your thumb to a new position at a 'check point' such as a path junction or some other obvious feature where you might stop or slow down so as to check your location.

Photo: www.pyb.co.uk

Part II

Navigation Techniques

2.1 Relating the map and the land to each other

One of the fundamental skills in map reading is transferring information gleaned from the ground to the map and vice versa. The most important and reliable information for the walker is provided by the contours, which allow the skilled mapreader to build a mental picture of a three-dimensional landscape. Other features can then be superimposed on top of this from the additional signs and symbols on the map. It should be remembered that these other features might change over time; paths or even streams re-route themselves. Field boundaries shown on larger scale maps can be a useful aid to navigation, but are sometimes confusing as they may no longer be visible at ground level, as walls crumble or have been plundered for new constructions.

Although maps are remarkably accurate, minor errors occasionally occur – the most common is swapping blue and black inks, for instance showing a stream as a wall or vice versa. In recent years many new fences have been constructed on British moorland and mountains, often after the most recent surveys and latest map editions. Because a map is only a pictorial representation of a section of ground it is open to interpretation and a certain amount of artistic licence when it comes to the positioning of symbols during its production. A good example of this is outcrop markings on mountain slopes. In rocky terrain where there are numerous outcrops it becomes almost impossible to mark each crag accurately. Often the best approach is to litter that particular area with such symbols to give an overall impression of the nature of the terrain. On OS maps at 1:50,000 it can sometimes be difficult to show the subtleties in the contour markings, requiring the user to be even more vigilant in complex ground.

2.1.1 Setting the map

The map is a plan view to scale of an area of ground and as such it should be possible to turn and hold the map so that the features seen around you are in their correct and relative positions on the map. This is known as setting or orientating the map. This is the most fundamental navigation skill and is often an integral part of any navigational task, in particular those that involve relating ground to map or vice versa. A good habit to adopt is to set the map before commencing any task and, if walking with the map, try to keep it orientated as you move. As the ground is encountered the navigator can observe the features passed and relate them to the map. By constantly comparing features on the map with those on the ground it should be possible to notice and counteract any errors before they become significant.

FIGURE 2.01   WALKING WITH THE MAP SET

2.1.2 Setting the map using a compass

It is possible to set a map quickly using a compass. This is achieved by placing the compass on the map and rotating them together until the needle is parallel to the vertical grid lines.

A correctly set map will have its northern edge pointing north. This technique is particularly useful in poor visibility or for relocating, when it can be difficult to identify features. Strictly speaking magnetic variation should be accounted

 3 NOTES FOR INSTRUCTORS **Setting the map**

Photo: Karl Midlane

As this is one of the fundamental navigation skills, it is important to introduce the concept of why and how to set a map at an early stage. Good use of exercises and verbal input when introducing these skills will help to establish understanding. A simple explanation as to the basic principle might work as follows: 'Position the map so that all the features are lined up with your own location as the central point. What is in front of you on the ground will be in front of you on the map; what is to your left on the ground will also be to your left on the map and so on. The writing on the map may be upside down or sideways. However having the map set is far more useful in relating the map to the ground than being able to read the writing. Think of the map as the last piece of a much bigger jigsaw puzzle; it will complete the puzzle and make sense with its surroundings if it is positioned in a certain way.'

Exercise

Classroom Maps: as a simple start point using a blank sheet of paper draw a bird's eye view (map!) of a room. Place letters on each wall to show North, South, East and West. Group members

can then annotate their drawn maps with these points and set the map accordingly. Exercises that involve moving around the room in different directions will allow people to practise a variety of basic skills including setting the map. Encourage them to 'drive their maps' turning them as they move in order to keep them set to the letters on the wall.

3 X 3: this simple exercise can be conducted anywhere with the aid of nine markers and some blank paper. Draw a 3 x 3 grid as shown above (these could be prepared beforehand and laminated to preserve for future use). Using appropriate markers lay out this grid on the ground to roughly the size of a tennis court. A route between various markers can then be plotted on the drawn grid (map) using straight lines and arrows to link points and indicate direction. People are then asked to navigate this route while keeping the 'map set' first at slow speed but then faster to give more challenge. Individuals can then design their own courses and swap maps.

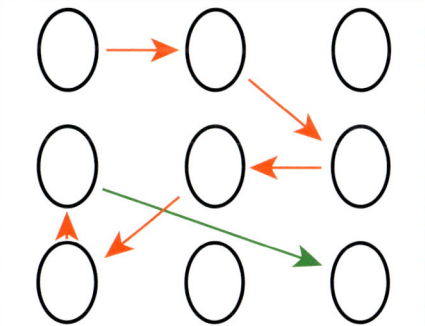

After completing a number of the courses with the maps held set, it is worth trying to complete a course by not holding the map set. This often fails and highlights the importance of setting the map.

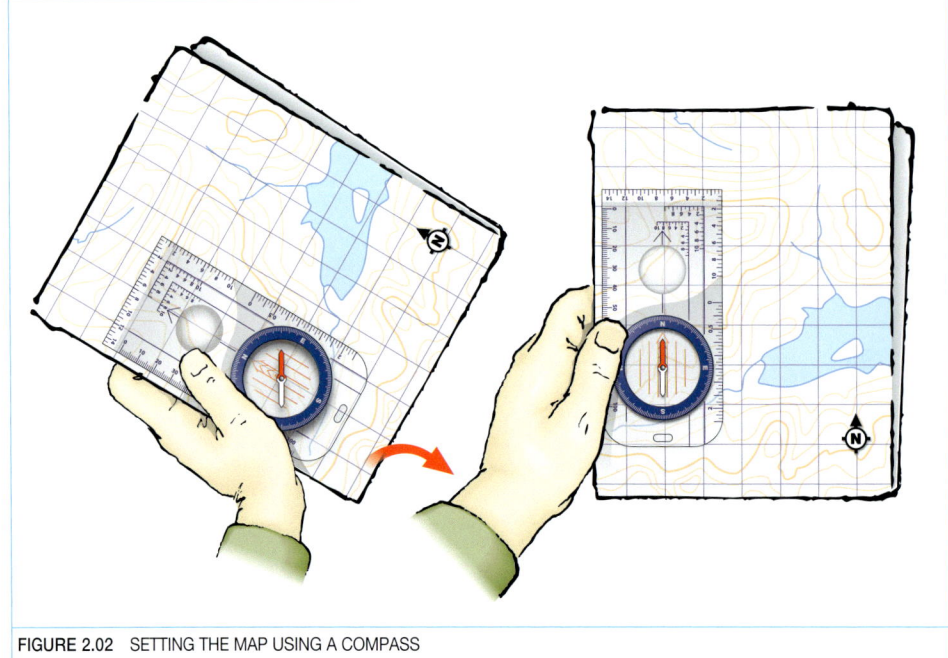

FIGURE 2.02 SETTING THE MAP USING A COMPASS

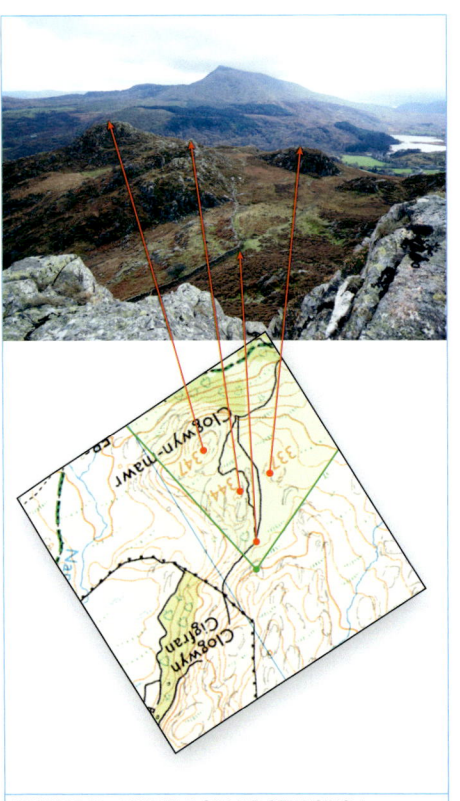

FIGURE 2.03 EXAMPLE OF MAP SET USING A
COMBINATION OF **SPOT** AND **LINEAR** FEATURES

for when using a compass to set the map, however in the UK because the variation is so small at present it can be ignored. When using foreign maps in regions where the magnetic variation is greater this is more of an issue and as a result the variation will need to be considered if the map is to be set accurately.

2.1.3 Setting the map using features

The alternative method is to use the features you may be able to see around you. The thumb can be placed beside the present position and the map rotated until the surrounding features line up with their counterparts on the ground. The best features to use for this are linear features such as roads, paths, streams, edges of woodland, boundaries or anything that runs more-or-less in a straight line. By turning the map so that the feature on the ground is parallel with its counterpart on the map it is possible to set the map with a good degree of accuracy. One pitfall to look out for might be that the map is 180° out. Using more than one linear feature or comparing with other features will often highlight and correct this mistake.

FIGURE 2.04 SETTING THE MAP USING FEATURES

2.2 Gathering information

Good observation skills are an important tool for any navigator. The ability to observe your surroundings and sense what the terrain is doing as you walk provides an endless stream of information that can be used to help confirm position and direction. Being able to pick out the detail in the landscape and relate this to the map and vice versa is an essential skill to try and fine tune. The same can be said for interpreting the terrain as you move; is it ascending or descending? Is it rising to the right or dropping away to the left? As you move your senses are bombarded with information that could be used to good effect when navigating. Developing an awareness of distance and size can help to relate the ground to the map more accurately. Examples from everyday life can be used to assist with this process:

- an average house is approximately 10 metres high, the equivalent of a 10 metre contour interval;
- 25 metres is a standard length for a tennis court and a common length for a swimming pool;
- a football pitch or running track could serve as a good gauge for 100 metres (*see Figure 2.05*).

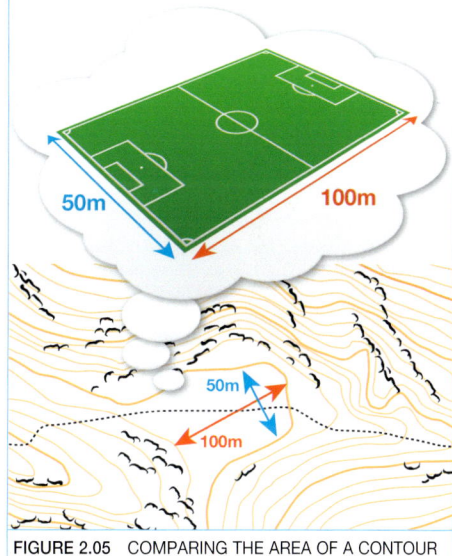

FIGURE 2.05 COMPARING THE AREA OF A CONTOUR FEATURE TO A KNOWN EXAMPLE OF SOMETHING WITH THE SAME AREA, IN THIS CASE A FOOTBALL PITCH

Using these examples it is possible to judge distances between features or their size more accurately. These skills are particularly useful when having to distinguish between various features in complex terrain.

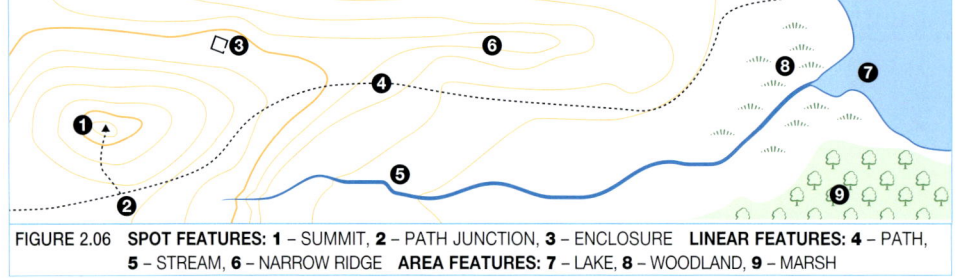

FIGURE 2.06   **SPOT FEATURES: 1** – SUMMIT, **2** – PATH JUNCTION, **3** – ENCLOSURE   **LINEAR FEATURES: 4** – PATH,
5 – STREAM, **6** – NARROW RIDGE   **AREA FEATURES: 7** – LAKE, **8** – WOODLAND, **9** – MARSH

High vantage points that look down on the landscape are excellent places from which to develop an understanding of the relationship between the map and the ground. Working with a variety of maps and scales also helps to build the ability to visualise the land and the cartographer's attempts to depict it in on a flat sheet.

Features we may observe as we move can be categorised as three types.

1 **Spot**
Single point features, for example house, boulder or cairn. These features pinpoint a particular location.

2 **Linear**
Anything elongated but narrow, for example a fence, stream, path, road or narrow ridge.

3 **Area**
These are features that do not necessarily have sharp edges, for example woodland, slopes or marsh.

When navigating it is all too easy to make the features on the ground match where you actually want to be on the map but the competent navigator learns to use every new piece of information to challenge the assumption that everything is OK. A useful technique when trying to confirm a particular location is to seek out five features that support the hypothesis that it is a certain place on the map (*see **Section 2.11 Relocation**, page 59 for further information*).

2.3 Contour interpretation

Contour lines are the conventional symbols used to indicate height. Being able to visualise the shape of the landscape by looking at the contour lines on a map is a very useful skill that can be developed with practice and experience. In remote and complex terrain where there is an absence of feature it is often only contour information that provides clues to our location. Since natural features don't change as quickly or easily as their man-made counterparts, being able to use them to navigate is essential. Creating a mental picture of a 3-dimensional landscape from a 2-dimensional map can be difficult initially; however understanding basic principles and applying simple knowledge will lead to improvement and refinement of these skills.

2.3.1 The basics
Understanding the basic principles provides a good starting point when trying to create a mental picture of the landscape from contour information.

Index contour lines are labelled with a number showing their height above sea level. The top of the figures are orientated pointing uphill, so by finding one of these figures it is possible to work out which is uphill and which is downhill.

The closer together the contour lines are the steeper the slope and the further apart they are the flatter the ground. This is all relative; however knowing this information allows for better understanding of shape and with practice it is possible to determine rough angles of slopes based on contour information alone. The experience gained from walking up and down slopes and comparing them to the contour information on the map will allow for more informed decisions about whether or not slopes confronted in the future are passable. This experience can also provide useful information during the planning stage.

Recognising the basic slope shapes from the map seems straightforward; however in practice the ground is rarely that uniform and the majority

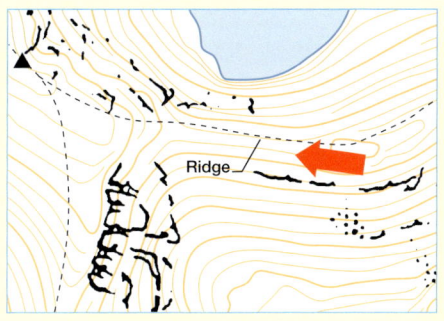

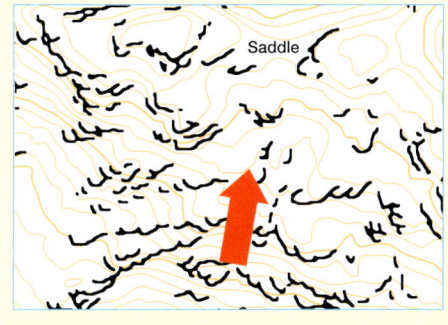

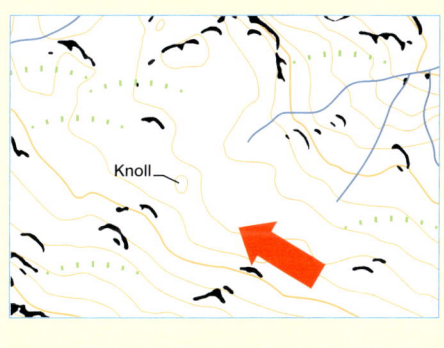

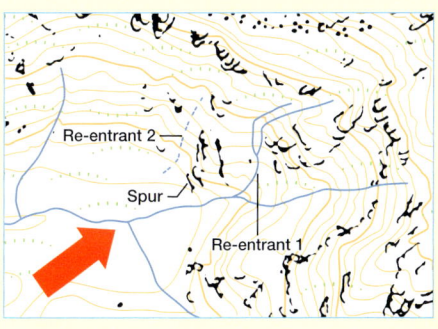

1:50,000 Thick contour lines per 1cm on map	Slope Angle	1:25,000 Thick contour lines per 1cm on map
—1cm—		—1cm—
2	10°	1
2.6	15°	1.3
3.5	20°	1.8
4.3	25°	2.2
6	30°	3
7	35°	3.5
8	40°	4
10	45°	5
12	50°	6
13	55°	7
16	60°	8
—1cm—		—1cm—

FIGURE 2.07 RECOGNISING SLOPE ANGLE FROM CONTOUR SPACING

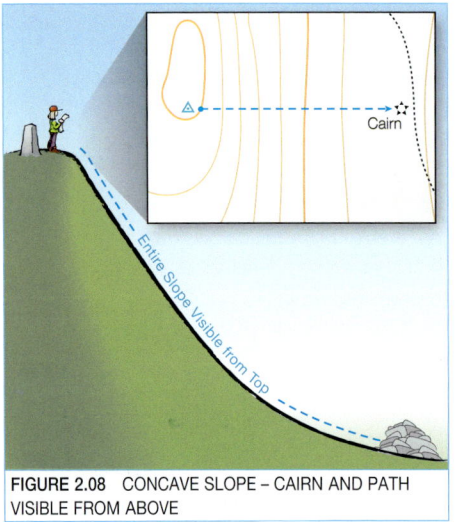

FIGURE 2.08 CONCAVE SLOPE – CAIRN AND PATH VISIBLE FROM ABOVE

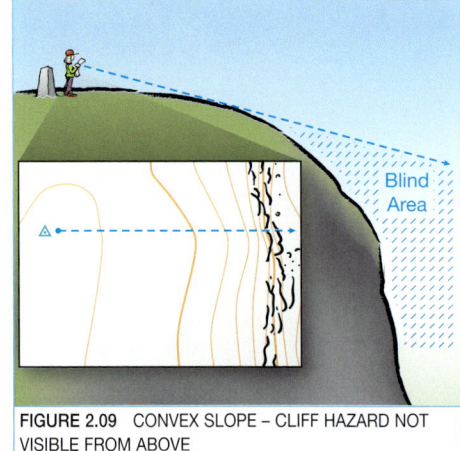

FIGURE 2.09 CONVEX SLOPE – CLIFF HAZARD NOT VISIBLE FROM ABOVE

of slopes will be *composite*, that is, made up of two or three of the basic types (*see Figure 2.10*).

As well as basic slope shapes, contour lines depict an array of other topographical features that can be seen in the landscape. Learning to recognise such features as *valleys*, *spurs*, *tops*, *ridges* and *knolls* on both the map and the ground will make contour interpretation easier.

Practical tips

Practice and experience are essential to becoming more proficient with contour interpretation. The following tips can be used to improve these skills when navigating.

- Always orientate the map before trying to interpret the contour lines. It will make more sense when relating map to ground and vice versa.
- When interpreting the contours for a particular navigation leg, place the line on the compass baseplate on the map linking up your location and destination (as when taking a bearing) and look along the line in the direction of travel. It should then be possible to look at the contour spacing along this line and picture the shape of the ground to be crossed. The more obvious changes in slope angle can be used as tick off features. Features can also be identified on the right or left side of the line and will appear on the same side on the ground as you travel. However, there is no point in interpreting the contours any further than the limit of visibility either side of your line of travel.
- Use the magnifying glass on the compass to pick out the contour detail underneath other markings. This is particularly useful when

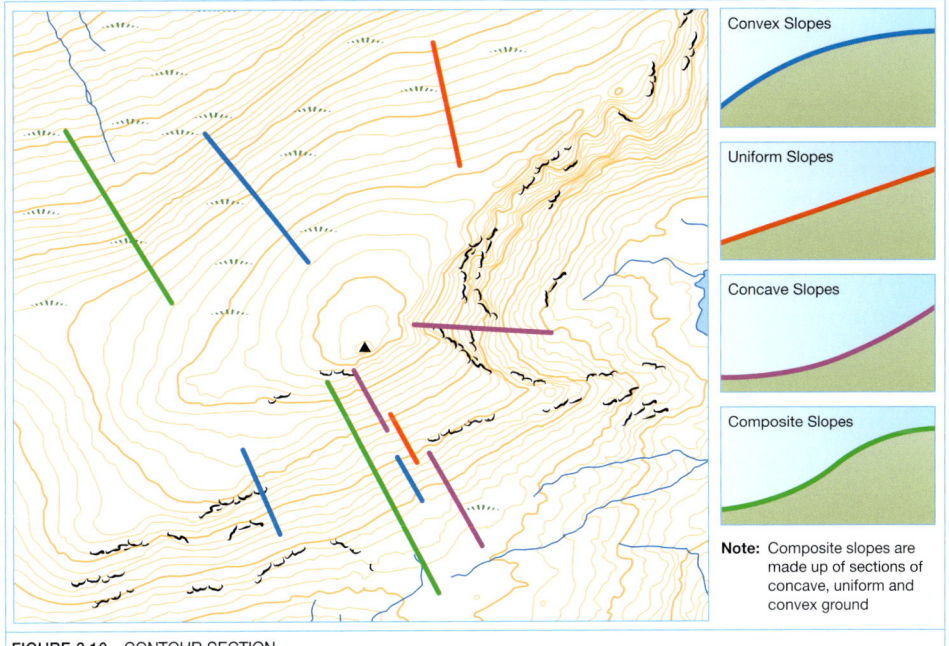

FIGURE 2.10 CONTOUR SECTION

there are a lot of outcrop markings obscuring the contour lines. (Harvey maps remove a lot of these outcrop markings by using a grey contour line to signify rocky ground.)

- If possible try to gain height above your location and look down onto the ground. This will feel like looking at an aerial photograph and can sometimes make it easier to see land shapes and picture contour lines.

- Consider measuring contour features to give an idea of scale and how big they might be on the ground. As an example if you measure a ring contour to be 2mm across on 1:25,000 map you will be looking for a feature that is 50m across on the ground.

- Practise using contours by using 1:10,000 orienteering maps with 5m contours. The features will be more consistently and accurately marked (because they have been systematically surveyed) than on the smaller scale maps.

One of the easiest ways to convert contour lines into a mental picture is to imagine the lines as high tide marks left by the sea. As the water level drops it leaves a '*shoreline*' every 5 or 10 metres on the landscape. This analogy can often be used when trying to interpret the ground

before consulting the map and is particularly useful when relocating (*see **Section 2.11 Relocation**, page 59*). As an example, if trying to identify the shape of the ground around a particular location, imagine standing on the shore with water lapping at your feet. Remember that water fills to a level. It should now be possible to trace out the shore-line left and right of your position. Sometimes drawing this information on paper can help to visualise the contour line more clearly. This information can then be transferred to the map.

2.3.2 Reading between the lines

It's worth bearing in mind that a contour line will only show the shape of the ground at that particular height. Smaller features may be missed by falling within the contour interval. If a feature is 9 metres higher than the previous contour line it may not appear on a map with contour lines at 10 metre intervals. This can be surprising when viewing the actual landscape as it may contain features you were not expecting to see. In some situations the terrain may undulate dramatically although this may not be shown on the map. With experience of the terrain you are walking through it is sometimes possible to 'read between the lines.' Indications on the ground around a current

Interpreting contours

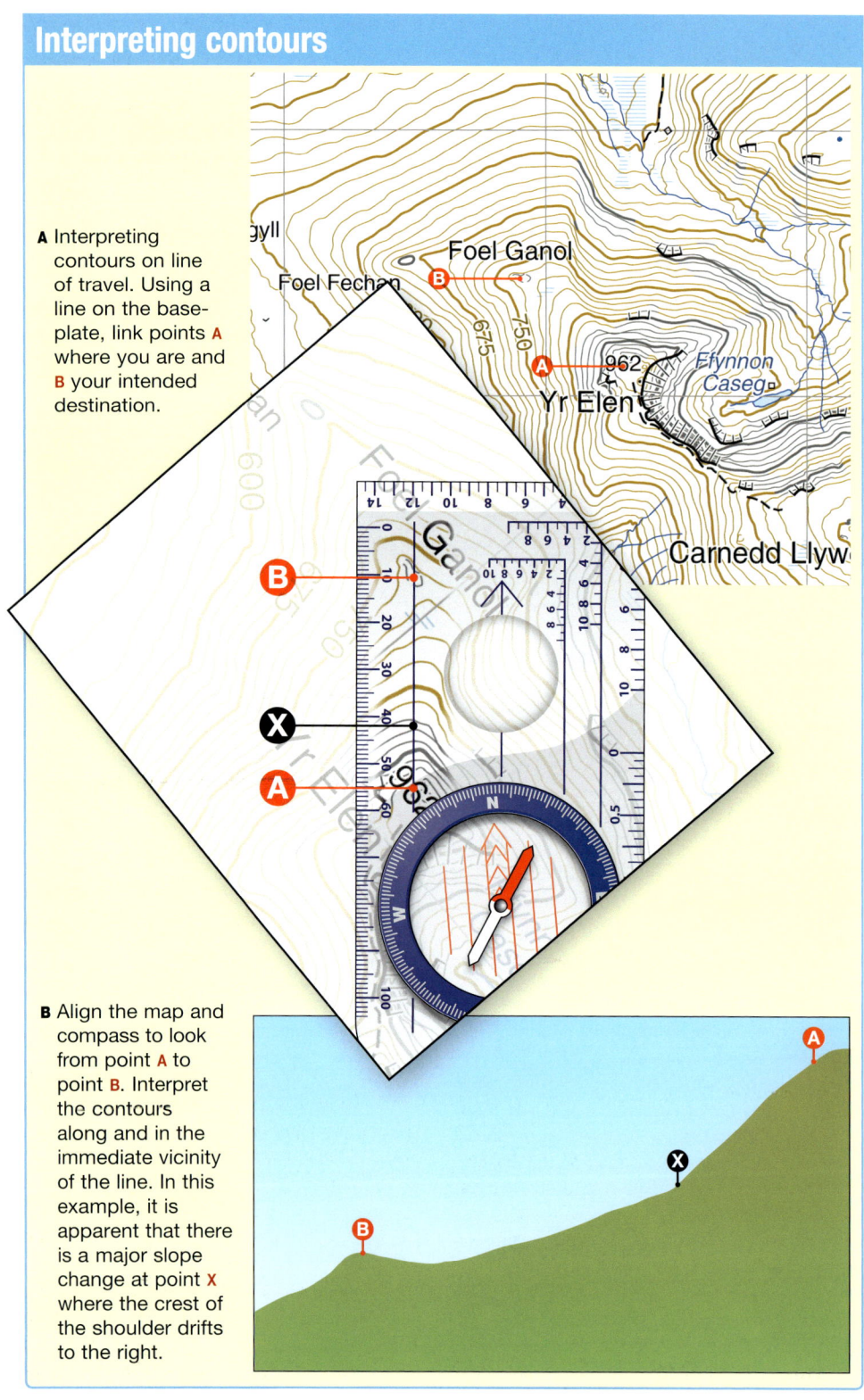

A Interpreting contours on line of travel. Using a line on the base-plate, link points **A** where you are and **B** your intended destination.

B Align the map and compass to look from point **A** to point **B**. Interpret the contours along and in the immediate vicinity of the line. In this example, it is apparent that there is a major slope change at point **X** where the crest of the shoulder drifts to the right.

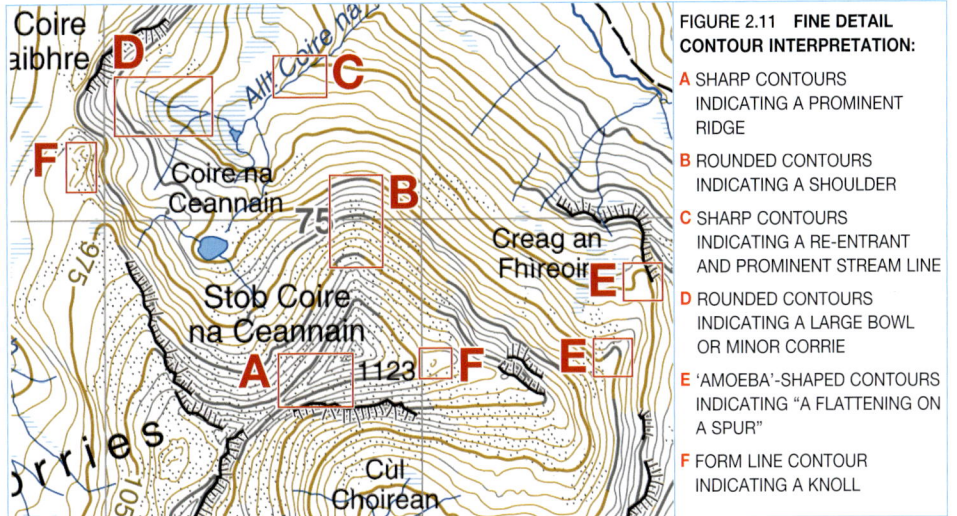

FIGURE 2.11 **FINE DETAIL CONTOUR INTERPRETATION:**

A SHARP CONTOURS INDICATING A PROMINENT RIDGE

B ROUNDED CONTOURS INDICATING A SHOULDER

C SHARP CONTOURS INDICATING A RE-ENTRANT AND PROMINENT STREAM LINE

D ROUNDED CONTOURS INDICATING A LARGE BOWL OR MINOR CORRIE

E 'AMOEBA'-SHAPED CONTOURS INDICATING "A FLATTENING ON A SPUR"

F FORM LINE CONTOUR INDICATING A KNOLL

location may provide clues that the ground ahead might be more complex than indicated by the map. Often the problem arises when the horizontal spacing between contour lines is large. Generally when the ground is steep there is less likelihood of there being features that do not appear on the map. Plateau areas, gentle slopes and undulating ridges provide more scope for the land to rise and fall within a contour interval. This problem can be exacerbated when using a map with a greater contour interval. Harvey maps use a 15 metre contour interval; although they use a *form line* to mark significant features that fall between contour lines, that is a dotted interim contour line (*see Figure 1.10, page 12*).

2.4 Following linear features

Many features can be used as **handrails**. These can be very easy to follow, or may require great skill, particularly in poor visibility. Suitable linear features include fences and walls, overhead cables or pipelines, streams, escarpments and sometimes landforms such as ridges or valleys. Sometimes a skilled navigator will use a pen to draw a line on the map between two points or use contour lines (nothing on the ground) as handrails to 'simplify' the navigation! Using this technique provides the navigator with a way of quickly identifying tick-off features and following them to a destination even though the handrail is

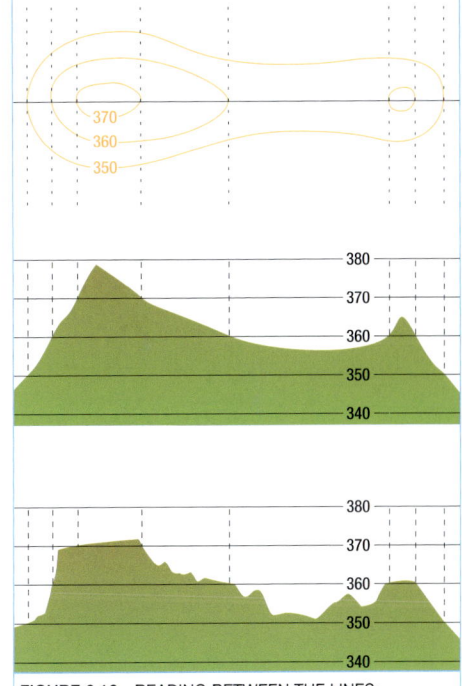

FIGURE 2.12 READING BETWEEN THE LINES: TWO DIFFERENT BUT EQUALLY POSSIBLE INTERPRETATIONS OF THE SAME MAP

not visible on the ground. With good visibility, popular paths are often easy to see, because of the footprints, erosion or even their man-made surface. In these conditions, navigation along handrails consists mainly of keeping track of the direction and distance travelled. Along the way,

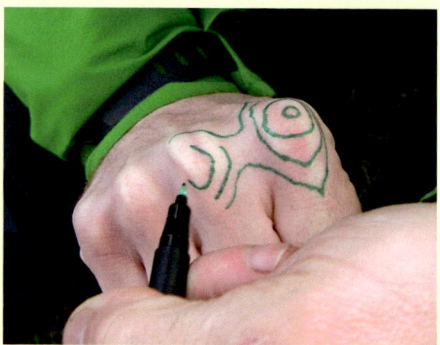

Using knuckles and a pen to help illustrate the basic contour principles

Introducing and developing contour interpretation skills can be a challenging aspect of teaching navigation. A carefully planned progressive approach is required for people to understand how to use all forms of contour information. A good starting point is to define what contour lines signify and the nature of contour interval. The basic principles of uphill, downhill and steepness need to be mastered before progressing onto considering relief and general landforms. As people develop their understanding and ability to use contour information the terrain can be changed to offer more subtle landforms. Using contours and in particular more subtle contour information is a conceptual process that may prove difficult for some people. Giving people simple analogies that link to existing knowledge can break down some of the barriers to learning. A good example of this is to use the shoreline analogy shown in section. Classroom sessions can help to introduce and reinforce these skills. Use of modelling exercises using sand or play dough can be a good fun way to introduce various concepts. The 3D and 'fly-through' facility on most digital mapping software products provides a very powerful resource to help teach these skills. A more realistic approach is to compare a map with photographs or slides of various locations. Practice is the key to improvement and various exercises focused on these skills will help to enhance the learning.

Exercises

Contour walk: simply use a contour line as an imaginary footpath: students should consider whether the path moves to the left or right as they move along.

Contour map: contour maps of small areas can be produced from mapping software by enlarging areas where there are only contour lines present. These maps can then be used for navigation and various other exercises.

Draw the contour: give group members a blank sheet of paper (laminated works well) and ask them to draw the contour line they are standing on. They can then repeat the process for the contour line below and the one above. This will construct a simple contour map of an area that can then be used to navigate with. People can mark points on these maps for other individuals to walk to.

Drawing a contour map of a small section of ground

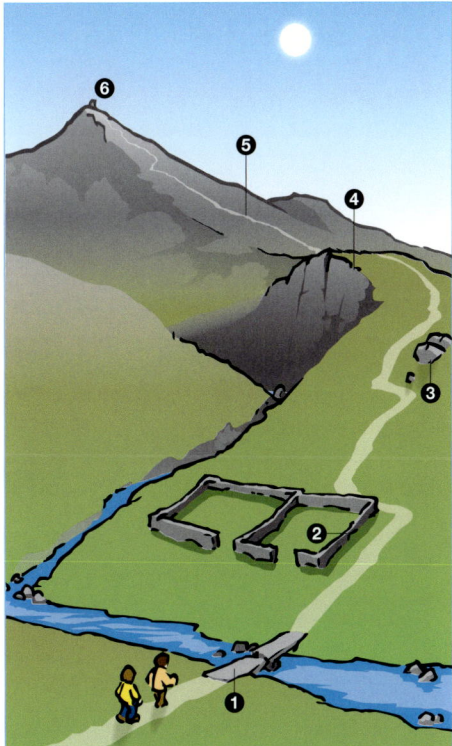

FIGURE 2.13 HANDRAILS AND TICK FEATURES CROSS THE BRIDGE *(1. TICK)*, THEN FOLLOW THE EDGE OF THE ENCLOSURE *(2. HANDRAIL)*, STRIKE OUT FOR THE BOULDERS *(3. TICK)* AND FOLLOW THE TOP OF THE ESCARPMENT *(4. HANDRAIL)*. ASCEND THE RIDGE *(5. HANDRAIL)* TO REACH THE TRIG POINT ON THE SUMMIT *(6. TICK)*.

5 Handrails

Handrail navigation is a basic skill that can be introduced at an early stage. By encouraging people to suggest simple ways of navigating they will soon appreciate the value of using such features. When introducing these skills for the first time, choose an area with obvious handrails; roads, paths and boundaries. As a person progresses the handrails can become more subtle; streams, ridges, re-entrants and contour lines (contouring).

Exercise

Handrail course: select a small area with lots of obvious linear features (paths, tracks, boundaries, etc). Allow students to plot a route following these handrails from a start point to a finish point (this could be the same place). If the environment is safe it may be possible for group members to navigate around the course independently. If people are encouraged to keep the map set as they move around the course it will help to consolidate these skills. Introducing handrails can also provide the opportunity to begin teaching navigational strategies.

a variety of features are likely to be passed, allowing navigators to re-affirm their position continually while travelling. These **tick-off** features can be likened to motorway junctions on a car journey. As long as the car stays on the motorway, junctions will always be passed in the right order. This everyday analogy can be easily applied to navigating in the mountains. **Tick-off** features are used almost subconsciously by good navigators, so that ticking off a wall, or a change in slope angle, or vegetation change becomes almost second nature. On distinct slopes, it is often possible to use a contour line as a handrail, by taking care to maintain the same height. Once again subtle changes in the contour line can be used as a tick-off feature, for example where it intersects with a stream or bulges around a spur. Linear features can become indistinct in places or may have even been moved since the map was

made, so it is important to continually assess the situation. When following a linear feature it is sometimes possible to overshoot the destination, point particularly in poor weather or if the handrail is indistinct. Having a **catching feature** *(see Figure 2.14 on page 36)*. in place will allow the navigator to recognise they have overshot the target and prevent them going any further.

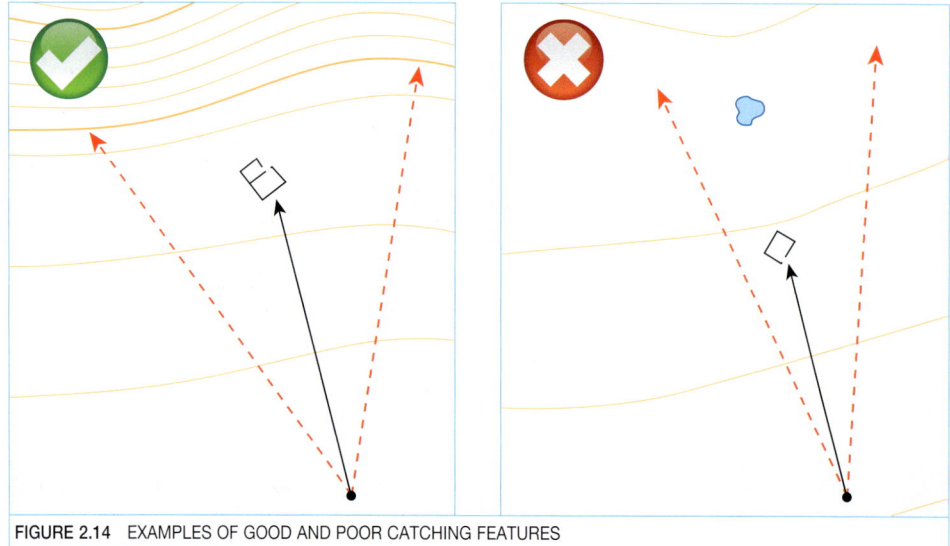

FIGURE 2.14 EXAMPLES OF GOOD AND POOR CATCHING FEATURES

Catching features are extremely important to prevent the probability of becoming lost when the destination has been missed. Selection of these features should form an inherent part of the planning process for every navigational leg (*see Section 2.10 Navigational strategy, page 53*).

The choice of a catching feature needs to be considered carefully. Ideally it will be an obvious linear feature running perpendicular to your line of travel. This way no matter how far you deviate from your intended course you will always stumble across the catching feature. Once on the catching feature you will have a better idea of your location and can then plan how to get to the intended destination. Some more subtle catching features may have to be considered. Changes in slope angle work very well as these are easy to see but can also be felt as the ground changes under your feet.

2.5 Distance judgement

In difficult conditions or in featureless terrain, observing features is often not enough to confirm a particular location. Keeping track of distance covered becomes increasingly important, whether following a path or a bearing. Techniques for estimating distance are useful at all times, but become crucial in poor visibility when otherwise identifiable features are obscured.

There are various methods of estimating distance, enabling an experienced navigator to achieve a high degree of accuracy (plus or minus ten per cent of the actual figure on most terrain). As with all navigational techniques, this information should be used in conjunction with other observed information.

2.5.1 Measuring distance

Being able to measure distance from the map allows for the calculation of how long a navigational leg or series of legs may take. It is an integral part of the planning process if timings are to be calculated to ascertain whether or not a journey is feasible in the allotted time. Conventionally measured distances are stated in the metric system rather than in yards and miles. Various tools can be used to measure distances ranging from a piece of string through to a specific map measurer or *opisometer* (*see Figure 2.17, page 38*). For planning purposes simply counting up the grid squares will give a quick rough estimate of the distance and help you decide whether the route is an appropriate length for the group you are walking with.

On the hill the most convenient method to measure map distance is to use the *romer scale* found on the base plate of some compasses. This is particularly useful when the distance is less than 1km, although separate romers can be purchased which can measure greater distances. When using a romer it is possible to measure

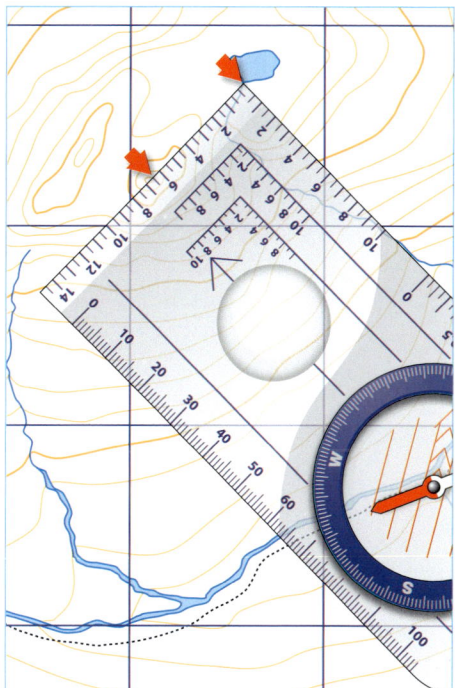

FIGURE 2.15 USING THE ROMER SCALE TO MEASURE BETWEEN TWO POINTS. IN THIS EXAMPLE THE DISTANCE MEASURED IS 650 METERS

2.6 Timing

Timing is a useful way of measuring distances travelled over the ground. By estimating your speed it is possible to use a distance measured from the map and calculate how long it will take to arrive at a chosen destination. Using modern variations of the formula published by W.H. Naismith in 1892 it is possible to calculate the time required for a journey and with skilful application the distance travelled can be estimated reasonably accurately.

> **Naismith's formula suggests:**
> **Average party will walk at 4kph and ascend at a rate of 10m/min**

Quite simply, walkers travelling at 4 kilometres per hour would cover 1km in fifteen minutes or 100m in one and a half minutes. However, there are many factors that affect speed: **weather**, **terrain**, **fitness** and **loads**. In practice the situation is usually more complicated, as walking speeds vary considerably and will fluctuate throughout the day. Most parties walk at between 3 and 5 kilometres per hour; some groups and families achieve an overall average of only 2 kilometres per hour.

The amount of ascent during any particular day will obviously affect a party's average speed. Steeper ground, perhaps requiring the occasional use of the hands for support, will require longer than one minute per 10 metres of ascent. Heavy vegetation, boulder fields, wet rock or snow will slow even a fit party travelling with light rucksacks. From this it is possible to see that it becomes difficult to apply a rigid formula to every situation. While Naismith's formula works as a planning tool for gauging the overall timing of a mountain day, it becomes less accurate when applied to shorter navigational legs. Therefore when calculating time for a single navigation task it is important to adopt a flexible approach, taking into consideration all the variables that may affect speed. Only by doing this will it be possible to achieve a high degree of accuracy. With experience, a kinaesthetic awareness of speed evolves – heart rate, leg rhythm and ease of breathing all relate to speed of travel and angle of slope. Comparing the time taken to walk set distances at different levels of effort can assist developing this 'feeling' of speed. *Figure 2.18* is an example of a crib card showing timings for

distances down to 50m on a 1:25,000. However, for greater accuracy on any scale of map it is preferable to measure using the millimetre scale. This achieves an accuracy of 25m when using a 1:25,000 scale map. For 1:50,000-scale map 1 millimetre will equal 50m, and half a millimetre equals 25m. Estimating distance on the ground is covered in the next two sections; however accuracy can only be achieved if attention is paid to measuring distances from the map. In certain circumstances a lack of concentration while measuring could give a 50m error which could mean the difference between hitting the target or missing it. Before measuring a distance try to estimate by eye as this will give some idea of what the distance should be. If a radically different distance is measured then it will force you to re-evaluate and probably measure again. A similar system is used before taking a bearing from the map to avoid any early errors (*see Section 2.9.1 Taking a bearing, page 44*).

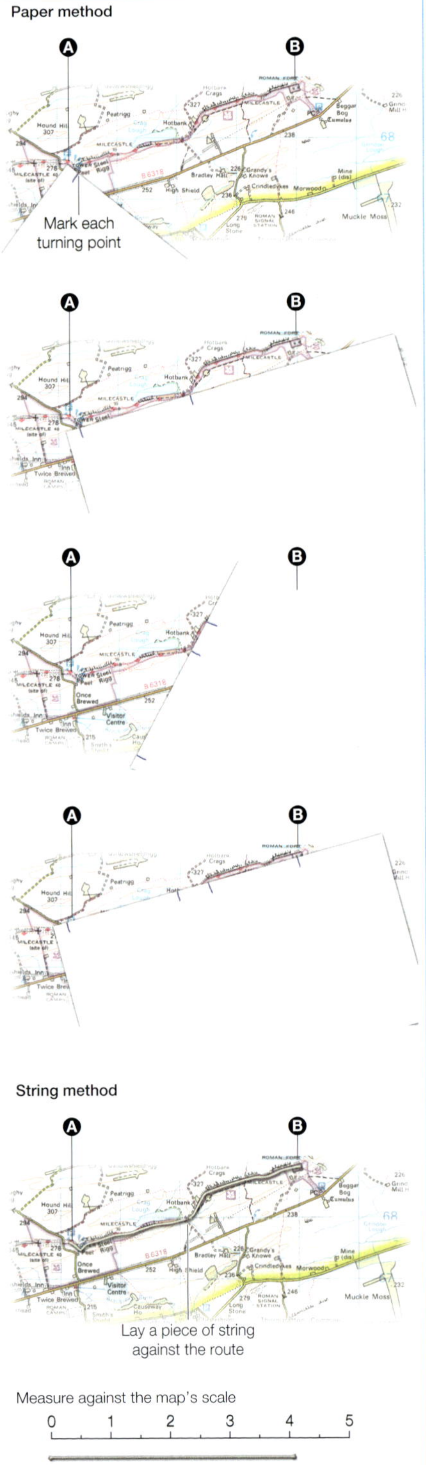

Paper method

Ⓐ Ⓑ

Mark each
turning point

Ⓐ Ⓑ

Ⓐ Ⓑ

Ⓐ Ⓑ

String method

Ⓐ Ⓑ

Lay a piece of string
against the route

Measure against the map's scale

0   1   2   3   4   5

FIGURE 2.16   MEASURING DISTANCE WITH STRING
OR PAPER

FIGURE 2.17   MAP MEASURING DEVICES

various distances at different speeds. Used by many navigators, these help to reduce the need for mental arithmetic on the hill.

2.6.1 Timing ascent

Ascent of any angle of slope will influence speed to a greater or lesser extent. Naismith's formula takes a basic horizontal travelling speed and adapts it to undulating ground by adding time for travelling uphill. Generally, a minute is added for every 10 metres of ascent. When using maps with contours at 10 metre intervals it is a simple matter of adding one minute for every contour crossed in an upward direction (*refer to Figure 2.19 for **Calculation of timing on an undulating ridge**, page 39*).

When measuring ascending slopes from the map it is worth remembering that any distance measured is only a two dimensional representation of the slope and on the ground this distance will be greater. For example, take a distance marked as 100 metres on the map; on a 45° slope you would have to walk 140 metres to cover the distance measured. It is also important to consider that it may not be possible to walk straight up a slope. Detours may have to be used to avoid hazards or zigzagging may be required to reduce the angle of the slope to make walking easier. Either way it will increase the amount of distance covered and therefore the time taken.

Adding one minute per 10 metres of height gain is not always appropriate and once again requires a flexible approach depending on the nature of the terrain. On a very steep slope it may be more accurate to use more than one minute per 10 metres and on less steep terrain it may be that 0.5 or 0.75 of a minute per 10 metres height gain is more effective.

As an alternative method, when ascending it is often possible to employ a simplified formula using only the vertical distance covered, that is the number of contours. For many walkers one and a half minutes per 10 metres of ascent with no addition for distance covered is quite effective. For a lightly laden fit group this may well be reduced to one minute per 10 metres. This system works best when calculating time for steep slopes where there is little horizontal distance being covered. Once the contour lines become more spaced and the horizontal distance increases it is more accurate to adopt the previous method.

2.6.2 Timing descent

Many people assume that downhill sections can be ignored as gravity takes over, meaning it is possible to walk at a faster speed. On gentle slopes and easy paths this may well be the case. As a rule of thumb on easy ground, one minute for every 30 metres of descent can be subtracted from any timing calculations. However, speed over a downhill section can be influenced by the same set of factors that reduce speed over an uphill section meaning it can often take longer than planned to descend a section. Steep descents may require a similar amount to be added to the total time and rocky sections can take even longer.

Timing is only effective for estimating distance if the party moves at a reasonably steady pace

Distance travelled ,metres	Speed kilometres per hour			
	5	4	3	2
1000m	12 min	15 min	20 min	30 min
900m	11 min	13½ min	18 min	27 min
800m	9½ min	12 min	16 min	24 min
700m	8½ min	10½ min	14 min	21 min
600m	7 min	9 min	12 min	18 min
500m	6 min	7½ min	10 min	15 min
400m	5 min	6 min	8 min	12 min
300m	3½ min	4½ min	6 min	9 min
200m	2½ min	3 min	4 min	6 min
100m	1 min	1½ min	2 min	3 min
50m	½ min	¾ min	1 min	1½ min

The timings have been rounded to the nearest ½ minute

FIGURE 2.18 SPEED/DISTANCE TRAVELLED CHART

and any time spent stationary should be excluded from the total. A stopwatch becomes a useful item of equipment when using timing. Used carefully

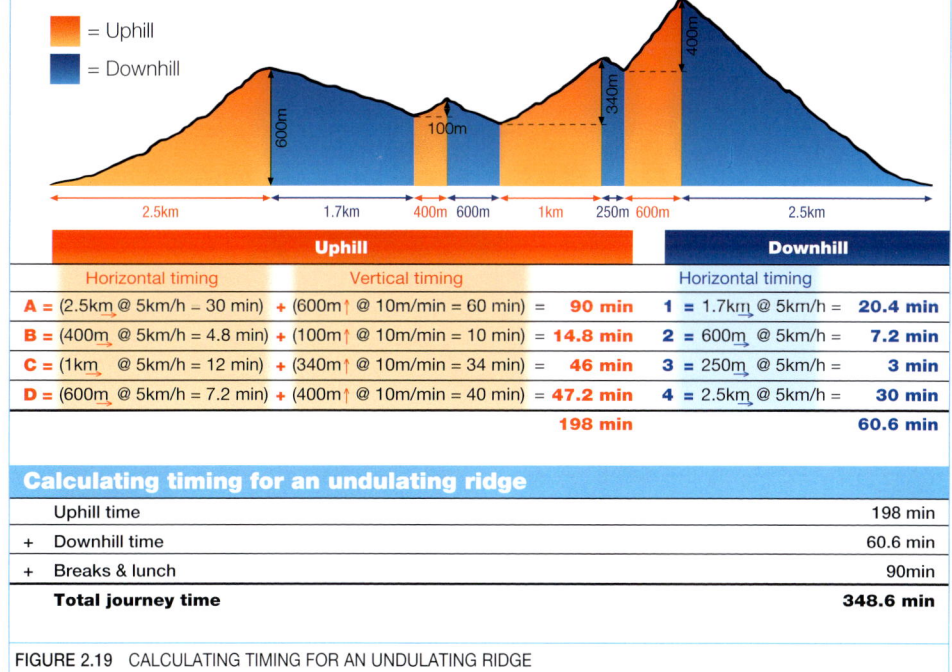

FIGURE 2.19 CALCULATING TIMING FOR AN UNDULATING RIDGE

it will allow the navigator to constantly compare estimates with the actual time taken for each section of a journey. By doing this it is then possible to make adjustments while travelling. This is particularly important if for any reason the speed changes due to unforeseen circumstances. The hardest part of timing can often be remembering to start and stop the watch! When timing, try to adopt the habit of starting your stop watch as you begin to walk and stopping it when you stop moving. In doing so you only record the time taken while you are moving (which is the calculated time) and not the time that you stopped. GPS receivers can often be setup to show a range of timing displays. (*See Section 5.8 Setting up a GPS unit on page 111.*)

2.7 Pacing

Counting steps is a well-established method of estimating distance and is known as 'pacing'. Imagine walking with the feet joined by a half metre of rope. Every time the left foot touches the ground, a distance of 1 metre will have been covered. This is the basic principle behind counting paces, although generally our stride length is not quite so conveniently sized. The length of a natural stride varies, mainly according to leg length. Everybody develops a stride over the course of their lives that is remarkably consistent for any given individual on level terrain as long as there are no obstacles and it is firm underfoot.

Normal practice is to measure 'double' paces, counting only when one designated foot touches the ground. To establish the counting rhythm, pacing should start by stepping forward with the other foot. Counting double paces simply keeps the numbers more manageable; the average for adults is about 64 double paces for 100 metres. Normally, pacing is used to count off 100 metre sections. This is a convenient unit of measurement; the same unit is used in 6-figure grid references. One hundred metres is long enough to allow a natural walking rhythm to be established, but short enough to sort out any errors without resorting to lengthy back-tracking.

There are various reminders available for keeping count of multiples of 100 metres travelled. One simple method is to pick up some pebbles and transfer them one at a time to another pocket or hand.

A useful customisation is to fix five plastic draw-cord toggles on the compass lanyard or even a separate cord attached to a rucksack shoulder

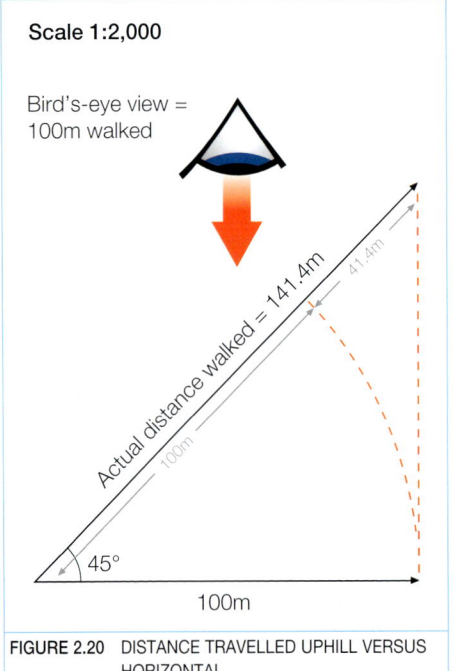

Scale 1:2,000

Bird's-eye view = 100m walked

Actual distance walked = 141.4m

100m

41.4m

45°

100m

FIGURE 2.20   DISTANCE TRAVELLED UPHILL VERSUS HORIZONTAL

FIGURE 2.21   USING COUNTING TOGGLES WHEN PACING TO HELP KEEP TRACK OF DISTANCE COVERED

strap. From a central starting point these can be slid individually to one end of the lanyard every 100 metres for the first half kilometre, and back to the other end for the next. An extra refinement is to use alternating colours to aid visual identification. If the compass lanyard is used, check that any springs in the draw-clips do not cause the compass needle to deviate from north!

Alternatively, there are various electronic pedometers available that record the number of steps taken and the distance covered. These vary in reliability and accuracy, with some prone to freezing in cold conditions.

Pacing is not an exact science since the length of stride varies with many factors. Wearing a heavy rucksack will result in shorter strides, as will terrain demanding more care in foot placement. Wet conditions, rocky ground, coarse vegetation and snow are factors that will significantly increase the amount of paces needed to cover a set distance.

Pacing is dramatically affected by slope angle. The third dimension of height results in greater distances being covered than the simple measurement on the map. This was mentioned previously in relation to timing, and similarly affects the number of paces required. Pacing uphill is further complicated by the need to take smaller steps and can also be exaggerated by rocky or eroded

ground. It is quite common to double the number of paces required to cover the 100 metres marked on the map. The ability to make suitable allowances comes with practice and requires a flexible approach to modify the number of paces totalled as the terrain changes. On long slopes it may be more appropriate and accurate to consider using timing over pacing, especially if the ground is complex requiring deviations from a straight course. In practice it is often possible to customise your pacing to a particular situation and therefore easily make it more accurate. In *Figure 2.22* the distance from the top to the ruined fence is almost identical to the distance from the ruined fence to the boulder and as it covers similar terrain you can just count your paces to the fence and then repeat the same number of paces to find the boulder.

In descent, gentle slopes may allow striding out with bigger steps, thus reducing the number of double paces required to cover 100 metres. However, complex ground will require more careful foot placements and thus extra paces. It is worth stressing that the greater the distance paced between two points, the greater the potential error. Greater accuracy can be achieved over shorter distances. As a general rule 500 metres is an optimum distance although this will be dependant on terrain and conditions.

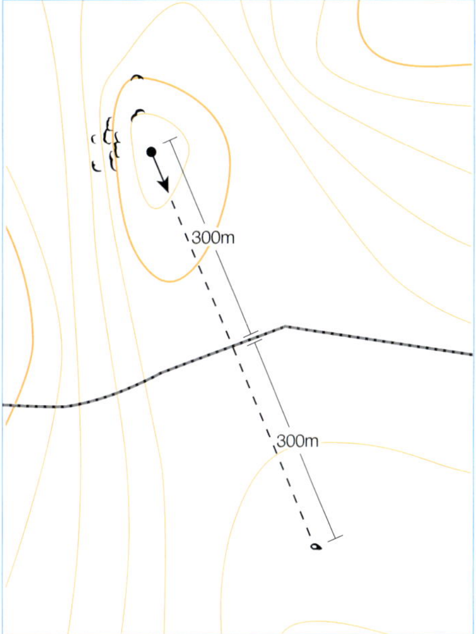

FIGURE 2.22   IN THIS EXAMPLE AN OBVIOUS HALFWAY FEATURE PROVIDES A USEFUL CHECK WHEN MEASURING DISTANCE

Double paces per 100m	Conditions underfoot		
	Good	Moderate	Poor
Flat	60	70	90
Uphill	80	100	120
Downhill	65	70	90

FIGURE 2.23   AS EVERYONE WALKS DIFFERENTLY AND HAS A DIFFERENT STRIDE LENGTH THESE FIGURES CAN ONLY EVER BE AN EXAMPLE. WITH A LITTLE PRACTICE ON A VARIETY OF TERRAIN IT WILL BE POSSIBLE TO CONSTRUCT A SIMILAR TABLE TO HELP WHEN USING PACING.

Pacing, as with timing, can be taught and practised anywhere, but initially a track with clear tick-off features conveniently spaced allows the technique to be matched to the map. Alternatively, 100 metres can be measured out in various types of terrain to compare variations; a 50-metre rope makes an effective tape measure.

Counting paces is particularly effective as a navigational tool in poor visibility but destroys the navigator's ability to talk. A leader may well choose to delegate this task to other members of the party and perhaps get somebody else to keep a running total of multiples of 100 metres. This requires considerable skill from these individuals and may require further coaching in how to make suitable adjustments when crossing varied terrain. In certain situations it may be easier to let someone else manage the group and for you to take responsibility for the navigation. Practise before you really need it.

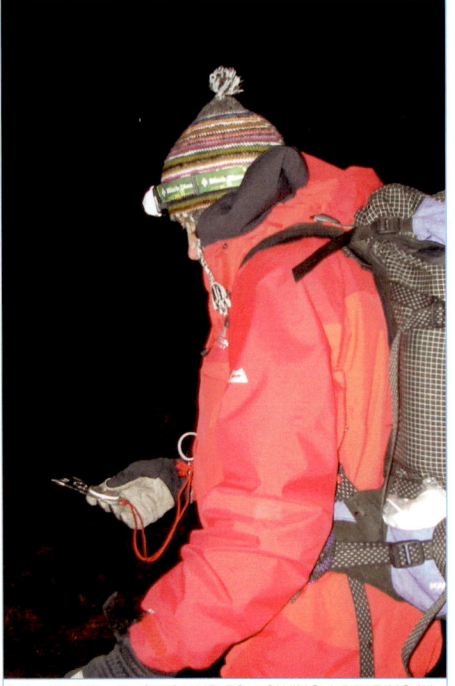

FIGURE 2.24 PACING AND FOLLOWING A BEARING IN DIFFICULT CONDITIONS

FIGURE 2.25 STEEP COMPLEX TERRAIN MORE SUITED TO TIMING THAN PACING WHEN COVERING LONG DISTANCES

Leaders can easily get a feel for the walking speed of their group by timing some simple legs at the start of the day. Speeds can be calculated over a measured distance and used as a reference when using timing at a later stage in the journey. Being able to judge how long a group will take to complete a particular route is a basic mountain leadership skill. These judgements should be used to plan the day but more importantly to adapt the route during the day so that the route covered matches the group's ability.

2.8 Choosing the right techniques

Experience allows the navigator to adjust distance estimation constantly by monitoring the ease or difficulty of progress. In good visibility, it is often possible to gain sufficient information by spotting the tick-off features and estimating the distances between them. Conditions and the composition of the party will influence the selection of the most appropriate technique for estimating distance.

Accurate judgement of distance travelled becomes particularly important when navigating through featureless terrain, where direction and distance become essential elements in navigating by *dead reckoning*, that is calculating location by estimating the distance travelled from a known point on a bearing.

Timing is often used for 'rough' navigation in easier conditions. For example, if a party has walked for ten minutes along a linear feature on flat ground, it is simple to estimate their position as within 600–900 metres of the starting point. Experienced walkers maintaining an even pace can estimate distance using timing alone and achieve much greater accuracy. A reasonable target for a walker travelling at a known speed is to be within ten per cent of the actual figure. Timing can be of limited use when an individual or group is constantly stopping for rests or crossing obstacles, although attentive use of a stopwatch can counteract this problem.

In very difficult conditions, a combination of all the methods listed above allows the maximum information to assist navigation. If the timing suggests that pacing is leading to over estimating distance then unless the party has sped up dramatically, the number of double paces representing 100 metres should be increased for similar conditions. If the pacing and timing are in agreement, then the unexpected appearance of a feature will not faze the navigator.

 6 NOTES FOR INSTRUCTORS **Pacing and timing**

Becoming competent with these skills takes time and practice. People need to be given the opportunity to use these tools in a variety of settings to build a good understanding of how best to apply them. Being able to measure a distance from the map is the first skill required. While it is important to be realistic about the 'accuracy' of a measurement, people should understand that if they cannot measure distances from the map they can never hope to be accurate when measuring on the ground.

Exercises

Guess the distance: pick a variety of points on the map and get students to guess the distances between them. In the same way as we estimate bearings before taking them as a back-up the same can be done with distances before they are measured.

Track calibration: pacing of 100 metres can be calibrated using a set distance on a good flat surface such as a track or road.

Vary the surface: once the person has set their paces to 100 metres, they should be given the opportunity to discover how this may vary in different terrain. A fifty-metre rope can be laid up, down or across a hillside to allow students to experience the effects terrain has on their pacing.

GPS: a GPS unit can be used to check both pacing and timing plus give an indication of walking speed at a particular time. This feedback can help people to build a kinaesthetic awareness of their speed.

Timing card: individuals can produce their own timing card to help with calculations. This activity will help gain a greater understanding of the maths involved making them more likely to use timing in the future.

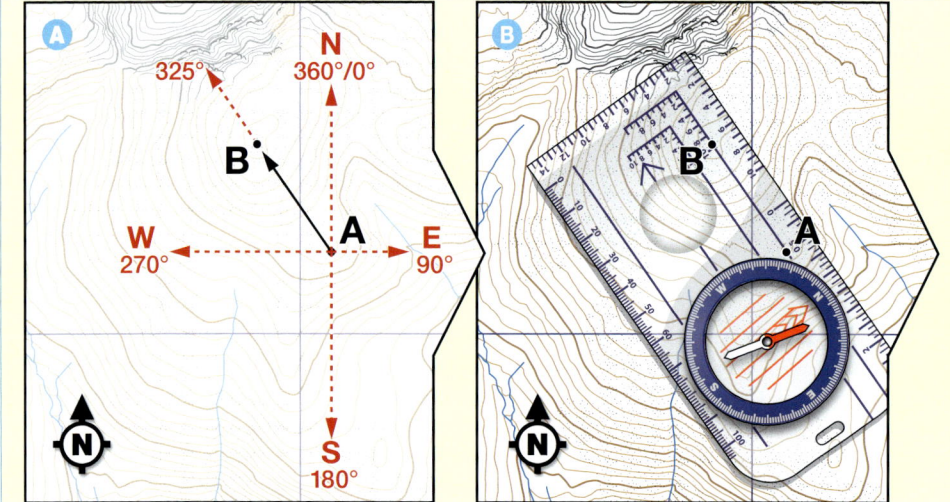

FIGURE 2.26 **TAKING A BEARING WITH A COMPASS: A** ESTIMATE THE ANGLE (GRID BEARING). TRAVELLING FROM **A** TO **B**, THE ANGLE IS JUST OVER HALF WAY BETWEEN 270° AND 360° – ROUGHLY 320° TO 330°. **B** USING A LINE ON THE BASEPLATE, LINK POINTS **A** (WHERE YOU ARE) AND **B** (YOUR INTENDED DESTINATION) WITH THE DIRECTION OF TRAVEL ARROW POINTING FROM **A** TO **B**. **C** ROTATE THE COMPASS HOUSING TO ALIGN THE ORIENTING LINES

2.9 Using the compass

2.9.1 Taking a bearing

Sighting a bearing

Taking a bearing from the ground has many applications and is particularly good for gaining information about the direction and aspect of features. It is possible to use sighted bearings to work out the direction of a path, the flow of a stream and the direction a slope faces. It is often possible to transfer the bearing back to the map to help confirm a position or hypothesis.

To take a sighting bearing simply hold the compass horizontal and point the direction of travel arrow toward the subject; either along it in the case of a linear feature, or straight at it in the case of a spot feature. Once fixed on a subject, without moving the base plate, rotate the compass housing until the orienting arrow is directly underneath the needle (*see Figure 2.29, page 47*). A bearing can then be read from the index line. This information can then be compared to the map, or if greater accuracy is required it can be converted to a grid bearing by making allowance for the magnetic variation before transferring onto the map.

Sighted bearings can also be of use when the visibility is constantly changing. You may catch a glimpse of the way ahead or a sight of some feature which you can identify on the map. By taking a quick bearing it could provide information to help confirm position or line of travel.

2.9.2 Following a bearing

Featureless terrain and poor visibility are common aspects of hill walking in the British Isles. The ability to follow a compass bearing accurately is therefore essential when landmarks are not visible. Once a magnetic bearing has been obtained the compass is then held with both hands immediately in front of the navigator's navel[1] with the ***direction of travel*** arrow pointing straight ahead. By locking elbows into the sides of the body it ensures the compass is maintained in a horizontal plane so that the needle can rotate freely. The navigator then rotates on the spot with the compass until the north (usually red) end of the magnetic needle floats over the ***orienting arrow*** on the compass housing. At this stage, the compass has been 'set' and the direction of travel arrow points along the bearing. Make sure the compass housing is not moved accidentally when holding or moving the compass as this will change the bearing.

---

1 Some sighting compasses are designed to allow the needle to be kept orientated accurately while sighting at eye rather than waist level. These can allow very accurate bearings to be taken, but this method should only be used with these specialised compasses.

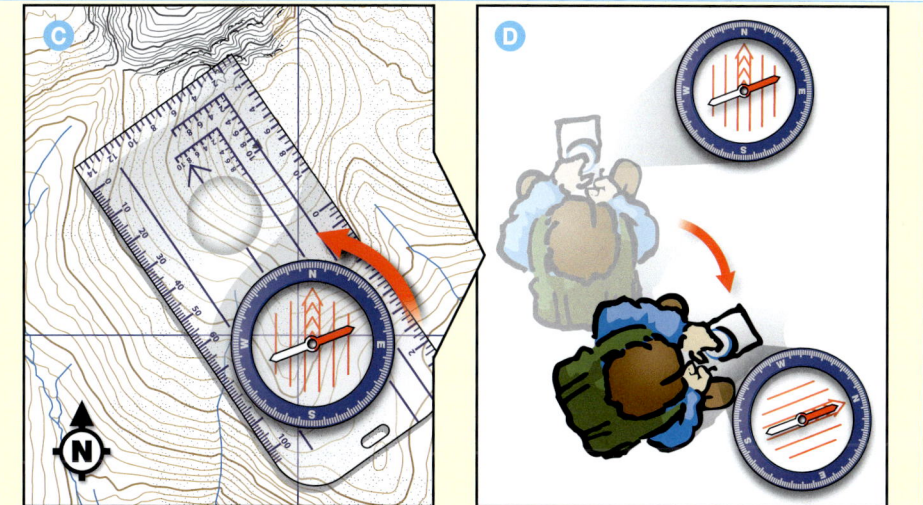

WITH THE NORTH—SOUTH GRID LINES ON THE MAP, WITH THE ORIENTING ARROW POINTING NORTH. ROTATE THE COMPASS HOUSING TO COMPENSATE FOR MAGNETIC VARIATION. **D** REMOVE THE COMPASS FROM THE MAP AND ROTATE THE ENTIRE COMPASS TO ALIGN THE NORTH (RED) END OF THE NEEDLE AND THE ORIENTING ARROW. KEEPING BOTH NEEDLE AND ARROW ALIGNED, FOLLOW THE DIRECTION OF TRAVEL ARROW

To walk along a bearing, the navigator sights along the direction of travel arrow towards a fixed object that is located on the bearing line. This is why the compass should be pointing straight ahead from the body, minimising any tendency to make an inaccurate sighting. Ideally the object should lie somewhere in the middle distance as objects on the far horizon may disappear in the mist or become hidden by intervening undulations. Having fixed on an object it may now be possible to put the compass away and walk to it via the most appropriate route. This will avoid having to walk in a straight line with the compass set although for certain situations (fog, darkness, white out) this is an essential skill to develop.

Having identified an object that lies on the bearing, the navigator heads towards it. Shortly before reaching it, the object can be used to sight through to another target and continue the process. With practice it is possible to re-sight the bearing on a new object by merely slowing down, reducing the need for prolonged stops or compromising any distance estimation (timing or pacing). Heading towards an identifiable object while en route also allows detours to be made, avoiding obstructions or hazards such as boggy or craggy ground. This can be done without losing track of the bearing or having to make complicated adjustments (*see Figure 2.31, page 49*).

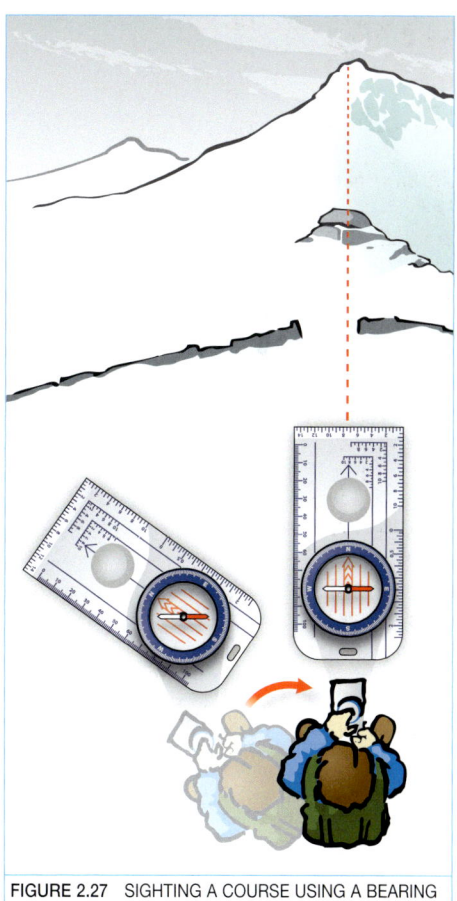

FIGURE 2.27 SIGHTING A COURSE USING A BEARING

7 Taking a compass bearing

For many people this can be a difficult skill to master. Initially this could be introduced with a blank grid rather than a map, so that people are not put off by the complex nature of some map detail. Using a blank grid mark two points that can then be used to take a bearing between. This will help fine-tune the skills of placing the compass base plate on the map and keeping it still while moving the housing.

Exercises

Guess the bearing: it is good practice to guess the bearing before taking it so as to factor in a small 'safety net'. People could spend time guessing bearing between one point and another. An element of competition can be introduced by working in pairs and seeing who is the closest when the actual bearing is taken. Taking bearings: there is no better practice than actually taking bearings for real; however opportunities should be created for

people to practise in a variety of different environments and conditions in order to develop a more robust skill. One simple way to vary the practice could be to use unfamiliar maps and compasses.

In very misty conditions, it can be difficult to find suitable objects for sighting ahead. A technique used by some navigators is to send members of their party out in front to act as sighting points. This usually requires signalling for communication and is very time consuming. In addition, the stop-start nature of this technique invariably leads to inaccuracies and furthermore, splitting up in this way may well compromise safety. However, it is very rare for no identifiable natural objects to be visible; even snow tends to have identifiable bumps and marks. Following a bearing in exceptionally poor visibility requires great concentration but it is possible to achieve without splitting the party. Careful attention must be paid to subtle variations of the ground within the field of vision, lining them up with the direction of travel arrow. A navigator should develop this skill to a high standard. *Refer to Section 3.4.3 Following a bearing in winter, page 71* on following a winter bearing for more details on following bearing in poor visibility.

FIGURE 2.28   USING A COMPASS TO SIGHT A BEARING DOWN A LINEAR FEATURE TO DETERMINE ITS DIRECTION

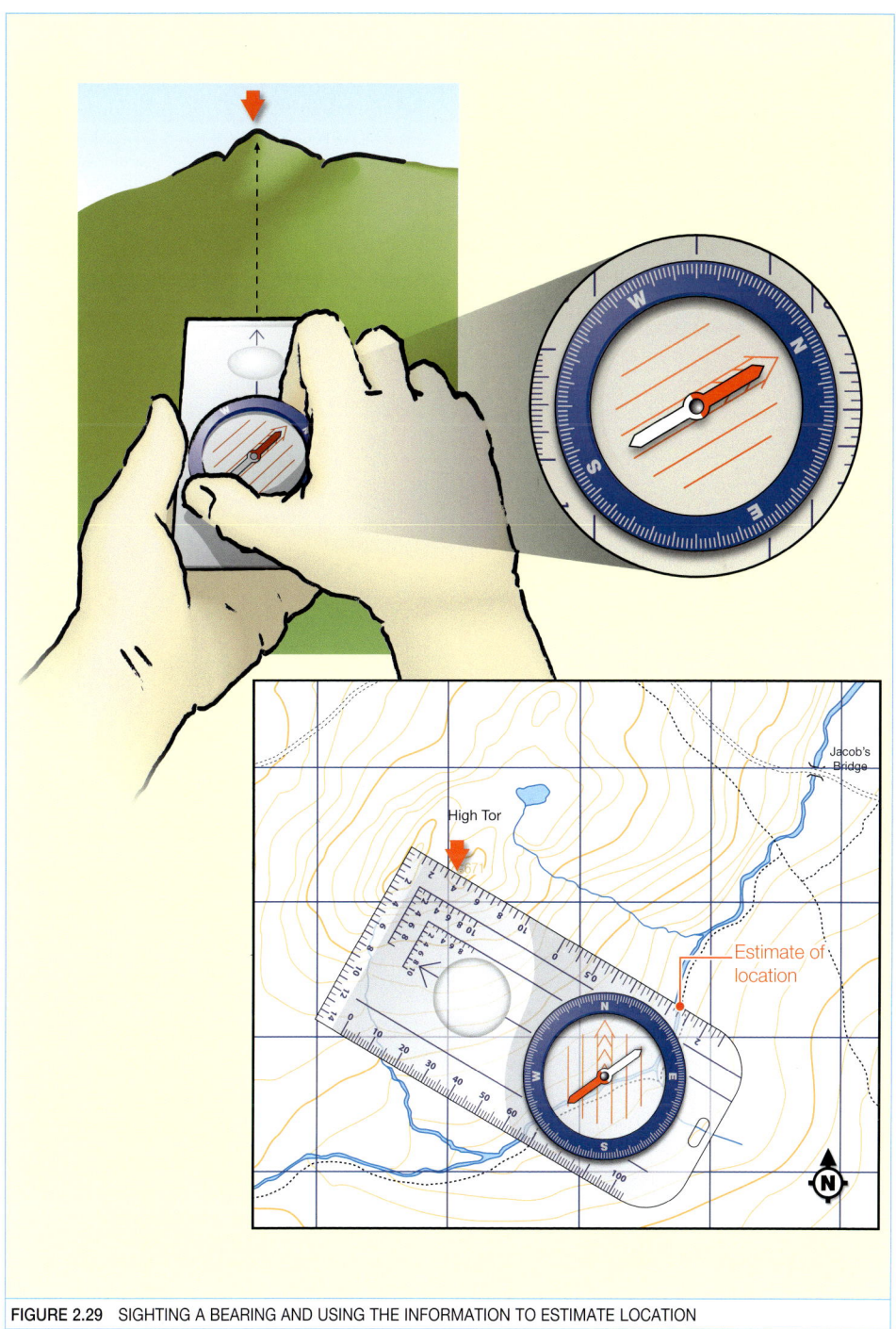

FIGURE 2.29   SIGHTING A BEARING AND USING THE INFORMATION TO ESTIMATE LOCATION

2.9.3 Transit points

In good visibility it is often possible to identify two features that are in line with each other, for example a building or a boulder or perhaps a distant wall running towards the observer. Only moving directly towards or away from these two

Being able to walk on a bearing and hold a straight line across a variety of terrain can be challenging for the novice navigator. Initially these skills can be introduced in easy terrain, even a park or playing field will suffice. However if people are to become truly proficient at this skill, then proper contextual practice is necessary.

As well as using bearings to help navigate to points these skills can also be practised in isolation. The following exercises require a safe area of terrain to operate on.

Exercise

Star burst: from a central point group members are sent out on a bearing for a set distance to leave a marker, for example their rucksack. On return to the central point they then swap the information with another person to then go and retrieve that person's marker.

Extended star burst: as for above; however the person sent out to retrieve the marker now moves it to a new location using a different bearing and distance. On return to the central point the information is swapped and the marker is then retrieved by having to navigate a 'dog-leg'. This can be extended further to include more legs, provided all the information can be remembered.

Searches: if markers are lost from the above exercises, search techniques could be introduced to find them. In the case of a spiral search using compass bearings and distances, this will help to reinforce these skills.

Photo: www.pyb.co.uk

FIGURE 2.30 FOLLOWING A BEARING IN MISTY CONDITIONS

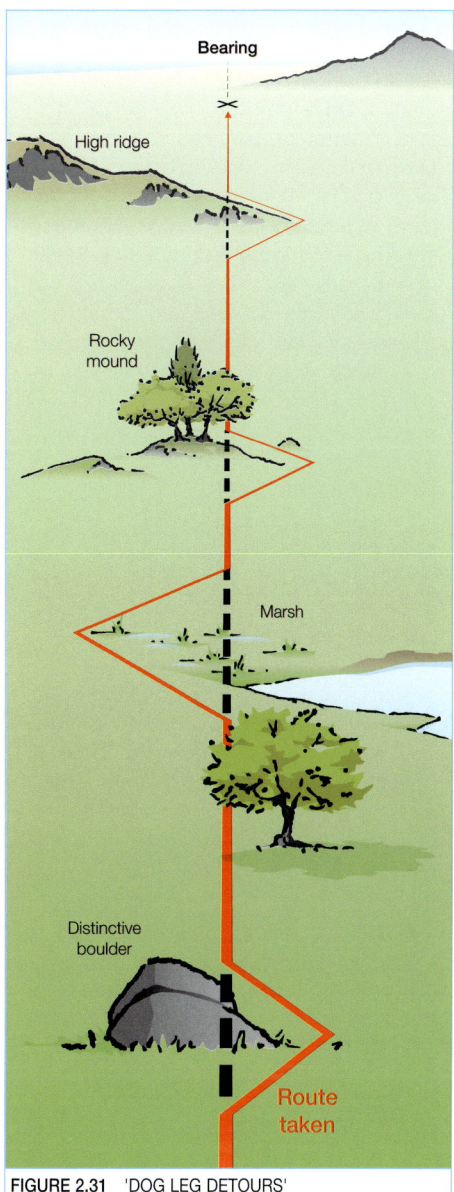

FIGURE 2.31 'DOG LEG DETOURS'

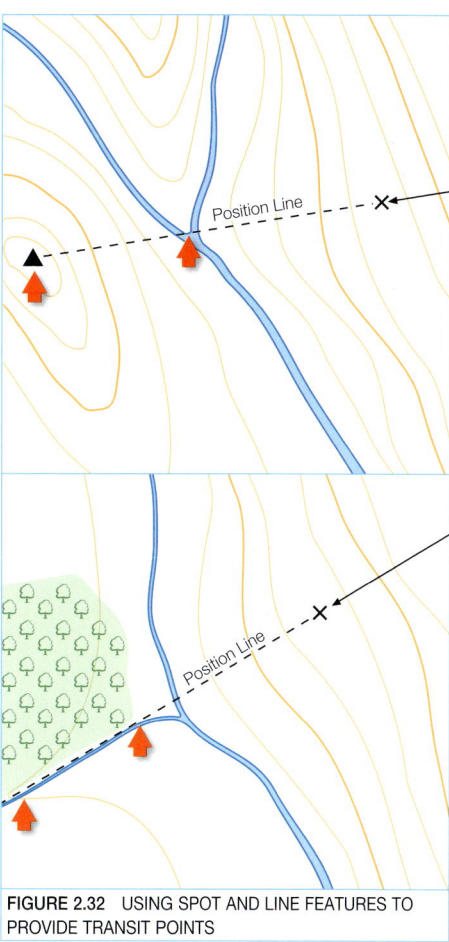

FIGURE 2.32 USING SPOT AND LINE FEATURES TO PROVIDE TRANSIT POINTS

features will keep them in line; otherwise, they will begin to drift apart visually. This is a simple and effective method of walking accurately in a straight line when following a bearing.

2.9.4 Back-bearings

Taking a bearing back along the route already travelled can often allow the direction of travel to be checked. This is a simple matter if the starting point can still be seen, but even in poor visibi-

lity, a back bearing can often be taken by aiming back along the other members of the party. The simplest way of obtaining a back-bearing is to rotate the compass so that the south end of the magnetic needle floats over the north end of the orienting arrow on the compass housing. It is also possible to add or subtract 180° from the bearing and alter the housing, but this is usually unnecessary work and more likely to lead to error. If drifting from the correct line has occurred, it may be possible to solve by turning at right angles and walking until the back-bearing has returned to the correct line (see *Section 2.9.7 Boxing* on page 52).

2.9.5 Slope aspect and shape

Observing changes in the angle and direction of the slope as a route is travelled is a useful skill to acquire particularly when walking in featureless

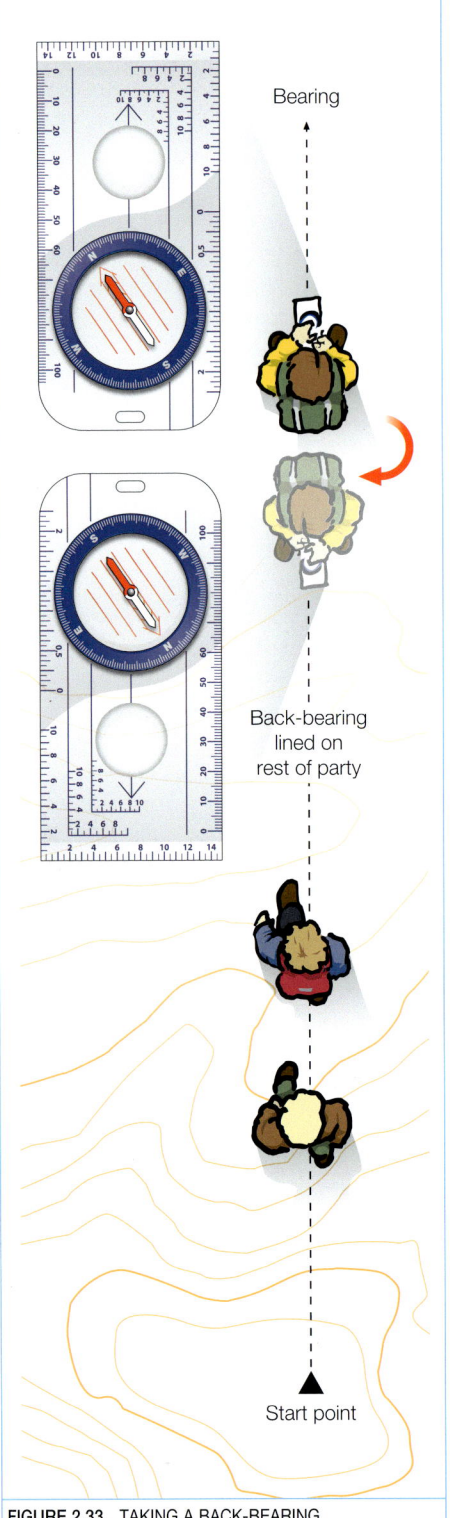

Bearing

Back-bearing
lined on
rest of party

Start point

FIGURE 2.33 TAKING A BACK-BEARING

Often this can be one of the most difficult skills to grasp. However with a little thought and cunning it can be made fairly straightforward. Consistent use of language is the key to success with this plan. At an early stage people can be introduced to using a compass to help check the direction of a stream or path. Essentially this is the same process as taking an aspect of slope and could be referred to as an 'aspect.' By using the same language in this way when aspect of slope is introduced for the first time a link can be made to a similar process they are already familiar with.

Exercise

Walk the line: from the map choose an open slope with different aspects and few features other than contour lines. Group members can then contour around the slope taking aspects of slope at set distances. In doing so they could practise pacing but also find out how the aspect changes as they move round. To help highlight how the bearing is transferred to the map try to use a feature that traverses the slope in the same way a contour line does (a path or boundary). Once students have grasped the concept and method their skills can then be developed in more complex terrain.

terrain. Often in these situations it is the shape of the ground and the direction it faces that provides the most useful information to help pinpoint a location. The direction a slope faces is referred to as its ***aspect*** and can often provide a vital clue when trying to relocate.

Slope aspect can be measured accurately by taking a bearing straight down the ***fall line*** – in other words the line down which a rolling stone would travel. In poor visibility, care should be taken to check that this is the main slope and not a small basin confusing the overall picture. The magnetic bearing shown will instantly give an idea of which way the slope is facing. For example, a bearing of 315° will mean it is a North West facing

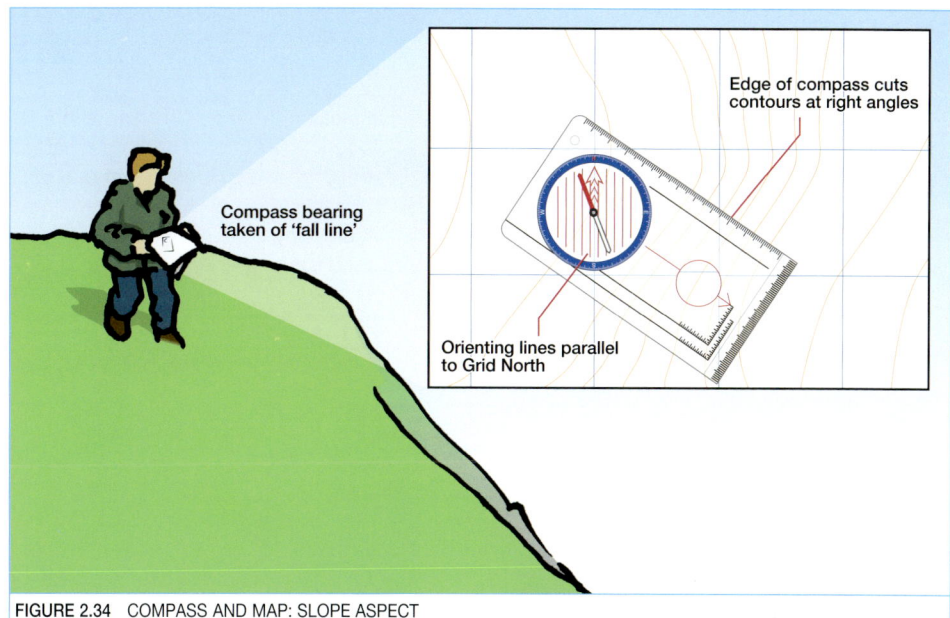

FIGURE 2.34   COMPASS AND MAP: SLOPE ASPECT

slope. This may be all that is required to confirm a location, however greater accuracy can be achieved by transferring this bearing to the map. After making the appropriate adjustment to the bearing from magnetic to Grid North, the compass is placed on the map and rotated until the ***orienting lines*** on the compass housing are parallel to the vertical grid lines. The compass can now be moved over the map, maintaining the same orientation. The edge of the compass will cross through the contours at right angles on any slopes with the same aspect – all other slopes are eliminated. If there is already a rough idea of location this information might provide a more accurate fix.

2.9.6 Aiming off

Drifting off from a bearing by as little as 5° will lead to an error of nearly 50 metres after walking only half a kilometre. This is a good reason for keeping navigational 'legs' relatively short, but also means that trying to walk on a bearing straight to a point feature such as a bothy is quite optimistic in thick mist.

Imagine trying to journey through featureless terrain in dense mist with the hope of finding a bridge over a stream. As long as the bearing cuts across the stream, it will not be very hard to find this line feature: but if the bridge is not visible, should the party turn upstream or downstream? Aiming off is a classic navigational technique,

FIGURE 2.35   TAKING A BEARING OF THE 'FALL LINE' OF A SLOPE TO GIVE THE DIRECTION IT FACES

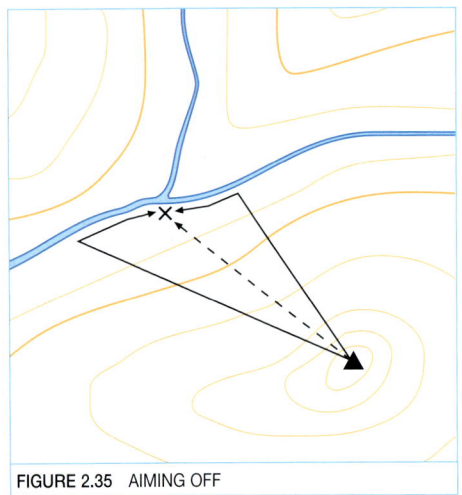

FIGURE 2.35   AIMING OFF

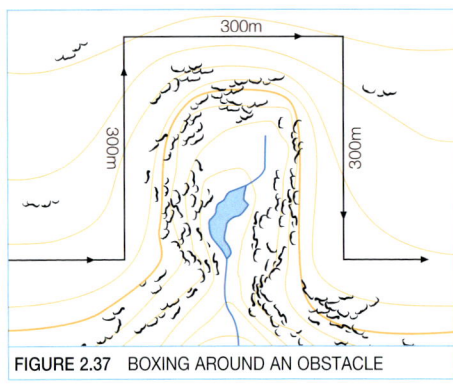

FIGURE 2.37   BOXING AROUND AN OBSTACLE

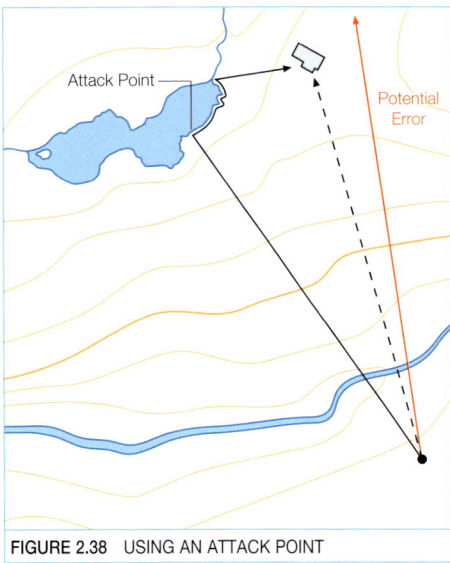

FIGURE 2.38   USING AN ATTACK POINT

which will eliminate this quandary. The party deliberately sets a bearing a few degrees to the side of the bridge – usually uphill if descending, then turns downhill upon reaching the stream, using it as a 'handrail' to reach the bridge. The uphill deviation is used to prevent dropping down too low and then having to regain height to find the destination. This technique is particularly useful for finding junctions or other points located on linear features.

2.9.7 Boxing

Sometimes when following a bearing it is necessary to make a detour around an unexpected obstruction that you cannot see the far side of, for example an unmarked enclosure, boggy ground

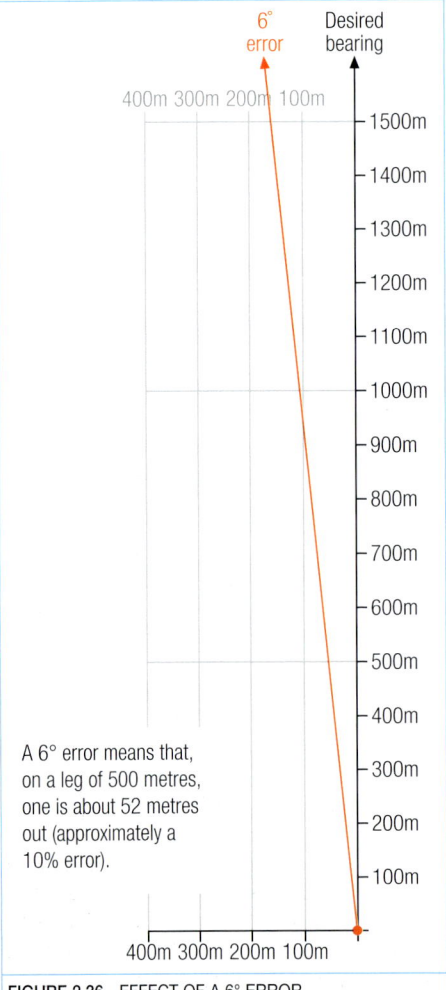

A 6° error means that, on a leg of 500 metres, one is about 52 metres out (approximately a 10% error).

FIGURE 2.36   EFFECT OF A 6° ERROR

or escarpment. It may be possible to make a series of turns around the object in order to get back in line with the bearing. This technique, known as boxing, is simplest when 90° turns are made.

The first step is to turn at right angles from the bearing, until the magnetic needle aligns with the East/West markings on the compass (according to the direction turned). The direction of travel arrow now shows a bearing at right angles, without having to make any calculations. This bearing is followed, while measuring distance until beyond the obstacle. The original bearing is then followed until it is possible to turn back beyond the other side of the obstacle. The navigator turns to move back towards the original line of travel, until the magnetic needle points to West or East (the opposite of the previous detour). This is followed for the same distance as the detour and thus the original line is reached, having followed three sides of a square – only the side that is parallel to the original bearing should be included in the total reckoning of distance travelled.

Whenever possible, a box with sides that are parallel or at right angles to the slope will make it easier to keep on course. *For further information see **Section 3.6.9 Dog-legs** and **3.6.10 Boxing** on page 77.*

2.9.8 Attack points

A useful technique in any conditions for seeking a poorly defined feature is to identify something clearly distinguishable within a few hundred metres of it. Having located this ***attack point***, a more cautious systematic approach can be used to pinpoint the required feature. This is often described as using two different styles; 'rough navigation' to locate the attack point, and 'fine navigation' to find the actual feature.

For example, in poor visibility it might be necessary to locate a sheepfold for shelter. In open moorland this would be a difficult task but with a clear feature 200 metres away, such as a large lake, it might be possible to use rough navigation to find the lake and then fine detail navigation for the final 200 metres. It is important to choose an attack point that can be found using rough navigation otherwise no benefit is achieved. In the same way 'reverse' attack points can be useful; when you are leaving a known point and want to head off in a particular direction you can use an attack point to check that you are walking on the right bearing.

10 NOTES FOR INSTRUCTORS Navigational strategy

Using good strategies is a skill that can underpin any navigational leg. Group members could be encouraged to think about the basic information required to navigate a leg. By developing their own versions of the 5 Ds or 5 Ws they are more likely to become familiar and use their own systems in the future.

Exercise

Map memory: allow people to plan a navigation leg using their strategy. Initially this information could be written down and as more experience is gained it should be confined to memory. Once the planning is over put the map away and try to navigate the leg either from the notes or from memory. Initially these skills should be introduced in terrain where there are good positive features to work with. As people develop the terrain can become more difficult, requiring the need to use the need to use more subtle features and so encouraging other aspect of navigation, for example contour interpretation.

Photo: www.pyb.co.uk

2.10 Navigational strategy

An effective navigator will make many strategic decisions in the course of a journey. Navigating in good visibility will usually be very different to navigation through difficult terrain in poor visibility. When conditions are challenging navigation

Using the 5 Whats

WHAT are you going to see en route?
Total distance is 800m.
1 Descending ground through rocky terrain with steep ground to the left.
2 Change in angle of slope at approx. 300m, becoming flatter.
3 Terrain levels, pass a small lake at 500m.
4 Cross a boundary at 550m and leave footpath.
5 Ground starts to rise gently at 600m.

WHAT are you going to see when you reach destination?
6 Top of high ground with terrain descending in all directions.

WHAT are you going to see if you go too far?
7 Ground will descend gradually at first then more steeply (convex slope).

WHAT are the potential hazards?
1 Steep rocky ground to the left.
3 Water hazard.
7 Convex slope with steep rocky ground.

WHAT are the appropriate skills to use?
Follow footpath, time or pace distance (depending on conditions), use a bearing to check general direction or more accurately if visibility is poor. Tick off features **1** to **5**.

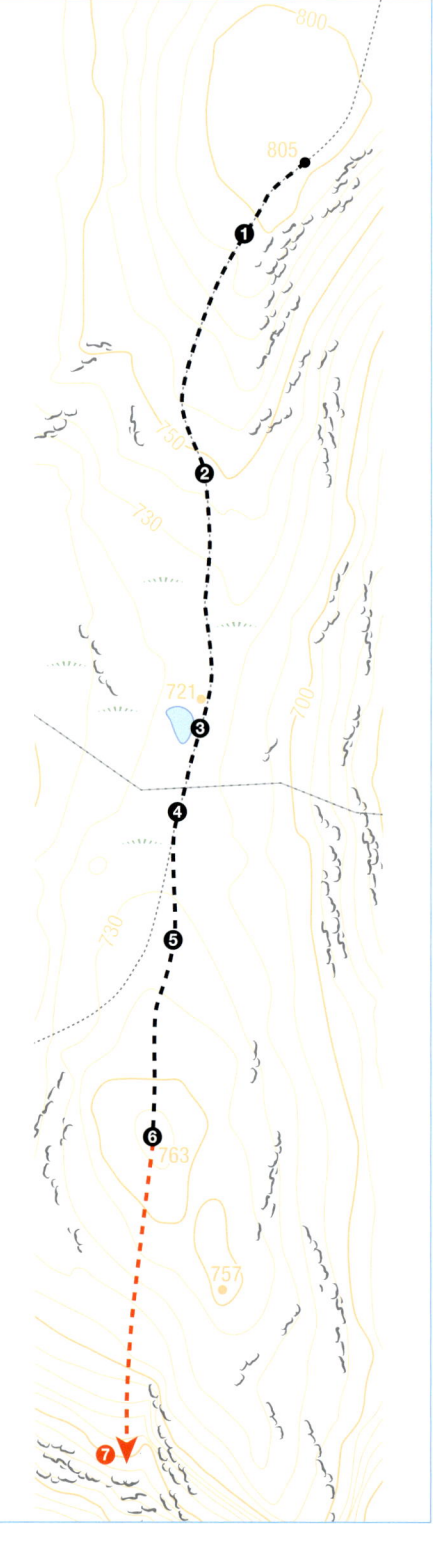

can be stressful with a real possibility of missing vital pieces of information. In these situations it is easy to become focused on one particular technique to the detriment of others. For example in poor visibility concentration may be so focused on taking a bearing that hazards, distance, tick-off and catching features are overlooked. A good strategy in any situation will bring together the most appropriate set of skills and techniques to solve any particular navigation problem and help to avoid any oversights. A check list can help ensure nothing is overlooked and the following two examples can be employed in any situation. By answering these questions the risk of forgetting vital pieces of information are reduced.

2.10.1 The 5 Ds

1 Distance
   How far to the intended destination?
2 Direction
   Which direction will you need to head in?
3 Description
   What are the tick off features and catching features en route, and what does the destination look like?
4 Duration
   How long will this leg take?
5 Dangers
   Are there any potential hazards en route?

2.10.2 The 5 Whats

This system uses a slightly different approach and places emphasis on looking carefully at the map to establish the nature of the terrain to be encountered on the journey. By considering the ground carefully beforehand it allows the most appropriate set of skills to be chosen.

1 What are you going to see en route?
2 What are you going to see when you reach your destination?

3 What would you see if you went too far?
4 What are the most appropriate skills to use on this leg?
5 What are the potential hazards en route?

The benefits of using a checklist or aide memoir are particularly important to less experienced navigators and anyone operating in challenging conditions.

2.10.3 Route planning

Inappropriate route planning, or a complete lack of it, is a common factor in mountain incidents attended to by mountain rescue teams. An experienced hill walker will choose a route for a day by obtaining a variety of important information from the maps, guidebooks, weather forecasts and other people in their group, if there is one. Planning a route in advance allows potential problems to be identified and corrective measures to be taken early, therefore minimising their impact. It allows for an estimate to be made of the amount of time required to complete the proposed trip. This can then be balanced against the available daylight hours and the weather

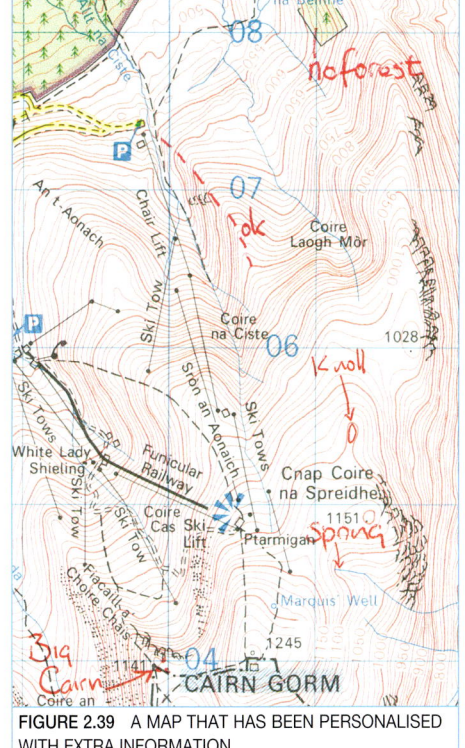

FIGURE 2.39   A MAP THAT HAS BEEN PERSONALISED WITH EXTRA INFORMATION

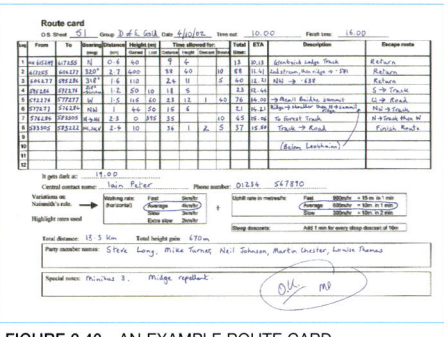

FIGURE 2.40   AN EXAMPLE ROUTE CARD

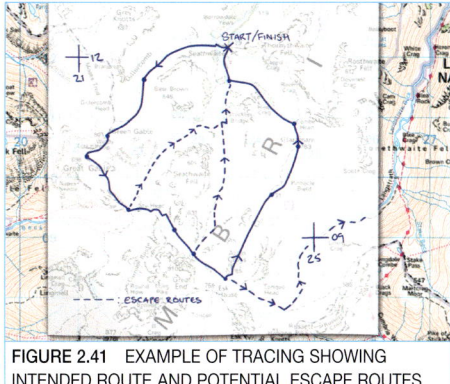

FIGURE 2.41   EXAMPLE OF TRACING SHOWING INTENDED ROUTE AND POTENTIAL ESCAPE ROUTES

Buachaille Etive Beag (summer)

Information

Travel Start Date and Time	08/01/2012 14:53:38	No. in Party		4
Start Place	Glencoe Car Park NN1883 5620			
End Place	Glen Etive (road bend) NN 1705 5145			
Objective	Traverse of Buachaille Etive Beag			
Name (Leader)	Carlo Forte	Phone		
Emergency Contact	01690 720 214	Phone		0773659000
Vehicle Registration	G818 LYB			
Parked At	Glencoe Car Park NN 1883 5620			

Points

Name	Coordinate	Bearing	Altitude	DTM Distance	Ascent	Date and Time	Note
start, carpark	NN 1883 5620	111.27°	256.6 m	0 m	0 m	08/01/2012 14:53:38	find suitable stream crossing
turn1	NN 1965 5584	172.93°	414.9 m	909.5 m (909.5 m)	158.3 m	08/01/2012 15:27:03	careful route finding to next point
flat spur	NN 1962 5563	126.16°	553.6 m	1,166.9 m (257.4 m)	297 m	08/01/2012 15:48:15	careful route finding required to next
Stob Nan Cabar spur	NN 1991 5539	129.97°	775.2 m	1,604.7 m (437.9 m)	518.6 m	08/01/2012 16:22:31	
Stob Coire Raineach 925	NN 1914 5480	132.33°	920.9 m	2,586.7 m (982 m)	664.3 m	08/01/2012 16:55:28	summit, munro
col	NN 1878 5450	138.38°	753.6 m	3,088.4 m (501.6 m)	664.3 m	08/01/2012 17:07:11	
902 top	NN 1845 5416	155.42°	895.1 m	3,589.5 m (501.1 m)	805.8 m	08/01/2012 17:32:24	ridge narrows to next points
col2	NN 1823 5373	132.01°	885.5 m	4,072.1 m (482.6 m)	805.8 m	08/01/2012 17:39:14	
spur	NN 1806 5359	117.73°	900.8 m	4,292.9 m (220.8 m)	821.1 m	08/01/2012 17:44:28	narrow ridge to summit
Stob Dubh 958	NN 1789 5351	137.54°	949.5 m	4,486.9 m (194 m)	869.9 m	08/01/2012 17:53:28	summit, munro
descent spur	NN 1763 5325	169.66°	832.8 m	4,877.3 m (390.4 m)	869.9 m	08/01/2012 18:01:33	careful route finding to next point
spur2	NN 1750 5268	-172.4°	559.5 m	5,523.1 m (645.8 m)	869.9 m	08/01/2012 18:22:37	steep slope to next
spur path junction	NN 1737 5195	159.33°	202.2 m	6,346.6 m (823.5 m)	869.9 m	08/01/2012 18:48:40	follow path to next
path junction	NN 1725 5167	140.27°	123.7 m	6,661.5 m (314.9 m)	869.9 m	08/01/2012 18:50:07	follow path SW to road
end	NN 1705 5145		99.5 m	6,959.1 m (297.6 m)	869.9 m	08/01/2012 18:53:34	road bend

MAPYX LIMITED
Digital Mapping Solutions

Quo

FIGURE 2.42 EXAMPLE OF ROUTE CARD PRODUCED USING MAPPING SOFTWARE

The enclosure wall *(1)* and the river *(2)*; the copse *(3)* and the escarpment *(4)* and finally the valley itself *(5)* all guide the walker onto the path, making them useful funnel features.

FIGURE 2.43 FUNNEL FEATURES

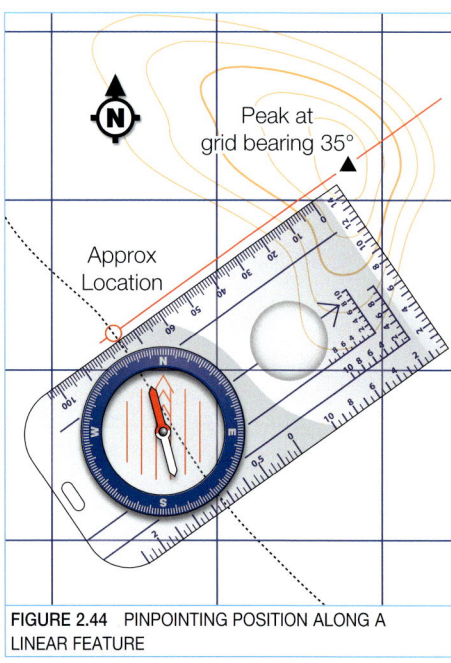

FIGURE 2.44 PINPOINTING POSITION ALONG A LINEAR FEATURE

forecast. A route plan can also be left with a friend or contact allowing constructive contingency measures to be taken if seriously delayed, however it is worth remembering that over rigid plans can stifle flexibility. Any route plan left with a friend or contact should also contain a number of extra pieces of information. As well as the intended route details, possible escape routes or extensions to the plan should also be included. The number in the party and any contact details are also useful (this is of particular importance if planning an overnight or extended expedition).

Recording a plan can be done in a number of ways. Route cards are a traditional format for recording this information during the planning process, however their tabular structure and lack of pictorial information makes them more time consuming and confusing to use for anyone wishing to evaluate the planned route. As a formal exercise route cards are a useful planning tool particularly for inexperienced people, allowing them to spend time studying the map and practising such things as measuring distances and taking bearings before commencing their journey. They can provide an aide memoir or useful reference if carried on the journey, although trans-

ferring information to the map when on the hill can lead to mistakes. With developments in modern technology and quicker more appropriate methods available, these traditional route cards are now more or less redundant. Nevertheless the process of producing a route plan is still very important particularly for longer journeys or prolonged expeditions. More pictorial ways of presenting the same information can make it easier for anyone wishing to view the intended route. More ideal formats for recording route plan information include:

- a tracing of the route, which can be overlaid onto a map;
- using a permanent marker pen to draw the proposed route on a laminated map including annotations where necessary;
- a map that can be photocopied or scanned with the route marked on using a highlighter pen.

Recent developments in digital mapping software have allowed for a more sophisticated approach to route planning. Used well this software can provide a wealth of information regarding the planned route all of which can be applied in a variety of ways. *Part VI page 121*, has more detailed information on the use of digital mapping software.

2.10.4 Breaking a route into sections
Dividing a long navigational leg into more manageable sections is a common technique for navigators to employ. Often in poor visibility, this will necessitate 'micro-navigation', that is moving from one small feature to another, relying on detail that would probably not be needed if conditions were clear. This is an important skill for navigators to develop to a high standard of accuracy if all-weather route finding is to be achieved.

Navigational requirements in difficult conditions often affect the choice of route. Sometimes a direct line to a destination takes the party through vague, indistinct terrain, whereas a circuitous route can link several identifiable features, allowing regular confirmation. Choosing a route that crosses or passes several features allows more than one opportunity to confirm that things are on course. Regular checks allow warning signals to be picked up rapidly if a mistake is made, helping to minimise the distance covered in the wrong direction. It may be also possible to link two sections together using *funnel* or *corridor* features, such as valleys, converging crags or walls. These form a natural boundary which leads the navigator naturally to a chosen point.

2.11 Relocation

Even the best navigators will experience moments of uncertainty in difficult conditions, possibly forgetting the number of paces or losing concentration at the wrong time. But many are able to relocate quickly enough so that their mistakes cost them seconds rather than minutes or hours! Continuing 'blindly' can easily compound the problem, so it is always best to stop and evaluate the situation and have a positive strategy for finding yourself.

2.11.1 Calm down!
Getting lost can be an unpleasant feeling and so the first job is to calm yourself down and make sure you are capable of rational decision making! Quite often people are not completely lost, they might not know exactly where they are or how to get back to their original route but often they can find a safe way off the hill or even retrace their steps. A good way to calm down and regain control is to simply describe out loud what can be seen, "I can see a stone wall, it is in a North South direction, etc".

2.11.2 Gather information
The first stage in relocation is to collect all the available information. Initially this should be done with a thorough inspection of the surrounding area. It is common for people to over examine the map and to neglect the wealth of information that can be gained from their surroundings. A creative mind can make any point on the map fit with their current location! However it is only the information gained from your surroundings that will help to confirm where you are; so look around before consulting the map.

- How much time has elapsed since leaving the last known point? How certain was that location? Answering these questions allows the present location to be narrowed down to an area based on your travel speed.
- Were there distinctive features, slope angles and aspects passed on route? This information can be plotted on the map to further narrow down the likely location.
- If walking along or close to a linear feature such as a wall or stream, a bearing can be taken along it and compared with the map. A sharp bend is particularly useful, as the shape of the bend and bearings on either side give additional information.

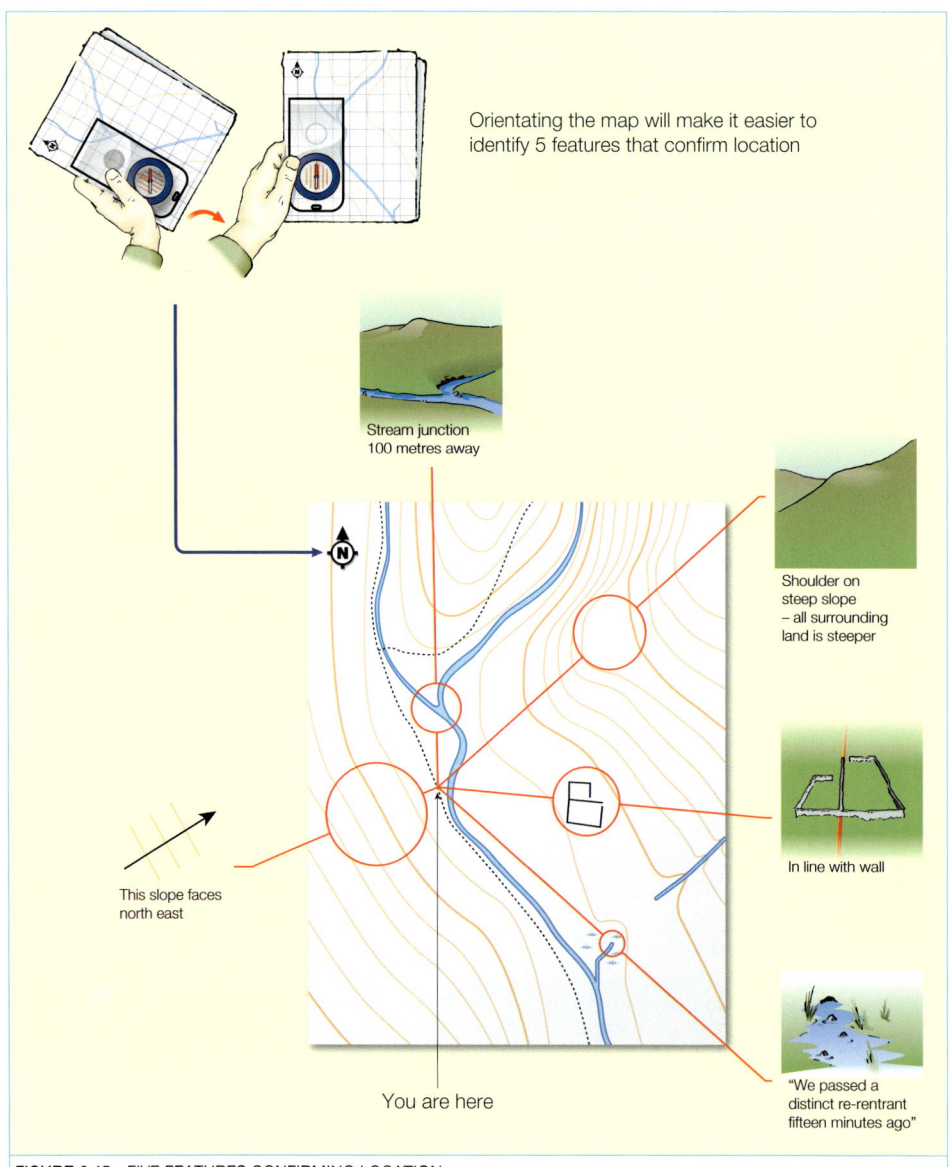

Orientating the map will make it easier to identify 5 features that confirm location

Stream junction 100 metres away

Shoulder on steep slope – all surrounding land is steeper

In line with wall

This slope faces north east

You are here

"We passed a distinct re-rentrant fifteen minutes ago"

FIGURE 2.45   FIVE FEATURES CONFIRMING LOCATION

- What is the current slope aspect and angle? This information effectively rules out most of the map, as long as a local hollow is not mistaken for the main slope.
- If any identifiable features are visible, a bearing can be taken and plotted on the map (remembering to make any adjustments for magnetic variation). Two or more features, preferably on bearings at about right angles to each other, allow the location to be narrowed down to an area around the intersecting lines in a technique known as **resection**. However, competent navigators rarely need to relocate when several landmarks are so clearly visible. Sometimes location along a linear feature such as a wall, ridge or even contour line can be pinpointed by taking a bearing on a spot feature and noting where the bearing crosses the line feature on the map.
- Seek out five features around you that confirm your position on the map.

The process of relocation

Trying to locate your position in unfamiliar terrain can be a difficult business. It is often small pieces of information that can be easily overlooked that will confirm the correct position. Using a simple checklist in these situations will mean information is gathered in a systematic way. A similar procedure to that highlighted in *Section 2.10.2* can be used in these situations with a little adjustment.

1 What did I see on the way?
Consider the following
- **Distance** from last known point
- **Direction** from last known point
- **Terrain** covered since last known point
- Major tick off features encountered

2 What can I see around me?
Gather information from surroundings try to work from ground to map first. Seek out at least **five features** around you. (*Section 2.11.2 and Figure 2.45*)

3 What can I see if I walk further?
Walk around location as this can often provide more information. In poor visibility you will need to use a structured approach such as *Mapping or Searching* (*Section 2.11.3 & 2.11.6*). Beware of potential hazards in this situation they are easy to overlook when attention is elsewhere.

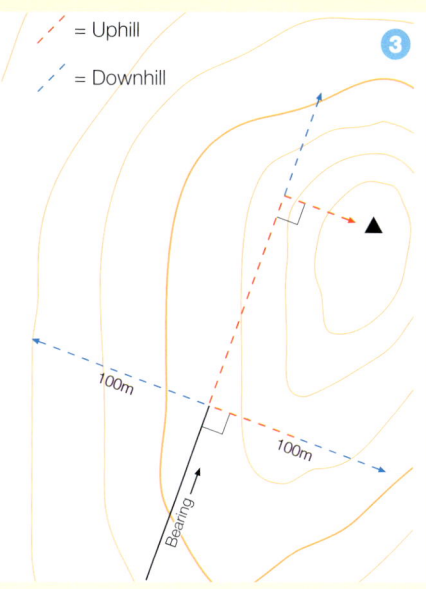

= Uphill

= Downhill

100m

100m

Bearing

4 What other techniques can be used to give more information?
Consider using the following techniques if conditions allow
- **Aspect of slope** (*Section 2.9.5*)
- **Back bearings** (*Section 2.9.4*)
- **Resection** (*Section 2.11.4*)

5 What if I cannot relocate?
It may be possible to head to an obvious feature seen from your location that can then be identified on the map. Your **catching feature** could be used in this situation. (see *Section 2.4 following linear features*). If all else fails you should retrace your steps to last confirmed location.

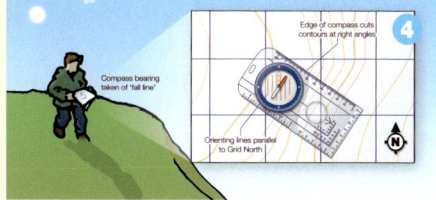

Compass bearing taken of 'fall line'

Edge of compass cuts contours at right angles

Orienting lines parallel to Grid North

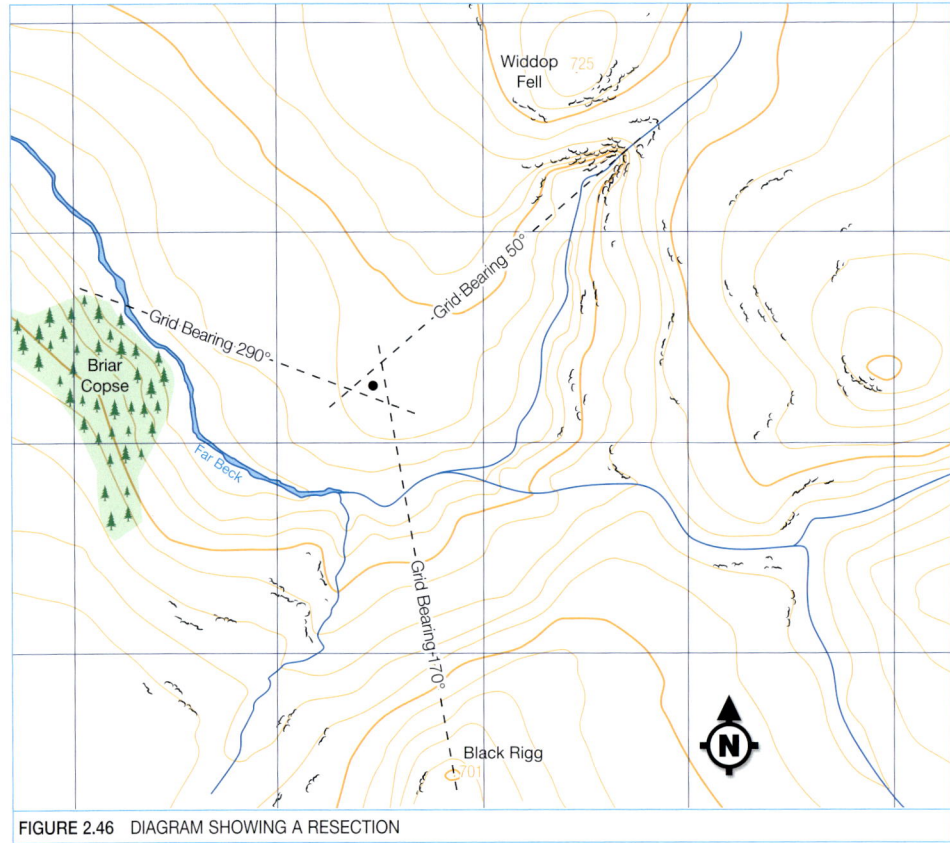

FIGURE 2.46 DIAGRAM SHOWING A RESECTION

- Using a GPS device or altimeter can provide very accurate information (*see **Sections 4.9 Using altimeters** on page 97 and **Part V, GPS** on page 103*).

Once all possible information has been gathered it is important to place more emphasis on that which you believe to be most accurate and reliable. If visibility is poor due to weather conditions or undulating terrain then it may be necessary to move location or use the technique of ***mapping*** to gather sufficient information.

2.11.3 Mapping

Sometimes it can be very difficult to form a mental picture of the surrounding land in poor visibility. In these circumstances, it is possible to map the area by walking a measured distance at 90° to the direction of travel, then returning to the starting point. On the way slope, aspect and shape are noted, along with any features passed. This allows information to be collected quickly and systematically, without needing to split up

the party. An excursion in the opposite direction can also be made if necessary. As information is gathered it can be transferred to the map to help establish the location.

2.11.4 Resection

Resection is a fairly time consuming procedure, and many would argue that if you can see clearly identifiable features then you are unlikely to have to use such a method to pin point your location. This is true to some extent; however it does have its place in certain circumstances. When navigating in featureless terrain such as open moorland or snow covered plateaus pin pointing a location can be tricky even on a clear day. In these situations you will roughly know where you are and in the absence of any other information resection may provide a more detailed idea of your location. The procedure relies on being able to definitely identify at least two or preferably three features. These features should be identifiable within the landscape and also

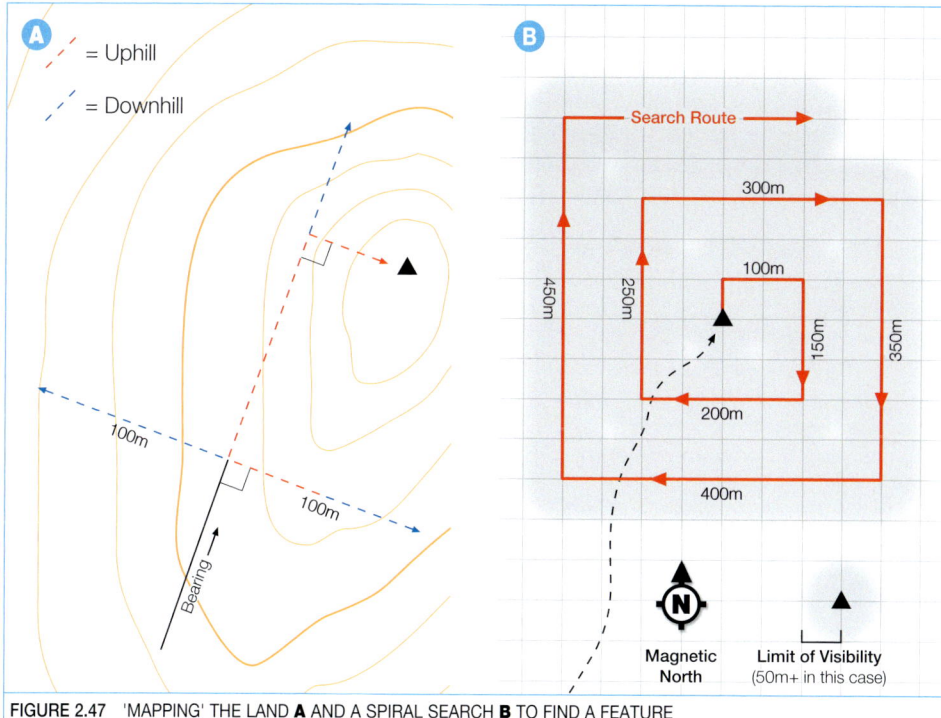

A
= Uphill
= Downhill
100m
100m
Bearing

B
Search Route
300m
100m
450m
250m
150m
350m
200m
400m

Magnetic North
Limit of Visibility
(50m+ in this case)

FIGURE 2.47   'MAPPING' THE LAND **A** AND A SPIRAL SEARCH **B** TO FIND A FEATURE

appear on the map. The greater the angle between these points respective to your position the greater the level of accuracy that can be achieved in determining your location. By taking a compass bearing to each feature and converting them to grid bearings it is possible to plot them onto the map (*see Figure 2.29 and refer to* **section on Sighting a bearing**, *page 44*). Depending on the accuracy of the bearings there will be a small triangle created where the lines intersect. Your position will be somewhere in this region and by using other information it may now be possible to pin point the location.

2.11.5 Plan of action

Having collated all the available information, it is now possible to formulate a plan of action.

*   It may now be possible to continue along a route, checking that the landform continues to match the map. If it does not, the party should stop immediately and relocate, using the techniques described above.
*   It may be possible to continue towards a clear bounding feature such as a road or ridge that will allow simpler relocation, assuming there are no serious obstacles in the way.

*   It may be necessary to retrace the party's steps to the last identifiable point and recommence from there.

If none of these options is possible it may be necessary to extend 'mapping' operations until sufficient information is found to allow the probable location to be determined. A series of excursions based on right angles from a particular bearing allows information to be gathered without straying even further from known ground.

2.11.6 Searches

Isolated features such as cairns on flat summits are notoriously difficult to find in poor visibility. Strategic use of party members can reduce the likelihood of passing the feature without spotting it. Party organisation is an essential pre-requisite for systematic searches both in terms of effectiveness and safety. The co-ordinator must ensure that all members understand their role and remain within communication range throughout the exercise. These methods are not suitable for crossing areas with craggy ground or similar hazards.

One of the most important navigational skills is the ability to relocate when lost or 'temporarily misplaced'. Developing a coping strategy for dealing with such situations is a fundamental part of learning to navigate. Group members should be given opportunities to develop these skills initially in easy terrain and so help build confidence and experience before dealing with more complex scenarios. A large part of relocation involves collecting information from your surroundings and these are skills that can easily be reinforced at every stage when students have to relate the ground to the map. People should understand the precise approach for relocation will be dependent on the circumstances. However there are strategies that can be employed in every situation that will serve as a starting point to this process. Building on skills already acquired it is possible to use a similar approach to relocation as they do to navigation. A strategy such as the **5 Whats** can be adjusted and used as a frame-work for starting the relocation process:

What did I see/do on the way?
What can I see immediately around me?
What can I see further ahead of me?
What other skills can I employ to help relocate? (Back bearings, slope aspect.)

Exercises

Follow me: quite simply ask the group members to put their maps away and walk them to a new location. Once at the new destination ask the students to relocate. Initially some help will need to be given with the process but as more of these exercises are repeated less intervention will be required.

Lost: capitalise on opportunities to relocate when genuine errors have occurred. There is nothing better than learning lessons from real situations.

Photo: BMC

2.11.7 Sweep search

This classic search technique adapts very well to seeking point features, for example a cairn or bothy. The party spreads out at right angles across the direction of travel and for the sake of effective communication the co-ordinator is probably best placed in the centre. The spacing between each group member can be varied according to the visibility but for safety, it is best for each to remain within the range of vision of the next person.

A sweep search requires careful leadership to retain party cohesiveness. All members should maintain a similar speed, so broken or craggy ground makes supervision particularly difficult. A communication system is best discussed before commencing the search; ensuring that any message is passed all the way along the line. If the line begins to break up, the leader should reorganise the party before communication is compromised. The party reconvenes when the feature is found or the leader calls a halt (when it is felt that the party has overshot its objective). In the latter case, the group can be moved sideways and a new search started on the back bearing.

2.11.8 Outriggers

A variation of the sweep search can be used to ascertain slope angle and aspect in poor visibility, when it is possible to distinguish shapes but not see any horizons. The search method is unchanged but by watching the relative height of party members on either side it is possible to observe the landform around the searchers. This technique works best with party members of similar height and can be particularly effective at night using head-torches. With practice, this method can assist in finding quite subtle variations in slope.

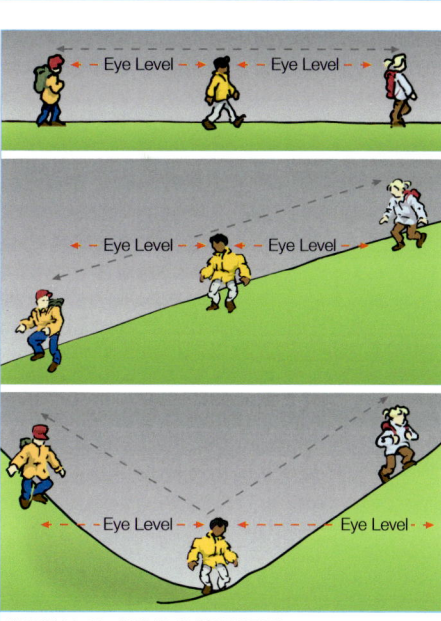

FIGURE 2.48   A SWEEP SEARCH

2.12 Other searches

Some navigators advocate a spiral of expanding right-angled turns walking multiples of the limit of visibility. This allows an exhaustive search but it is time consuming and it can make it difficult to return to the starting point. The technique involves walking two sides of a square with sides of 100 metres (if the visibility is 50 metres), followed by the next two sides at 150 metres, and the next two at 200 metres. This allows any objects within 50 metres of the line of travel (i.e. the limit of visibility) to be spotted.

FIGURE 2.49   USING OUTRIGGERS

Putting it together

Having looked at all the skills and techniques it is important to see how they might fit together so as to navigate safely between two points. The example below shows how you might navigate from point A to B in good visibility. Page 82 shows how a similar example may be navigated in poor visibility.

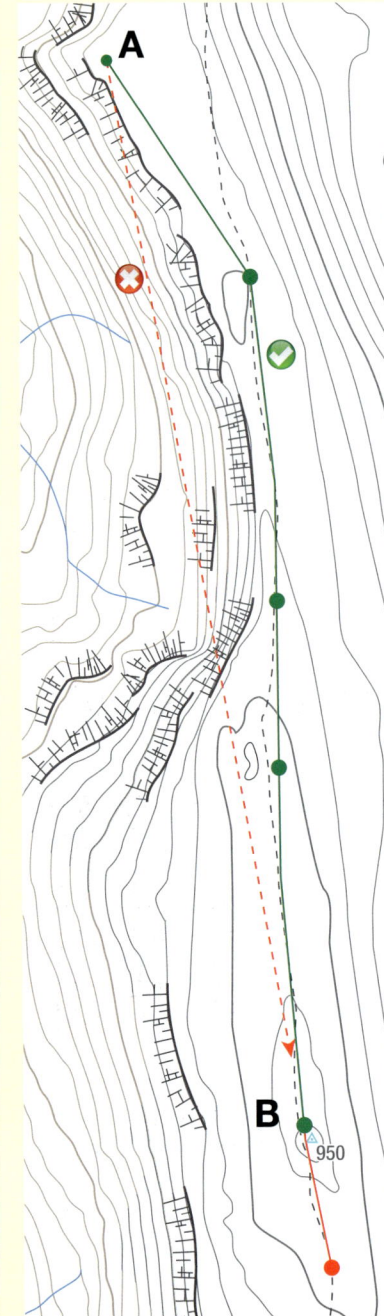

Set the map and confirm your current location. Select a suitable navigation target; Trig point 950m. Can you see this from your current location? If so you may be able to walk there by just using the ground in front of you to route find to the destination. Assess the weather/visibility and terrain. Work through **'5 Whats'** or **'5 Ds'** to gain information about the route. With good visibility it is now possible to walk the route keeping track of the ground and features identified between the two points.

From the start walk 500m across flat ground rising slightly (10m max) to first feature. ❶ **Ring contour**. To continue note the slight change in direction and descend no more than 10m (one contour) following ridge with steep ground to the West and broad convex slope to the East.

❷ After a further 400m ground rises gently, the ridge also broadens to the West as the crag line turns away. ❸ Continue to climb gently passing a **small ring contour**.

❹ ⚠ Reach trig point, set map and confirm destination by mentally working back through strategy and indentifying the features surrounding location; ground descending on all sides. ❺ The **catching feature** of descending ground can also be used to confirm destination.

Part III

Winter Navigation

FIGURE 3.01   CROSSING A SNOW BRIDGE

To be able to navigate effectively and confidently to the base of a specific climb up to or down from a high peak through a winter storm is probably as demanding a task as mountain navigation ever gets. The penalties for an error can be very serious and many winter accidents are the result of a navigational mistake. Winter brings with it such problems as reduced visibility, shorter daylight hours and the absence of many summer navigational features. You must do all the things required to navigate in summer conditions, only better! However, there are extra skills and strategies that can be employed to cope with winter conditions.

3.1 Winter hazards

Hazards include avalanche prone slopes, corniced edges, collapsing snow bridges over streams, frozen lochans, iced up paths as well as the normal crags and cliffs that may have dangerous edges or convex lead-in slopes above.

Good knowledge of winter hazards is fundamental to enjoying safe days in the mountains in these conditions. Snow and avalanches are complex subjects and go beyond the scope of

this book. However, it is important to have an understanding of these hazards, in particular making use of any avalanche forecast information and knowing how to assess the level of risk through gathering information as you travel.

Observations during the day, such as an increased volume of drifting snow or wet rock from a sudden rise in temperature, may indicate an increase in avalanche danger. Try to anticipate where the avalanche prone aspects are and use appropriate route-finding skills and judgment to avoid them. Working out slope angles and aspects from the contours (the most common angle for avalanches to occur are 30° to 45°) and avoiding convex slopes are obvious first steps.

3.1.1 Freezing temperatures
Freezing temperatures can have a major effect on your ability to perform seemingly simple tasks such as taking a bearing. Numb fingers and frozen gloves can make it difficult to manipulate a map and compass. Ice may cause the compass to slip on the map and obscure details on both. Eyelashes can become iced so making it difficult to see clearly and zippers and buckles can freeze making it difficult to access other equipment.

3.1.2 Snow cover
Complete snow cover can dramatically reduce the number of useable navigation features.

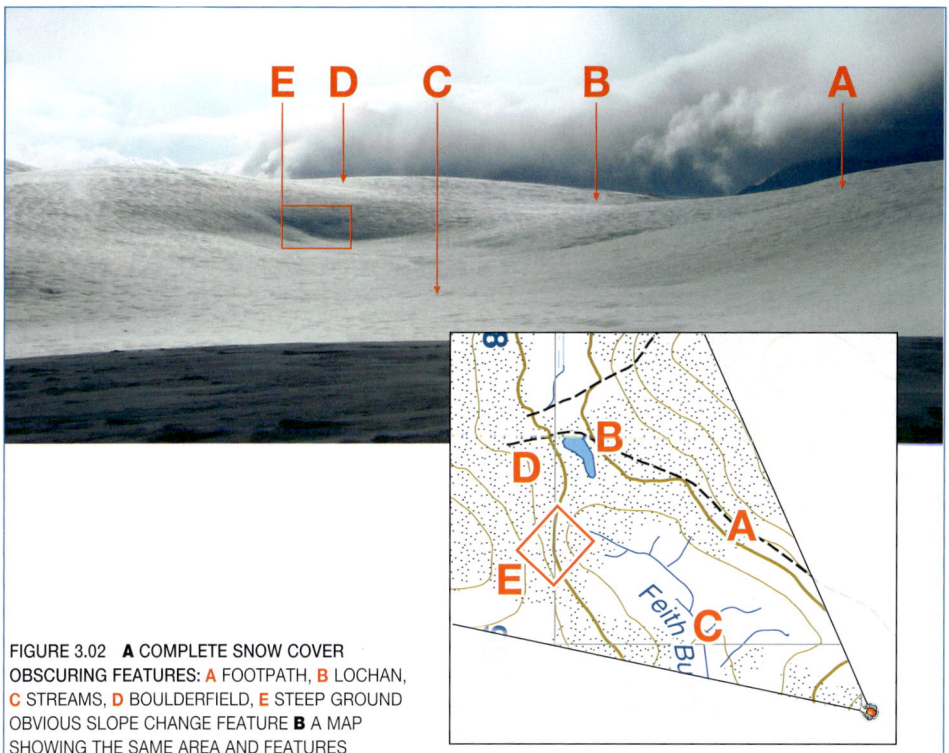

FIGURE 3.02 **A** COMPLETE SNOW COVER
OBSCURING FEATURES: **A** FOOTPATH, **B** LOCHAN,
C STREAMS, **D** BOULDERFIELD, **E** STEEP GROUND
OBVIOUS SLOPE CHANGE FEATURE **B** A MAP
SHOWING THE SAME AREA AND FEATURES

Features such as cairns, footpaths, streams (their junctions and intersection), small lakes, scree slopes, boulder fields and small contour features such as knolls and re-entrants may be under snow and so hidden or unrecognisable. Changes in slope angle may be obscured by deep snow making ground shape and contours more difficult to interpret.

3.1.3 Strong winds
Strong winds can cause drifting off course and make it difficult to hold a map and compass steady. Spindrift can make seeing difficult and a headwind can slow you down. The strength and direction of the wind can influence direction of travel and navigation options. For instance, it may not be safe to follow a corniced edge if the wind is blowing you towards it, or it may be impossible to walk in to the wind.

3.1.4 Poor visibility and white-out
In the worst case, the above conditions can produce a full white-out where you may experience disorientation, affected concentration, numbness and loss of confidence. Prolonged exposure to such conditions can produce feelings of nausea and problems with balance similar to sea-sickness. This is because there is nothing to focus on and some people can feel so bad they have to lie down for a while to recover!

3.2 Coping with the winter environment

Be thoroughly prepared before you start out. General route planning, weather forecast, and if available, avalanche forecasts must be considered, but also make sure that your winter clothing and equipment does the job.

3.2.1 Map
The map should be kept to hand and stored in an accessible pocket and not in your rucksack! It can be modified in a number of ways as suggested in *Section 1.3.1 Choosing the right map* but also consider the following points:

FIGURE 3.03   WELL PREPARED FOR WINTER NAVIGATION   Photo: Mo Lawrie

FIGURE 3.04   EXAMPLE OF A FOLDED MAP

- Fold or cut your map to a manageable size. Although cutting may be a drastic measure as it is often easy enough to fold a map to the area you intend to visit. If your route crosses a fold, then prepare the map so that you do not have to re-fold it while on the hill.
- If you are anticipating some technical navigation with small margins of error then consider printing off a section of map at 1:10,000 for that area so that measuring distances and taking bearings is easier and more accurate.

Some people even measure the important bearings and distances and record them on the map before they go out on the hill.
- Some waterproof maps, such as those that have been laminated, are difficult to fold but strong rubber bands can be used to hold the folded map more conveniently and also make it easier to grip.
- Beware of some types of map cases as in high winds they can blow about and be unmanageable or become stiff and brittle in the cold. The best types are those of soft plastic which can be folded and placed in a pocket.

3.2.2 Compass

This should be accessible, preferably attached to the zipper of a jacket outer pocket and stored with the map. Avoid keeping the compass round your neck or attached to your wrist as in high winds, opening your jacket lets in snow and a compass hanging from your wrist will encourage tangles. Practise operating the compass with gloves on; this will be beneficial when confronted with the rigours of a winter day. *(See Figure 3.06.)*

FIGURE 3.05   WINTER NAVIGATION IN GOOD CONDITIONS   Photo: www.pyb.co.uk

3.2.3 Wristwatch

When timing is used to measure distance on the ground, a digital watch with a stopwatch, a large easily viewed face, easily manipulated function buttons and a backlight to help during night navigation is recommended. One that can be worn on the outside of the jacket, on the wrist or rucksack strap is convenient. (See Figure 3.06.)

3.2.4 Altimeter and GPS

Both these should be regarded as aids to navigation. An altimeter is used as normal, but in winter the speed with which the weather and air pressure alters can be greater than at other times of the year. The altimeter must be re-set regularly to be accurate. Refer to *4.9 Using altimeters*, *page 97* and **Part V**, *page 103* for more comprehensive information on using these two items of equipment.

3.2.5 Clothing and equipment

The metal of your ice axe, particularly the head, can affect the magnetic needle when it is held too close, so keep the axe clear of the compass when

FIGURE 3.06   SHOWING HOW **A** A COMPASS SHOULD BE ATTACHED TO THE JACKET AND **B** WEARING A WRIST WATCH OVER JACKET

FIGURE 3.07 WELL PREPARED WALKER WEARING GOGGLES TO PROTECT EYES FROM BLOWN SNOW

Photo: Lou Beetlestone

3.3 Know where you are

In winter, relocation is more difficult as there are fewer features to be found and major ones may be further apart. Some techniques such as resections have limited use, as for much of the time it is not possible to see and identify two or more features to take back-bearings onto. Observation is continually required with the emphasis being on knowing where you are at all times. The speed with which weather and conditions can change makes this more important than in summer and the option of being able to return to your last known point and start again should be kept open. Ticking off features on the way provides important confirmation that you are on the correct route. In winter there are fewer points for this so less pronounced features can be used such as subtle depressions in the snow that can cover streams or less pronounced slope angle changes.

Having the ability to visualise the shape of the ground when covered in snow by interpreting the contour detail is vital. If the ground does not fit your interpretation or mental image as you walk the leg, then it either means you are not on the intended route, or perhaps you have missed something in the map reading. Either way, *you should stop and re-assess the situation*.

3.4 Winter navigation strategies

In winter conditions, the number of techniques available for navigation may be reduced, as some slopes can be too dangerous to use or cliff and ridge edges too corniced to approach. Using attack points and aiming off can be of limited use because the snow cover can obscure these features. Convex slopes are more likely to be avalanche prone while concave slopes may have corniced tops. However, there are several variations on summer techniques that can be employed.

3.4.1 The winter navigational leg

Following a procedure such as the *5 Ds* or *5 Whats* as shown in *Sections 2.10.1 and 2.10.2, page 54 and 55*, can greatly assist with navigating in winter. It is possible to feel under greater

sighting and following a bearing. Good footwear and where appropriate crampons allow you to concentrate on the navigation rather than what is underfoot.

A shell jacket with a spacious hood, a stiff wired visor and a high main zipper will maintain the shape of the hood in strong winds and pro-tect the face from spindrift. Removable hoods are for occasional use are not adequate for demanding conditions, they can sometimes become detached in strong winds or when pulling the jacket from a rucksack leaving you holding a hood while the jacket flies off in the wind! Cord attached to zip pulls allows for easier use. The map pocket should be on the outside of the jacket and have easy access above your waist belt or harness. Gloves are better than mitts for manipulating the map and the compass particularly when iced up.

Goggles help when navigating into a heavy wind and spectacle-wearers may have no other option but to protect their eyes. It has been known for contact lenses to be blown out by the wind! In winter, navigating in darkness is common. A powerful head torch is recommended, with a strong beam that can penetrate snow and cloud cover.

pressure due to the harsher environment and therefore sometimes miss vital pieces of information. Particular attention should be paid to potential hazards, especially snow conditions that may give rise to avalanche prone slopes and corniced edges. Annotating the map with an arrow to show the prevailing wind and weather conditions may help to focus your attention on this aspect when considering the hazards and trying to identify the areas of greatest risk.

Although map reading under-pins all aspects of navigation, the calculations of bearings and distances are generally done first and the inter-pretation of contour detail is then an on-going process. However, very detailed map reading is less useful if smaller features are hidden under snow.

3.4.2 Winter compass bearing

The procedure for taking a bearing in winter is no different to that of taking one in summer. However the conditions and equipment can often make taking and following a bearing more diffi-cult. Striving for accuracy is important and there are some simple additional measures that can help to ensure accuracy.

FIGURE 3.08   ANNOTATED MAP SHOWING WIND DIRECTION AND POTENTIALLY HAZARDOUS AREAS TO SERVE AS A REMINDER. **REMEMBER THESE MAY CHANGE DURING THE DAY**

- Set the compass to your estimate before you take the bearing. Assuming the estimate is correct, this means that there will be less movement of the housing and potentially reduces any slippage of the compass on the map while taking a bearing.
- When you are taking a bearing, use the marked line on the base-plate that is parallel to the compass edge to line up the two points, rather than the edge itself. This is more accurate since you can see clearly through the base plate that you are correctly linking the two points (there may be measurement lines along the edge obscuring the view of the map below and also light refraction through the edge can affect accuracy).
- Continual build up of ice on the map and compass can be a problem so wipe both clear before taking a bearing.
- Since a bearing can be taken in any position (you do not need to orientate the map), seek shelter to take the bearing or at least face down wind. A kneeling position will allow a knee to be used as a solid base.

3.4.3 Following a bearing in winter

The procedure is the same whenever following a bearing but in winter there may be fewer points to sight on.

3.4.4 Sighting

Usual sighting points such as rocks, boulders and distinctive vegetation can be hidden in winter. However, even with complete snow cover there may be other marks that can be used: old foot-

FIGURE 3.09   TAKING A BEARING IN WINTER CONDITIONS   Photo: Andy Cunningham / Allen Fyffe

Move compass out
and square to body
when sighting

FIGURE 3.10 FOLLOWING A BEARING: SIGHTING THROUGH A MARKER   Photo: Andy Cunningham / Allen Fyffe

steps; different shapes or shades of snow; lumps of ice or pieces of blown vegetation. This will require much more practice to become aware of what can be used. The worse the conditions and visibility, the more it becomes necessary to sight on nearby features and follow a bearing accurately. The greater the snow cover the more difficult following a bearing becomes and in a white-out when there is mist, cloud or blowing snow accuracy can be extremely difficult to achieve.

Unfortunately, there is no real alternative to having something to sight on to when trying to follow a bearing accurately. Simply holding the magnetic needle in the orienting arrow and trying to keep the two in line while walking is unlikely to be sufficiently accurate for any significant distance, particularly in bad weather. With practice though, dead reckoning over short distances is possible until something appears in sight.

In white-out conditions you may be able to produce markers by throwing snowballs or kicking snow out. This needs fairly specific type of conditions to work and is time consuming and laborious. Filling a helmet (if you have one) with snow and clipping it to a rope could provide a more visual aid when thrown out in front. Throwing anything else in front for this reason is more likely to result in lost equipment!

It can be useful in poor visibility to identify a visible feature even if it is *not* on your line of

travel and estimating where the correct position is to the side of that object. In this way there is a physical reference point that enables you to maintain the line of your bearing to the left or right of that particular point.

3.4.5 Sighting on a person

As suggested in ***Section 2.9.2 Following a bearing***, *page 44*, in poor visibility it is possible to send someone, usually the second best navigator, out to the limit of visibility and use them as a sighting point. Before leaving they must know the bearing, the length of the leg and the feature you are seeking. A clear communication procedure must be established using signs or sounds (usually whistle blasts), and the person in front must not go beyond the limit of visibility. Signals should include 'go', 'stop', 'go left', 'go right' and 'come back'. Although effective this is slow and the extra time may not be available in winter. While this can produce a stop start style of navigation it is possible to manage this more effectively to reduce the time spent standing around making adjustments. Two competent navigators using the same bearing can walk in single file with the person at the back using their bearing to check the person in front is maintaining course. This can be done while both people move at a steady pace allowing for more continued progress. Slow navigation with a

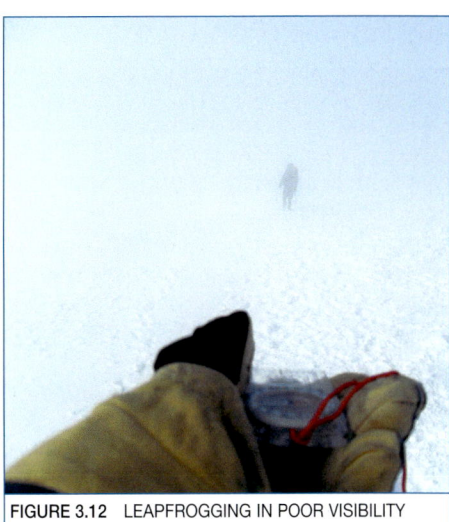

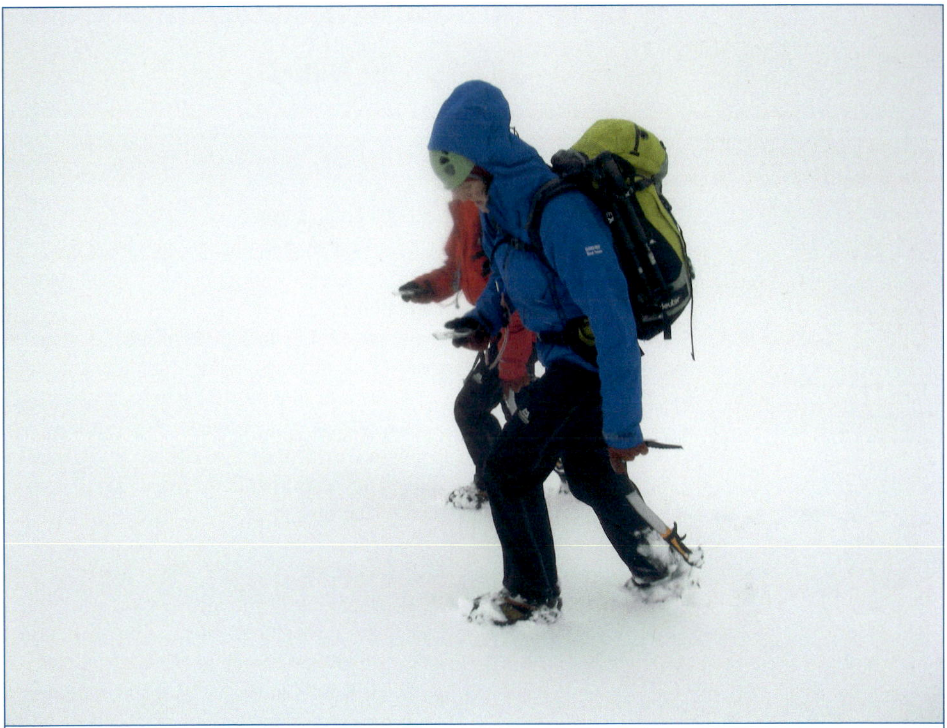

FIGURE 3.11 FULL CONCENTRATION WHILST NAVIGATING IN A WHITEOUT Photo: Lou Beetlestone

group can lead to members getting cold and disinterested.

A variation is ***leapfrogging*** in poor visibility, where there are two navigators of equal competence and they alternate leads out to the limit of visibility, being directed from behind. When swapping leads, remain on the same side each time, otherwise you may 'crab' sideways off the bearing.

3.4.6 Using footprints

In certain types of white-out, especially with soft snow a person can be sent in front to leave steps which can be used as sighting points. The step maker does not try to walk on a bearing but rather in a wavy manner, crossing the bearing line fairly regularly. It is the steps that coincide with the bearing that can be sighted on. The person in front needs to look back regularly and try to cross the bearing regularly. Communications must be established before starting but this method does permit continuous movement.

When using these methods, the person in front will be the first to encounter any serious hazards, such as corniced edges or a semi frozen water courses. Due care and attention needs to be taken to ensure their safety. In extreme circumstances a rope tied between members of the party will help to provide suitable security for the person in front. *See **Section 3.7.2 Using a rope**, page 80 for more details.*

FIGURE 3.12 LEAPFROGGING IN POOR VISIBILITY

FIGURE 3.13 USING FOOTPRINTS TO ASSIST NAVI-
GATION IN VERY POOR VISIBILITY   Photo: Andy Teasdale

3.5 Timing and pacing

Whether timing or pacing (or both) is most appropriate for the leg will depend on factors such as distance, conditions underfoot, weather, accuracy required and how much communication is needed as this can limit the usefulness of pacing which requires counting and concentration. In winter snow the conditions and wind can have a profound effect on speed and someone's ability to pace consistently. In these conditions it is important to exercise good judgment when choosing a navigation technique and to be realistic about how conditions will affect your speed and ability to pace. Timing for example, can vary considerably and may be below 2kph in deep soft snow with two or even three minutes for each 10m of height gained. Alternatively, on good firm neve, it can sometimes be possible to walk faster over the same ground than in summer.

3.6 Navigation considerations in winter

3.6.1 Use safe, large-scale features
Navigating to and from large obvious features will aid poor weather navigation and also in relocation should you need to reverse a leg.

3.6.2 Short legs
Try to keep your navigational legs as short as possible as this will reduce compounding any error made during either the calculation stages or while following a bearing. Since winter navigation can involve featureless terrain, it may be difficult to keep legs shorter than 1km between obvious features.

3.6.3 Contours
Close inspection of the map is crucial for interpreting the finer contour detail. Every bend in a contour signifies something and depending on the scale it may mean a change in aspect or a small feature. The better you are at interpreting contours the more tick-off features you will be able to use while following a bearing. As an example, if walking in featureless terrain and you sense that a slope is becoming steeper then that would be one contour feature to look for on a map, which could be used to locate your position. *Section 2.3 Contour interpretation, page 28* outlines how to interpret contours and while the environment is very different the skills are the same. Indeed many people would argue that because many of the other features are covered by snow, contour interpretation is made easier. Hence the reason for using a map with fewer markings as these will often obscure contour information. An OS 1:50,000 or any of the Harvey series are therefore good choices.

Being able to identify windward and leeward slopes is a part of travelling safely in snow covered terrain. Close inspection of the contour detail can provide information regarding the *aspect* of a particular slope and even the *shape* and *angle*. These are important pieces of information if potential avalanche terrain is to be avoided and should be considered carefully when planning a navigation leg. With this in mind, it is useful to develop an awareness of the steepness of slopes as represented by the density of

Winter route choice and tick-off features

Although route **A** is a long leg at 1.5km (estimated 32 minutes), there are many tick-off features and it is the better route choice. Route **B** is broken into two shorter legs, via the saddle at point **C**. It is less efficient than route **A** because it will take longer overall, it may prove difficult to locate point **C** in the middle of a broad saddle and in this example is more exposed to the wind.

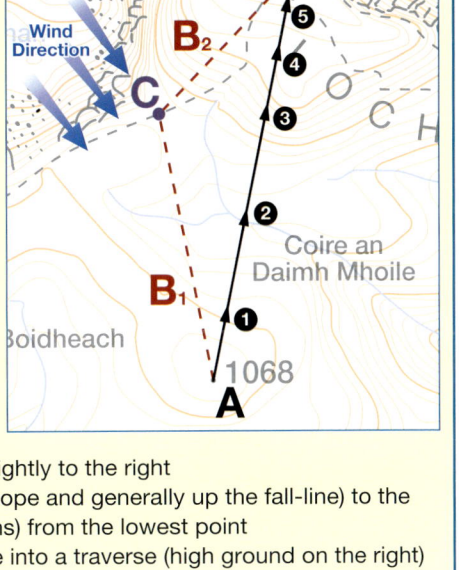

Route Tick-off Points:

1 A gentle descent (more or less on the fall line) from point 1068 leads into a wide depression on slightly steeper ground, with a broad spur on the right
2 After 600m (7–8 mins), the lowest point of the leg is reached (the line of the stream) in an open area with ground descending slightly to the right
3 The ground gradually steepens (concave slope and generally up the fall-line) to the steepest section of the leg at 350m (10 mins) from the lowest point
4 The ground has significantly eased in angle into a traverse (high ground on the right) below a minor knoll ('amoeba' contour) and a vague re-entrant on the left. There may be a very slight descent into the re-entrant on the left
5 A gentle, uniform slope up the fall-line leads to the open summit of Cac Carn Mor.

the contour lines. While it will never be completely accurate, being able to estimate if a slope is passable and whether or not an avalanche risk is present is a useful skill to acquire. *Figure 2.07 on page 30* shows how the distance between index contour lines on various scale maps relates to slope angle. While there is a potential for an avalanche to occur on any angle slope, statistics show that most avalanches run on slopes between 30° and 45°. On a 1:50,000 map with a 10 metre contour interval the lines between the index contours start to be removed at approximately 30°. Unfortunately up to this point the lines look crowded giving the appearance of a very steep slope but as a rule of thumb if you can only just distinguish all five contour lines then you should consider this as a potential avalanche slope.

3.6.4 Winter route choice

Don't break a long distance leg into shorter sections unless there are clearly identifiable features to tick-off, aim for, or use as attack points. In other words avoid setting yourself up to struggle by attempting difficult navigation to vague points

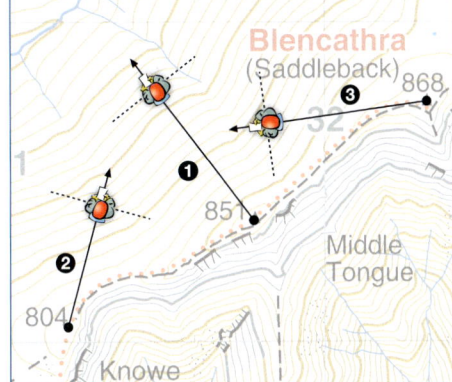

FIGURE 3.14 **CONSIDER THE ANGLE OF THE BEARING TO THE FALL LINE:** (1) THE BEARING LEADS DIRECTLY DOWN THE FALL-LINE WITH LEVEL GROUND ON EITHER SIDE (AT 90° TO THE BEARING) (2) THE BEARING LEADS TO THE RIGHT OF THE FALL-LINE. HIGH GROUND IS ON THE RIGHT-HAND SIDE AND LOW GROUND ON THE LEFT-HAND SIDE (3) THE BEARING LEADS TO THE LEFT OF THE FALL-LINE WITH GROUND RISING TO THE LEFT AND DESCENDING TO THE RIGHT

purely to shorten the distance of a longer leg (see *Winter route choice and tick-off features*).

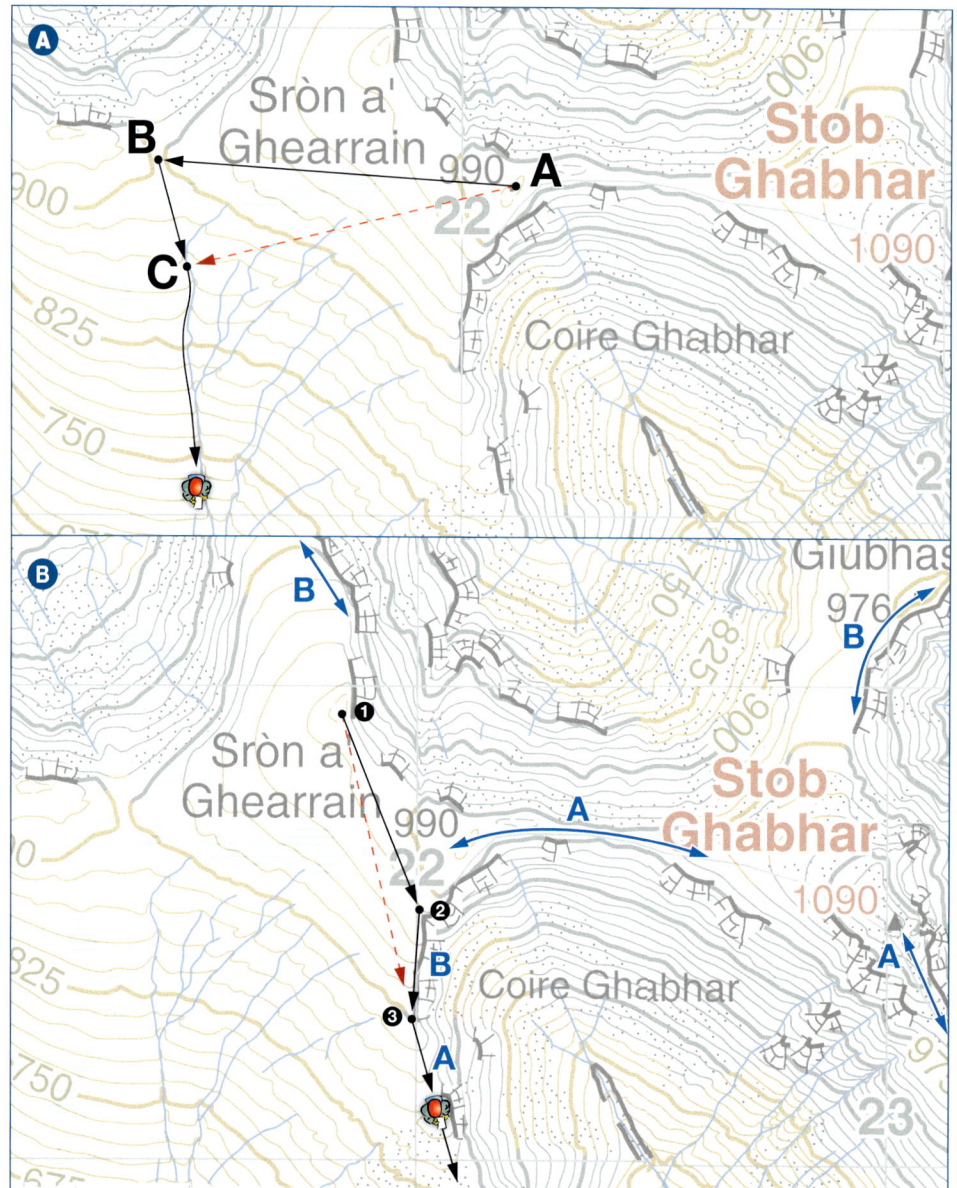

FIGURE 3.15 **A AN ATTACK POINT:** THE SADDLE AT POINT **B** IS USED AS AN ATTACK POINT TO LOCATE AND DESCEND A STREAM LINE FROM POINT **C**. THE NARROW SADDLE IS AN OBVIOUS LARGE SCALE FEATURE AND IS MUCH CLOSER TO POINT C THAN IS POINT **A**
B AIMING OFF ONTO A LINEAR FEATURE: INSTEAD OF TAKING A DIRECT BEARING FROM POINT **1** TO THE RIDGE AT POINT **3**, TO AVOID THE POSSIBILITY OF BEING DRAWN ONTO THE SLOPE ON THE RIGHT, A BEARING IS TAKEN TO POINT **2**, AIMING OFF TO THE LEFT OF THE DIRECT BEARING AND ON TO THE CORRIE EDGE. THE EDGE IS FOLLOWED DOWN TO POINT **3**. **LINEAR FEATURES: A** A RIDGE, **B** AN EDGE, **C** A STREAM LINE AS INDICATED ON UPPER MAP

3.6.5 Slope changes

Major slope changes such as defined edges are good features to use in winter. A flat spot on a broad shoulder, a saddle before a top, or a small highpoint are less obvious features that can also be used. On a wide flat saddle or a broad shoulder, navigate to a recognisable change in slope which would indicate that you are on one side of the

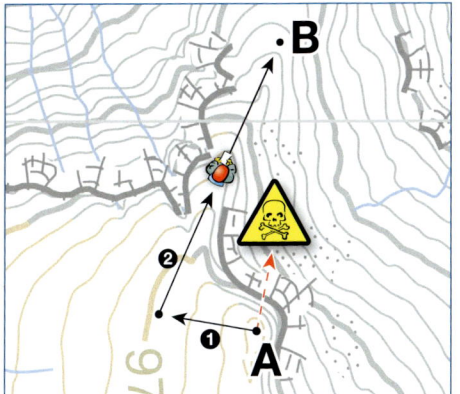

FIGURE 3.16   A DOG-LEG: A DIRECT LINE FROM POINT A TO POINT B IS NOT POSSIBLE AND A DOG-LEG IS APPROPRIATE TO AVOID THE EDGE. LEG 1 IS A SHORT DISTANCE DOWN THE FALL-LINE TO A POINT THAT WILL ENABLE LEG 2 TO BE A DIRECT LINE DOWN THE RIDGE TO POINT B

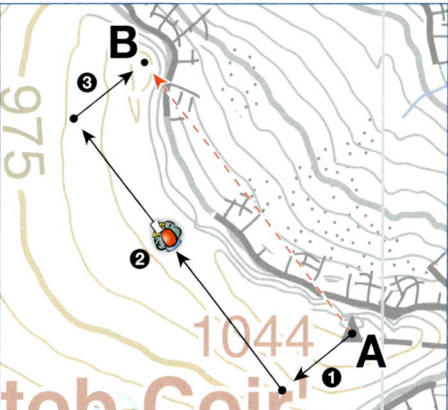

FIGURE 3.17   BOXING A CORRIE: A DIRECT LINE BETWEEN POINTS A AND B IS NOT POSSIBLE, AND TO AVOID THE EDGE, A SINGLE DOG-LEG IS CONSIDERED INAPPROPRIATE. TO BOX THE CORRIE, FIRST TAKE A DIRECT MAGNETIC BEARING FROM POINT A TO POINT B AND MEASURE THE DISTANCE BETWEEN THE TWO POINTS. (1) SUBTRACT 90° FROM THE DIRECT BEARING AND ESTIMATE THE DISTANCE ON THE NEW BEARING NEEDED TO AVOID THE EDGE ON STAGE 2. FOLLOW THE BEARING FOR THE ESTIMATED DISTANCE (2) ADD 90° TO REGAIN THE ORIGINAL MAGNETIC BEARING AND FOLLOW THIS FOR THE CALCULATED DISTANCE BETWEEN POINTS A AND B (3) ADD 90° AND PACE THE DISTANCE CALCULATED ON STAGE 1 UP TO POINT B

feature rather than at a vague point near the middle. This positions you more clearly on the map.

3.6.6 On a slope

When ascending or descending a slope, try and note the angle to the fall-line: are you travelling directly up or down a slope? Or are you crossing a slope diagonally? It is then possible to relate this information to the contours. Use your compass base-plate line to link up the two points (start and finish points) and check the angle this is to the contours. At 90° you will be on the fall-line and if at an angle to the contours, note on which side will be high ground and low ground as you follow the bearing up or down the slope. The most difficult bearings to follow are ones which head diagonally across a slope.

3.6.7 Aiming off and attack points

Use obvious features you know will be visible on the ground. Aiming off onto large scale linear contour features such as an obvious slope change is worthwhile, while trying to use a path may be a mistake (see Figure 3.15).

3.6.8 Linear features

Linear features may be used to follow as a handrail but take into account safety considerations such as cornices, visibility and wind direction if following an edge. Consider convexities relating to avalanches if you use a slope change feature (see Figure 3.15).

3.6.9 Dog-legs

One technique common to winter is walking on a dog-leg. Travel on one bearing for a set distance and then turn on to another bearing to walk a further distance to the main objective. In fact, coming down the most popular route off Britain's highest mountain Ben Nevis, requires exactly this technique. As a general rule keep the first leg as short as possible as this reduces any error at the end (see Figure 3.16).

Select a point on the map for the dog leg and measure distance and bearing to it. This point may be one which is a physical feature that may not be visible such as a stream junction, or it could be a point which is only on the map such as grid line and contour intersection. Importantly, it is something you can measure to and from when taking the distance and bearing. When planning a dog-leg, remember it is easier to walk at right angles to the contours – the fall-line.

3.6.10 Boxing

Boxing is basically a double dog-leg and can be used to good effect in poor visibility to avoid a

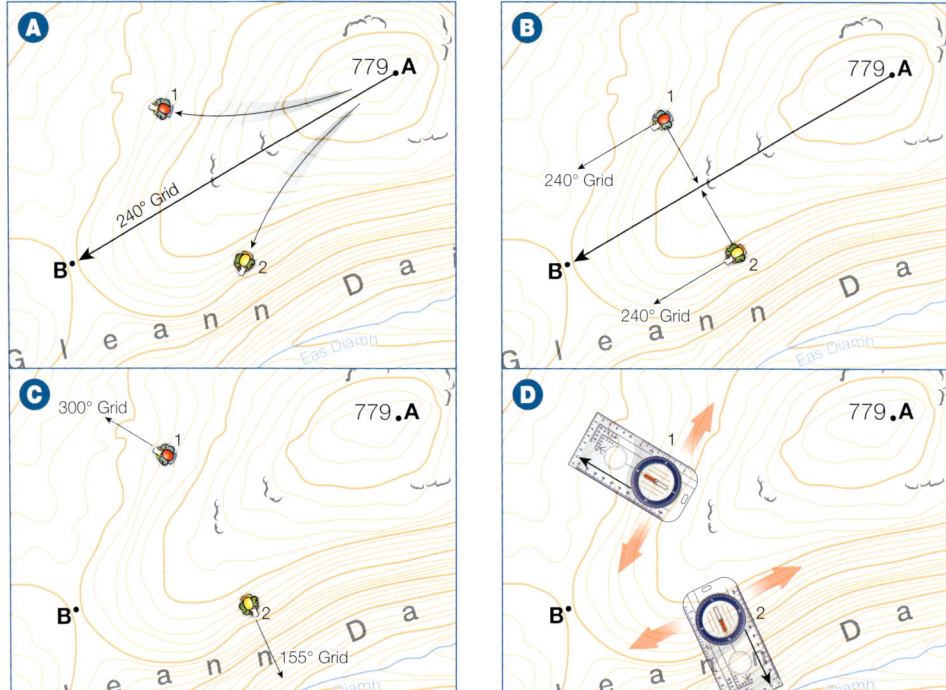

FIGURE 3.18 **SLOPE ASPECT: A** RELOCATING USING SLOPE ASPECT. THE NAVIGATOR HAS DRIFTED OFF COURSE ONTO A RELATIVELY STEEP SLOPE AND IS UNAWARE ON WHICH SIDE OF THE SHOULDER, EITHER AT POINT **1** OR POINT **2**. **B** BY ALIGNING THE COMPASS, IT IS APPARENT THAT THERE IS HIGH GROUND TO THE LEFT AT POINT **1** INDICATING A POSITION RIGHT OF THE INTENDED LINE WHILE AT POINT **2**, HIGH GROUND IS TO THE RIGHT, INDICATING A POSITION LEFT OF THE INTENDED LINE. **C** CALCULATE THE SLOPE ASPECT BY TAKING A MAGNETIC BEARING DOWN THE FALL-LINE AND CONVERT TO A GRID BEARING. **D** KEEPING THE ORIENTING LINES PARALLEL TO GRID NORTH AND THE ORIENTING ARROW ALIGNED NORTH (NOT THE NEEDLE), MOVE THE COMPASS ACROSS THE MAP AROUND THE ESTIMATED POSITION UNTIL THE BASEPLATE LINE CUTS THE CONTOURS AT RIGHT-ANGLES

corniced cliff edge with dangerous in-cuts such as gullies (*see Figure 3.17*).

3.6.11 Slope aspect

Finding the fall-line in winter can be difficult under poor visibility, full snow cover and flat light. Depending on the conditions, rolling a snowball or using the group to show the shape of the ground can help (*see Figure 3.18*).

3.6.12 What happens if…?

Interpret and visualise how the shape of the ground will differ if you travel off the bearing or overshoot the objective. Is there a catching feature at the point you are heading to? If there are areas which you need to avoid at all costs then make sure you know what the ground will look and feel like as you approach the hazard. If you have

planned ahead carefully then alarm bells should start ringing before you get into danger. Ironically accidents and major navigation errors often happen in relatively benign conditions or on easier ground. Human nature shows that we find it easy to concentrate when there is real danger or the task is clearly demanding but tend to relax and lose concentration when things are more routine. Reaching the top of a strenuous climb in winter is an obvious case when it is easy to relax because you are no longer on steep ground but actually the serious decision-making might just be beginning. Similarly being out with a group of experienced peers can lead to mistakes simply because no one person assumes responsibility for the navigation and the whole group falls into the trap of collective incompetence (*see Figure 3.20*).

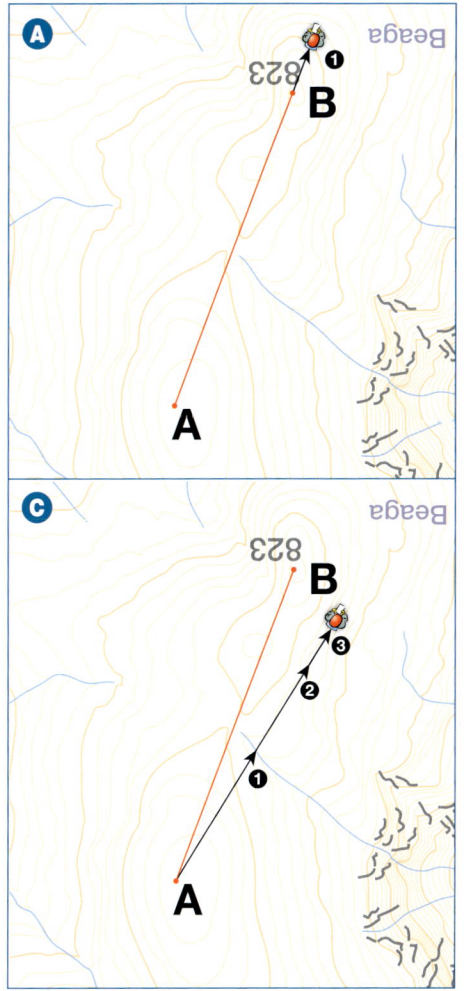

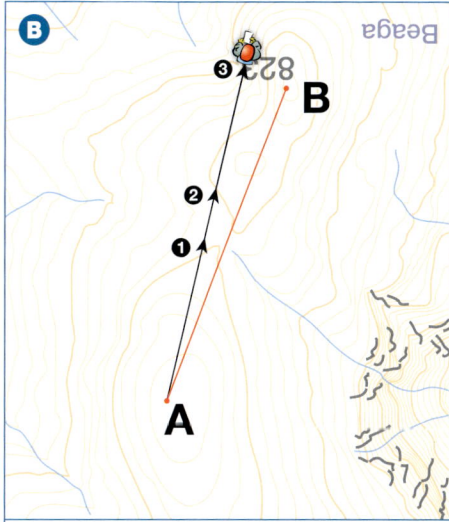

FIGURE 3.20 **THE SHAPE OF THE GROUND – CONSIDER THE ALTERNATIVES: A** OVERSHOOTING THE DESTINATION. CONTINUING ON THE BEARING AFTER POINT **B**, THE GROUND DESCENDS RELATIVELY STEEPLY – A GOOD CATCHING FEATURE: POINT **1**. **B** TRAVELLING 10° LEFT OF THE BEARING. AT POINTS **1** AND **2**, THERE IS HIGH GROUND TO THE RIGHT WHEREAS THE CORRECT LINE TRAVELS ALONG THE CREST OF THE FEATURE. AT POINT **3**, THE LINE DESCENDS ONTO STEEP GROUND AT A RE-ENTRANT WITH STEEP HIGH GROUND ON THE RIGHT. **C** TRAVELLING 10° RIGHT OF THE BEARING. THE LINE OF TRAVEL IMMEDIATELY LEAVES THE CREST AND DESCENDS TO A RE-ENTRANT AT POINT **1**, WITH GROUND RISING TO THE SADDLE ON THE LEFT. THEREAFTER, THE LINE RISES OUT OF THE RE-ENTRANT, TRAVERSES BELOW THE CREST AND KNOLL AT POINT **2** AND CONTINUES THE TRAVERSE TO POINT **3** WITH INCREASINGLY HIGH GROUND ON THE LEFT

12 NOTES FOR INSTRUCTORS Winter

Assuming that most people will have a good level of summer navigation experience, a quick revision of basic skills may be productive. Practical experience gained in the hills under winter conditions is invaluable. Practise following bearings and accurate timing and pacing in difficult winter conditions. Revise contour interpretation and be observant while navigating and let people adjust to limited contour features under winter conditions. Stress that there is little use in interpreting contours outside visibility limits. Training should also include points that encourage visualisation skills such as map memory exercises.

Photo: Keith Ball

FIGURE 3.19   USING GROUP MEMBERS TO SHOW
SHAPE OF THE GROUND   Photo: Keith Ball

FIGURE 3.21   USING A ROPE TO SAFEGUARD PARTY
IN DIFFICULT CONDITIONS   Photo: Andy Teasdale

3.7 Observations

Continually observing the ground and any features that can be distinguished is vital in poor conditions. There is no room for lapses of concentration. If the cloud lifts, however briefly, then stop and gather as much information about the terrain as possible and use it to confirm your position. Taking a bearing on significant features that sometimes appear briefly in gaps in the cloud can provide useful information in helping to determine location and direction. Clearings in the cloud can appear and disappear very quickly, even in the time it takes to reach for your compass. Using a trekking pole, ice axe or another member of your party to mark the direction of the feature you caught a fleeting glimpse of will allow you time to locate your compass and take an accurate bearing.

3.7.1 Using the group
Group members can be used to assist sighting while following a bearing or to show the shape of the ground. Placing people on the bearing on either side of the navigator will give an impression of slope angles. Keeping an eye on a group that is walking in line behind the navigator can reveal a high or low points on the ground.

Using the group in a sweep search can be useful but the leader must have complete confidence in the ability of the persons on the outside of the sweep. To place inexperienced people out of sight in difficult conditions can have serious consequences. Other search techniques that can keep the group together may be more appropriate in these situations. *See **Section 2.11.6 Searches**, pages 62 for information on search techniques.*

3.7.2 Using a rope
Using the rope is a last resort and should be avoided through planning, route choice and good navigation. However, there may be times when using the rope might provide the safest option. Operating in a small group or even as a pair it is possible to employ the rope in a simple manner to safeguard each other. In very poor conditions it may provide the best way of sticking together. Corniced edges are normally avoided but there may be occasions when it is necessary to approach or follow one, for example when looking for a

FIGURE 3.22 PROTECTING TRAVEL NEAR AN EDGE

descent route or using an edge as a handrail. *Figure 3.22* shows how best to organise a group of people when using a rope to safeguard a person approaching an edge. Individuals are tied onto the rope around the waist using a loop created from a simple knot. If the leader should fall through the cornice the rope will cut into the snow and with a weight on the other end they will be counter balanced and prevented from falling further.

Putting it together in winter

The example below shows how you might navigate from point **A** to **B** in poor visibility. Whilst this example focuses on dealing with winter conditions the strategy and skills used could be employed in summer conditions if the visibility/weather were poor.

❶ Set the map and confirm current location. Identify suitable navigation target. Remember in winter some features on the map will be covered with snow and may be difficult to find. Assess conditions paying particular attention to snow/avalanche hazard. This leg has been broken down into 3 sections so as to avoid the potential hazards (steep ground & cliffs).

A wide margin for error is given on each leg and catching features are identified for each section. Work through **'5 Whats'** or **'5 Ds'** to establish a strategy for each section. Whilst the ultimate goal is to reach point B, it is important to concentrate on the first leg to point **❷**. The first two legs will test **'Dead Reckoning'** skills as there are no features to confirm location. The last '0' of 1100 is used to help take an accurate **bearing** and **distance** from the map.

❷ The changing nature of terrain is noted as "the" **compass bearing** is followed. When **pacing** and **timing** are complete, stop and confirm position. In the event of overshooting the point the ground descends more steeply. Work through strategy for next section. If conditions remain the same it is likely the same set of skills will be required.

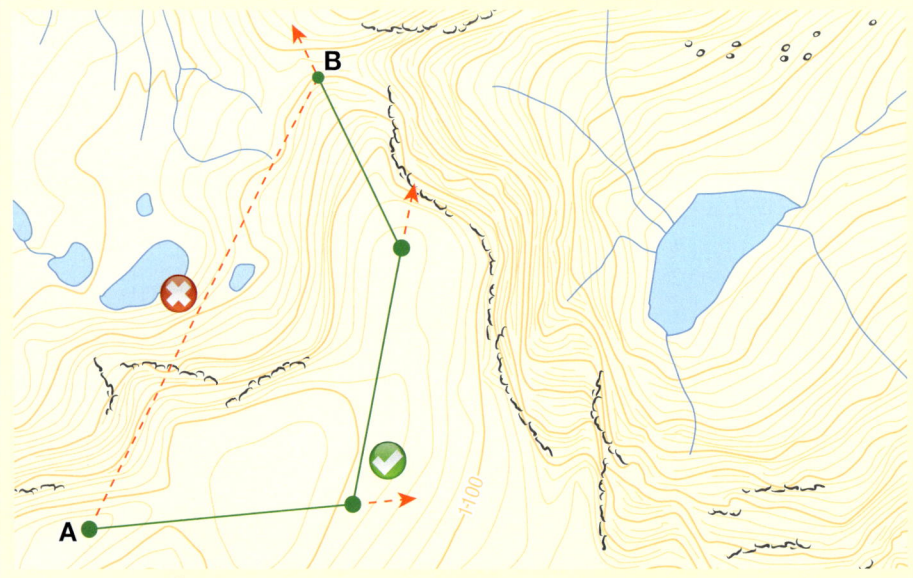

❸ As before, follow **compass bearing** until **pacing** and **timing** are finished. Stop and confirm position. Take note of the **catching feature** as this is very close to an edge. Take new bearing to point B; allow a margin for error with regards the edge to the East.

Follow bearing carefully; pacing may be difficult on the steeper ground. Stop when timing and pacing are complete and confirm position. As the gradient levels the destination should be close. **Relocation** techniques may be required to confirm destination.

Part IV

Overseas Navigation

FIGURE 4.01 NAVIGATING AWAY FROM THE PATH WITH AN UNFAMILIAR MAP CAN BE CHALLENGING

4.1 Maps

The quality of mapping throughout the British Isles is some of the best in the world. In some parts of Europe the quality of the maps leaves a lot to be desired. And this can be worse in developing countries where the maps can be a combination of imagination along with some input from local inhabitants rather than from a detailed survey.

Trying to source maps before a trip is important in order to allow time to become familiar with the scale, symbols and the amount of information available. This is an obvious necessity when planning and can prevent surprises when faced with an odd looking map for the first time in country. Familiarity with the map prior to its use will provide more confidence.

Obtaining maps for foreign countries can also present its own issues. Generally, the further afield the destination, the longer the period required for preparation. Sourcing relevant maps and guides should be a priority. Various agencies can supply maps for most regions across the globe and purchase can often be made over the internet but it is sometimes not possible to obtain the best maps via this method and more appropriate maps may need to be sourced while in country.

For remote countries, military maps offer a good deal of information. However, tracking these down is often only the first problem. Many countries still regard their maps as official state secrets: being caught with one in your possession could land you in trouble. Fortunately some countries are more liberal with this information and with a little research it may be possible to obtain a more detailed map for the area you are visiting. Embassies or consulates may be able to advise as might trekking companies and individuals who visit areas on a regular basis. As well as providing a wealth of other useful information they may be able to assist with details on mapping for the area.

Often when operating near borders it may be possible to obtain maps from two different countries for the same area of land, for instance Spain and France. This can provide more information and, on occasions, a more accurate map better suited for purpose. Before departure, laminate the map to preserve it through the

Navigating in other countries can present a variety of problems beyond mountain navigation. Throughout the course of a trip the terrain may vary greatly, from jungle to mountains to high desolate plateaus all of which will require a slightly different approach. On occasions the navigation may be straight forward, especially when following popular trails or well-marked route itineraries. Many of these are established paths used by locals which negate the need for fine detailed navigation and may not even necessitate the use of a map or compass. However, having skills and equipment you can fall back on is fundamental in the mountains and incidentally is often reassuring when facing the challenge of navigation in the large towns or cities encountered en route!

FIGURE 4.02 TAKE TIME TO STUDY AN UNFAMILIAR MAP CAREFULLY BEFORE USE

FIGURE 4.03 LAMINATED FOREIGN MAP BEING USED IN THE FIELD SHOWING ANNOTATIONS

various conditions it may be subjected to. This will make it easier to annotate the map as you travel, allowing adjustments to be made as inaccuracies are discovered.

4.2 Grid systems

When using foreign maps it is likely you will encounter many different grid systems and map datums (*see Section 4.2.3. Map datum, page 89*). Two of the most useful and widely used systems are latitude and longitude and the more modern and user friendly UTM grid (Universal Transverse Mercator system).

4.2.1 Universal Transverse Mercator grid system

The UTM projection and grid system was adopted by the US Army in 1947 for designating co-ordinates on large scale military maps. Still used by the US military and NATO it can also be found on many overseas maps and is often shown alongside the longitude and latitude grid system.

The UTM system divides the earth into 60 zones each six degrees of longitude wide. These zones extend from latitude 80° South to 84° North. Neither pole is included in the UTM system; instead a separate grid known as Universal Polar Stereographic (UPS) is used.

UTM zones are numbered 1 to 60, starting at the International Date Line, longitude 180°, and proceeding east. Zone 1 extends from 180° West to 174° West longitude and so on.

Each zone is divided into horizontal bands spanning eight degrees of latitude. These bands are lettered South to North, beginning at 80°

South with the letter C and ending with the letter X at 84° North. The letters O and I are skipped to avoid confusion with the numbers one and zero.

A square grid is superimposed and aligned so that grid lines are parallel to the centre of the zone, called the central meridian.

The UTM system is designed so that you read horizontal distances eastward and vertical distances northward from reference lines. This is the same as using the Ordnance Survey grid reference system. Not surprisingly, a distance in metres east is referred to as the 'easting', and a distance in metres to the north is referred to as the 'northing'.

As with the OS system it is possible to use both sets of co-ordinates to create a reference number unique to a particular location on the map. A complete UTM reference includes the UTM zone number and band letter followed firstly by the 'easting' and then by the 'northing.'

Eastings are made up of six digits as opposed to northings which are made up of seven. The convention is to add a 0 at the start of the eastings. This is particularly important when entering this information into a GPS

Some UTM northing values are valid in both the northern and southern hemisphere. In order to avoid confusion the full co-ordinate needs to specify if the location is north or south of the equator. This is usually done by including the letter for the latitude band.

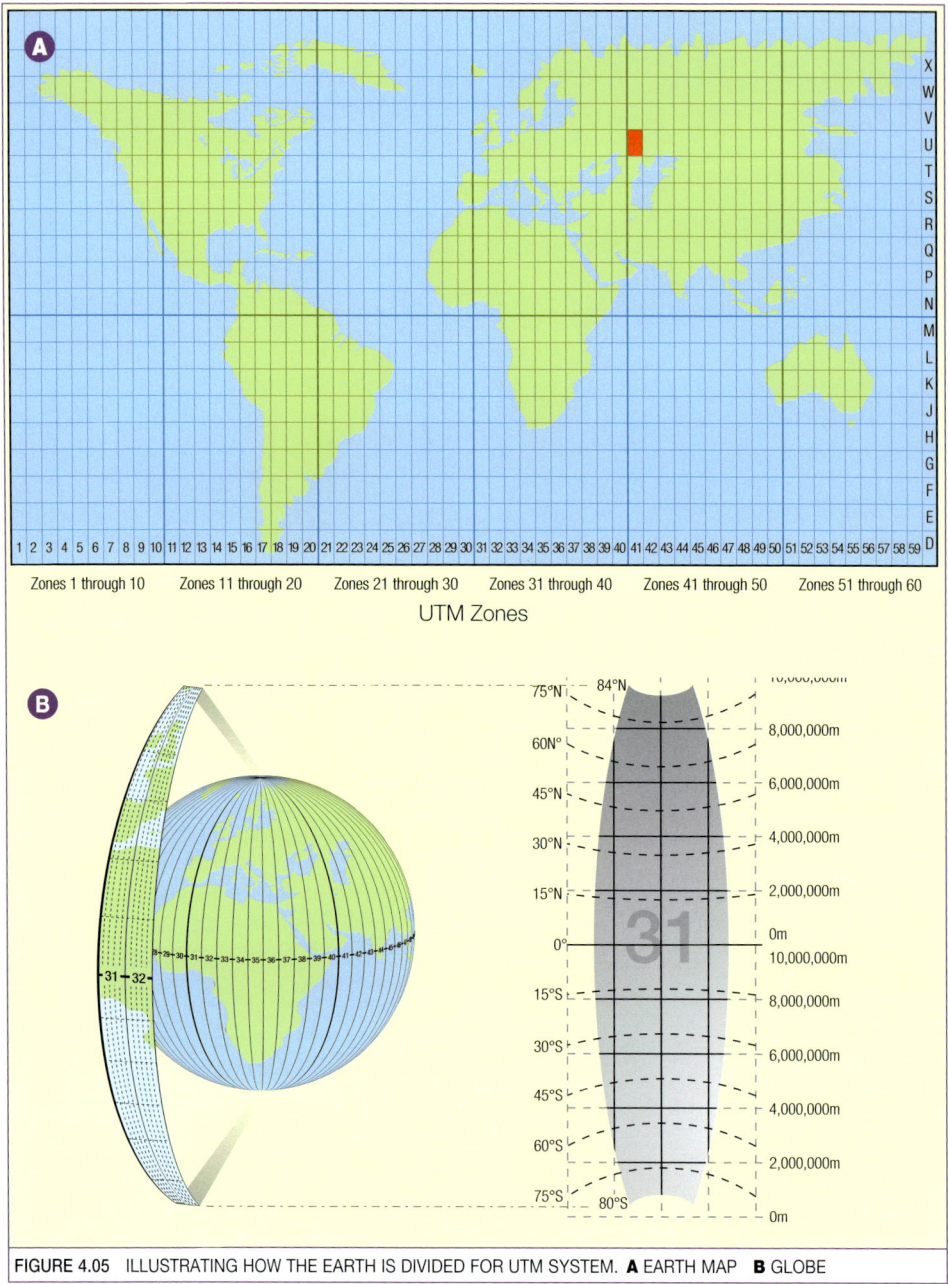

FIGURE 4.05   ILLUSTRATING HOW THE EARTH IS DIVIDED FOR UTM SYSTEM. **A** EARTH MAP   **B** GLOBE

4.2.2 Latitude and longitude

Developed and implemented by mariners and explorers in the middle ages to help guide them across the oceans, latitude and longitude is the oldest co-ordinate system. It divides the earth into lines of latitude, which indicate how far north or south of the equator you are, and lines of longitude, which indicate how far east or west you are of the prime meridian.

Latitude lines are always parallel to the equator and are known as 'parallels'. They become smaller in diameter as they reach the poles but the distance between them remains the same wherever you are on the globe. Longitude lines are

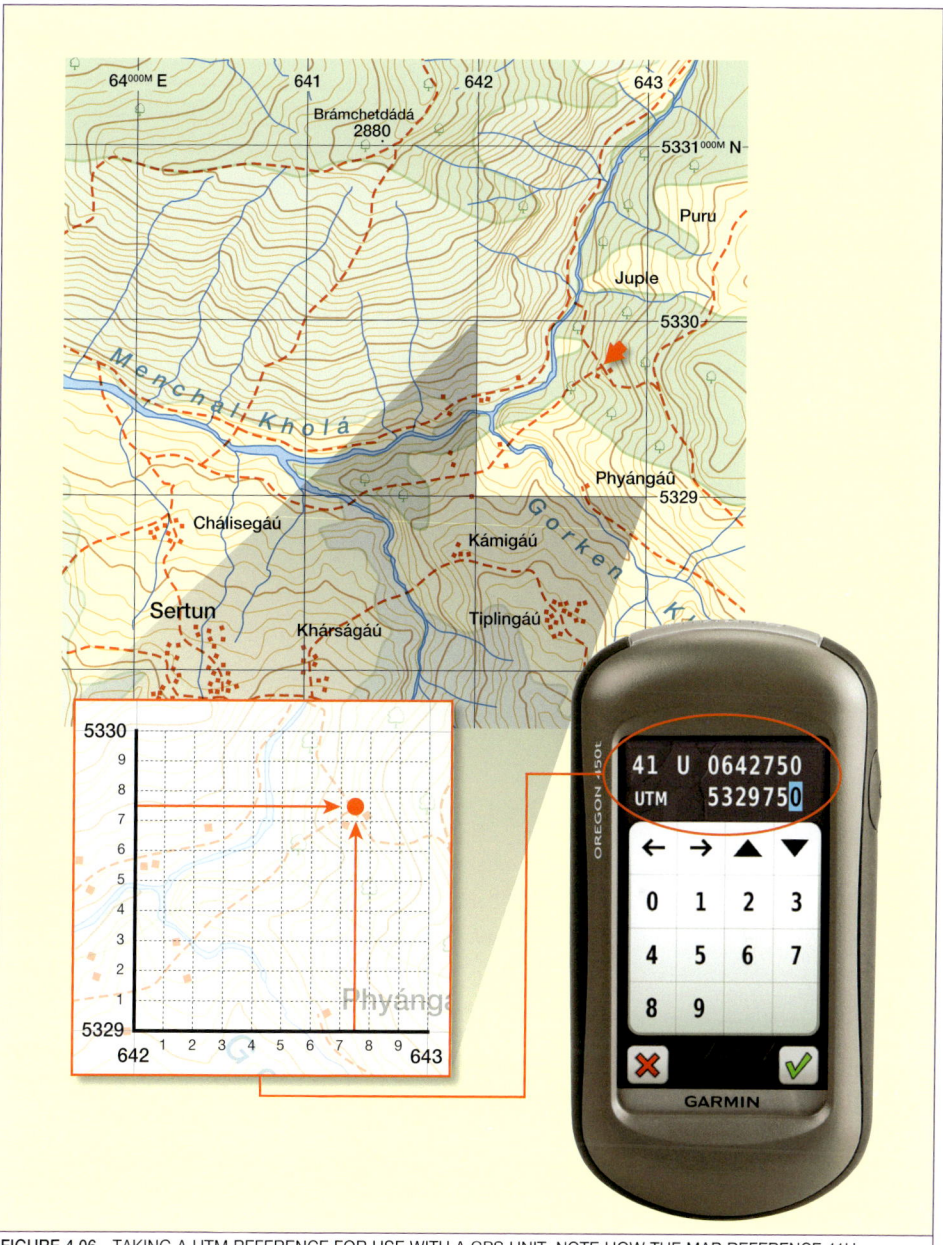

FIGURE 4.06 TAKING A UTM REFERENCE FOR USE WITH A GPS UNIT. NOTE HOW THE MAP REFERENCE 41U MATCHES THE HIGHLIGHTED BOX IN **FIGURE 5.05** AND PREFIXES THE REFERENCE NUMBER

known as meridians and circle the globe from pole to pole, perpendicular to lines of latitude. Unlike lines of latitude they are all the same diameter and do not run parallel, but converge at the poles. Longitude does not have a natural reference point such as the equator so the 0° line known as the prime meridian is an arbitrary designation. In the 18th century it was the British, being the most dominant navigators, that decided to define this as the line that runs through the Royal Observatory in Greenwich.

The combination of meridians of longitude and parallels of latitude establishes a grid by which exact positions can be determined: for example,

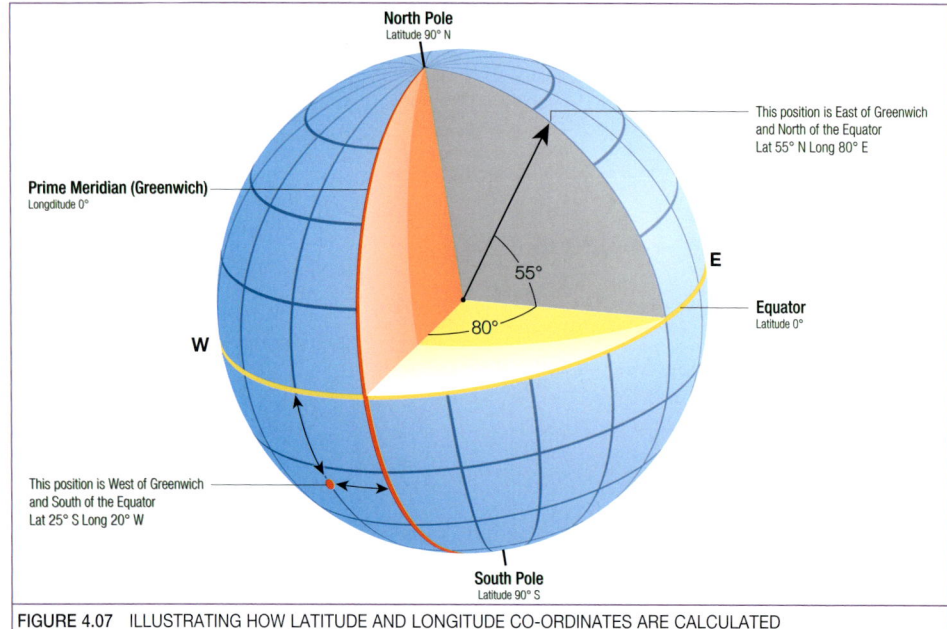

North Pole
Latitude 90° N

This position is East of Greenwich
and North of the Equator
Lat 55° N Long 80° E

Prime Meridian (Greenwich)
Longditude 0°

55°

E

Equator
Latitude 0°

W

80°

This position is West of Greenwich
and South of the Equator
Lat 25° S Long 20° W

South Pole
Latitude 90° S

FIGURE 4.07   ILLUSTRATING HOW LATITUDE AND LONGITUDE CO-ORDINATES ARE CALCULATED

a point described as 40°N, 30°W is located 40° of arc north of the equator and 30° of arc west of the Greenwich meridian.

To precisely locate points on the earth's surface, degrees of longitude and latitude are divided into minutes (') and seconds ("), which relate to the geometry of a circle as opposed to time. There are 60 minutes in each degree with each minute being divided into 60 seconds. Seconds can be further divided into tenths, hundredths, or even thousandths

- 1° of latitude is 111.12km (69 miles)
- 1' of latitude is one nautical mile (1.85km or 1.15 miles)
- 1" of latitude is approximately 100 feet (30 metres)

Because lines of longitude converge at the poles the distances between them decrease as they move further from the equator:

- 1° of longitude is 111.12km (69 miles) at the equator, but only 78km (49 miles) at 45° N or S
- 1' of longitude is one nautical mile (1.85km or 1.15 miles) only at the equator

There are three ways of expressing longitude and latitude for any given location:

1 Hemisphere degrees minutes and seconds,

as explained above hddd°.mm'.ss.s"

2 Hemisphere degrees and decimal minutes hddd°.mm.mmm'

3 Hemisphere decimal degrees hddd.ddddd°

The most commonly used method is hemisphere degrees and decimal minutes hddd°.mm.mmm'.

As an example of how these systems may be expressed:

YES TOR ON DARTMOOR = SX 581 902	OSGB GRID REFERENCE
N 50° 41' 36.3" W 4° 0' 37.6"	hddd°.mm'.ss.s"
N 50° 41.6' W 4° 0.616'	hddd°.mm.mmm'
N 50.69333 W 4.01027	hddd.ddddd°

Most maps show latitude and longitude scales running along their edges; however their ease of use will depend on how the map has been printed. On some maps even though the scales are shown in the margins there is no grid overlaying the map making it difficult to pinpoint the co-ordinates of a location. (see *Section 4.3.1 Establishing a grid* on page 89).

It is possible to measure co-ordinates with your eyes but the easiest and most accurate method involves using a specifically calibrated minute/second ruler.

4.2.3 Map datum

The subject of map datums is complex and can be confusing. Put simply when producing a map, mathematical models are required to convert the spherical shape of the earth into two dimensions. Before the map can be produced, a reference point is then adopted, known as a datum, from which all measurements are made. The datum point for OS maps lies slightly west of the Scilly Isles, for example.

Every map has a datum although mapmakers may use a different model to chart their maps, so position co-ordinates will differ from one datum to another. As an example co-ordinates expressed with reference to the WGS 84[2] datum can be as much as 150 metres away from the same co-ordinates referenced to OSGB[3] datum.

Information regarding a map's datum is usually shown in the title or in the key and is of particular importance to GPS users when comparing co-ordinates to a map. In these situations it is important to make sure the map datum in the GPS is set to match the map's datum for accurate comparison.

4.2.4 Symbols

Signs and symbols on overseas maps can often be difficult to decipher particularly if the key is written in an unfamiliar language. Occasionally maps may not even have a complete key defining all the signs and symbols used (in some cases a separate document can be purchased). Although common sense may help in deciding on the meaning of a particular symbol, it may only be possible to see the feature physically first before confirming how it is marked on the map. This may require the user to make a key as they are travelling!

4.3 Finding North on an unmarked map

Most maps follow the same convention of being orientated to North (Grid North). Many will show a grid devised from a datum line, usually Grid North. This is an artificial concept designed for communicating positions; it is the northerly direction of the North-South grid lines on a map. Maps will often show in the margins how the grid is constructed and the relationship between the three North Poles – Magnetic, Grid and True. This information is used when determining the magnetic variation and for orientating the map.

Knowing where North on the map lies allows the user to set the map. The norm is for this to be the top, that is the map reads like a book; top is North, bottom is South, left is West and right is East. Having said this, some maps do not follow this convention. While a map can be used without these features it makes sense to determine them beforehand, especially when operating in complex terrain or when having to take bearings. The accuracy of any bearing is based on how effectively it is lifted from the map and this can only be achieved with a quality grid in place. If a grid is not shown, and there is reference information shown around the margins of the map, then it may be possible to link corresponding co-ordinates with straight lines so as to overlay a suitable grid. This will create a series of northings and eastings. If no information is shown toward the sides of the map it becomes a much more laborious process to establish a useful grid.

4.3.1 Establishing a grid

A distinctive feature of British maps is the grid structure of lines superimposed over the whole country. These grid lines form the basis of a numerical reference system, which allow any point to be described. Grid lines can also be used to set the map and to help achieve a high degree of accuracy when taking bearing with a compass. If a grid has been used to produce the map it is likely that its orientation to north will be shown in the margins. Some maps may not use a grid system that is of any use so the user will have to establish one. This will allow bearings to be taken to help reference locations, particularly important if a duplicate is to be left back at base. To do this effectively there needs to be a series of identifiable features shown on both the map and the ground. This will allow the map to be set using ground features. Once orientated, a compass set to Magnetic North can be laid onto the map. This will define North on the map and allow

---

2   WGS 84 datum – World Geodetic System 1984
3   OSGB datum – Ordnance Survey Great Britain 1936

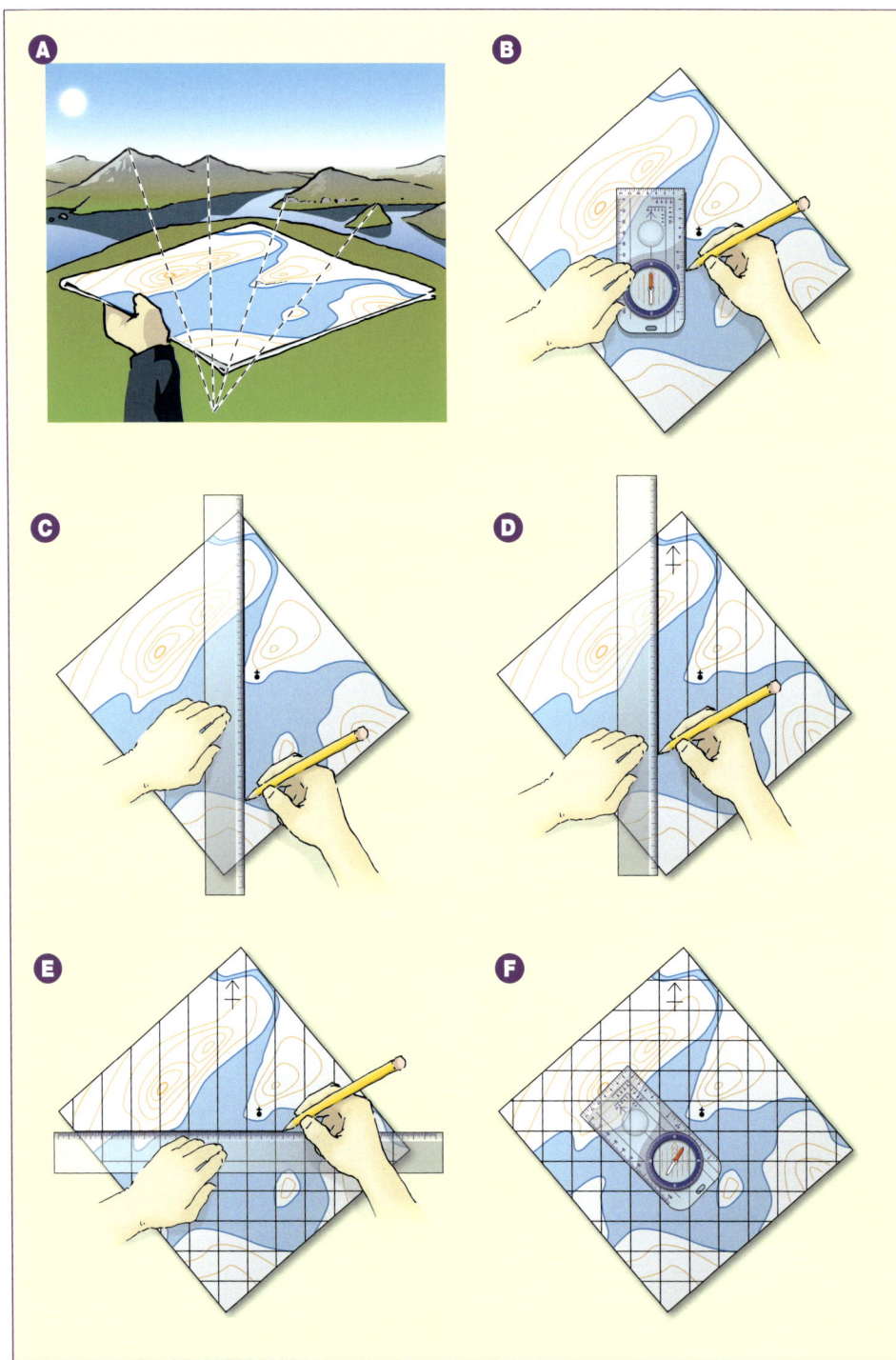

FIGURE 4.08 DRAWING A GRID ON A MAP THAT HAS NO GRID LINES: **A** ORIENTATE THE MAP USING IDENTIFIABLE FEATURES. **B** SET COMPASS TO MAGNETIC NORTH AND USE EDGE TO START DATUM LINE. **C** USE A RULER TO DRAW A DATUM LINE. **D** DRAW PARALLEL LINES EQUAL DISTANCE FROM DATUM. **E** DRAW LINES AT 90° TO DATUM TO CREATE A GRID OF SQUARES. **F** MAP CAN NOW BE USED TO TAKE BEARINGS.

FIGURE 4.09 A MAP SHOWING DIFFERENT CONTOUR INTERVALS EITHER SIDE OF A BORDER **A** CONTOUR INTERVAL THIS SIDE OF THE BORDER IN FRANCE IS 10M WITH AN INDEX CONTOUR LINE SHOWN EVERY 50M. **B** CONTOUR INTERVAL THIS SIDE OF THE BORDER IN SWITZERLAND IS 20M WITH AN INDEX CONTOUR LINE SHOWN EVERY 100M.

FIGURE 4.10 USING A WORLD COMPASS TO TAKE A FROM MAP

a line to be marked. It is important to note that this line refers to Magnetic North and not Grid North. The advantage of using this method means there is no requirement for needing to add or subtract magnetic variation when taking bearings and working from ground to map and vice versa. However, because magnetic variation changes over time this grid will have a limited life span before it becomes inaccurate for use with bearings. This line can then be used as a datum from which other lines can be marked at equal spacing. A complete grid can be produced from this by adding lines set at 90° to the original datum. Finally by adding in co-ordinate numbers a reference system for any location can be given. Using 1km spacing between lines will allow for easier use of a co-ordinate system giving similar accuracy to that on OS maps. This may seem crude; however it may well be of great assistance to anyone monitoring progress from a base or co-ordinating a rescue provided they have a corresponding map and knowledge of the grid used.

4.4 Contour interpretation

The use of contour lines to show relief on maps from other countries varies dramatically. Some maps may well have areas that show contour lines as well as other areas where they are absent due to a lack of accurate information.

If the shape of land is to be fully understood the user needs to make themselves familiar with both the scale of the map and the contour interval. Most maps give an indication of this interval either on the map, in the key, or on the grid margin.

As discussed in *Section 2.3 Contour Interpretation*, page 28 a change in contour interval can give a very different impression of the terrain. A common problem for UK navigators walking in Europe for the first time is to underestimate the scale of the mountains and it is always a useful exercise to work out the total climb of your journey and then compare it to the total climb you would normally cover on a day out in the hills in the UK (a reality check). Gaining a lot of height obviously takes time and effort but perhaps more surprisingly many people struggle to adapt to the long steep descents common in Europe and other countries and this needs to be taken into account in your journey planning.

In the absence of accurate contour information or a low contour interval, shading and/or colour are sometimes used to help define relief. The maps can appear very different, in some cases it adds to the level of detail making them appear almost three dimensional, in other examples it can confuse and hinder one's ability to relate ground to map and vice versa.

Finding direction without a compass

A reliable compass is an essential tool for finding direction, however there are many other methods that can be used to find or help confirm direction. These techniques are based on observing our natural surroundings and can provide an interesting new set of navigation skills. Numerous methods have been handed down over the centuries; this is a selection of some of the more simple methods:

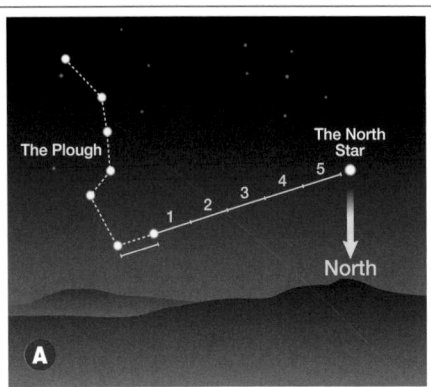

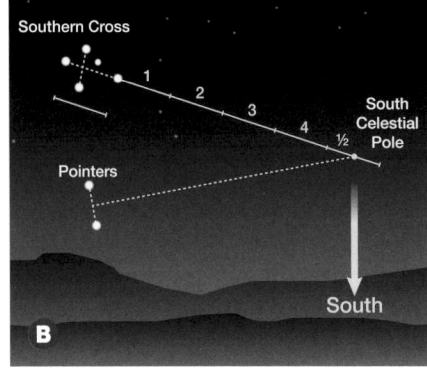

Using the Stars
(**A**) *Northern hemisphere:* Look at the Big Dipper (Plough), draw an imaginery line between the two stars that form the front of the Plough and continue it about 5 times the distance of those stars to find the North Star. This star lies over North on the horizon.
(**B**) *Southern hemisphere:* Use the Southern Cross to find approximate South. Draw an imaginary line from the cross piece, about 4½ times its length. South should be on the horizon below this point. Two bright stars below the cross can be used to help find the right point.

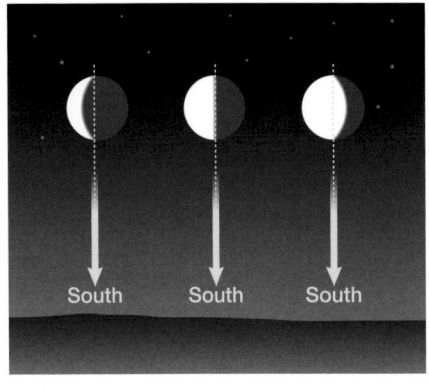

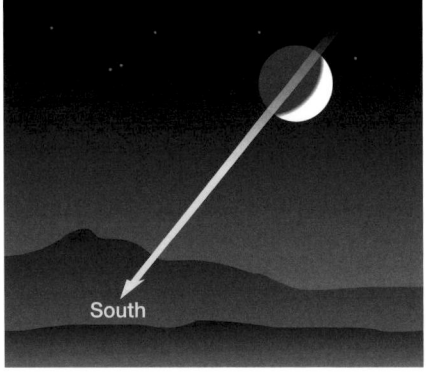

Using the Moon
As the moon travels across the sky it tilts, enabling the horns to always indicate South. The horns may be joined regardless of which phase the moon is in. This method becomes increasingly inaccurate the closer the moon gets to the horizon.

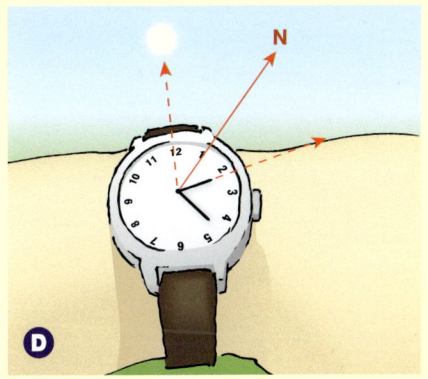

Using the Sun
(**C**) *Northern hemisphere:* Point the hour hand at the sun. Imagine a line halfway between the hour hand and 12 o'clock. South will be at the head of that line.
(**D**) *Southern hemisphere:* Point the 12 o'clock mark on the watch at the sun. North lies halfway between 12 o'clock and the hour hand. (**E**) *Sun stick method:* Stand a stick about 1m length on level ground. Mark the end of the shadow. After at least fifteen minutes mark the end of the shadow again. A line drawn through these markers will give you an East-West line. In the Northern hemisphere the first mark will be West.

4.5 Compasses

Refer to *Section 1.5.3 Using a compass in other parts of the world*, page 18 using compasses abroad.

4.6 Strategies for navigating waymarked routes

Many popular trekking areas have established walking itineraries where there is good mapping and good information with regard to the route. Some areas may have designated methods of marking routes using signs or symbols that correspond with the map or guide book information. As an example, this is predominantly the case for a lot of the linked hut walks and popular trails throughout the Alps. In Switzerland such a system is used extensively not just to guide walkers but also to inform them of the nature of the terrain. Different colour coding on signs and waymarks allows people to plan a journey appropriate to their ability, and because this is a system adopted throughout the country, the maps also show this information. Various countries, national parks and other organisations adopt similar systems to help inform and guide the public.

In good conditions, navigation along these paths consists mainly of keeping track of the direction and the distance travelled. Along the way a variety of features are likely to be passed allowing the navigator to confirm their position.

FIGURE 4.11   SIGNAGE AND WAYMARKING OF A ROUTE

In poor conditions, more effort should be made to note these features and possibly the distances between them and the direction travelled. This is particularly useful when arriving at decision points, (junctions, etc) and having to relocate before deciding the route to the next objective. Signage can provide great assistance at these points; however it is always worth a quick check of the map to confirm the correct location. Paths change over seasons especially if terrain is subject to movement, such as land slips. In these circumstances, signage and maps may not correspond. This can lead to confusion, and therefore time taken to confirm position and the direction to the next destination can save time and effort later on.

4.6.1 Strategies for navigating non-waymarked routes

In the absence of good mapping and waymarking a more structured approach to navigating and route finding on the ground will be necessary. Prior planning is essential and gaining as much information from as many sources as possible is

FIGURE 4.12   OTHER EXAMPLES OF WAYMARKING MAY INCLUDE WRITING OR SYMBOLS PAINTED ON ROCKS

FIGURE 4.13   IN THE ABSENCE OF A MARKED PATH A FEASIBLE ROUTE ON THE MAP IS SOMETIMES ACCOMPANIED BY A VISIBLE TRACK ON THE GROUND
Photo: www.pyb.co.uk

vital. Often what looks like a feasible route on the map is actually accompanied by a visible path on the ground. These are generally the logical lines local inhabitants and fellow trekkers have chosen in order to avoid hazards and for ease of travel. If you suspect your route to be a popular trail, looking for obvious signs of erosion will help. This is of course only a 'rule of thumb' and while beneficial it is worth considering the approach required when a path does not exist on the ground. When in unfamiliar terrain it is important to seek out the easiest option while always keeping an eye on the 'bigger picture'. Use the map and the terrain ahead to plan the best route before you become too committed, as this will minimise any back tracking or encountering any serious hazards. As an example, consider the ground 2 kilometres away as well as the terrain in the next hundred metres as this will prevent you from committing to more difficult terrain. It is important to continually consider how easy it would be to retrace your steps should the need arise.

4.6.2 Timing

Apart from the usual factors that can influence speed and time there are some others. Trips lasting a long period of time could mean speed is slowly reduced over that period due to ongoing fatigue. Altitude and acclimatisation also need to be borne in mind, particularly at higher elevations

	Makalu Basecamp Trek		
Day	Start	Finish	Altitude gain
1	Fly Kathmandu - Tumlingtar [460m]	Khandbari [1040m]	580m
2	Khandbari [1040m]	Fururu [1900m]	860m
3	Fururu [1900m]	Num [1490m]	410m
4	Num [1490m]	Sedua [1460m]	30m
5	Sedua [1460m]	Tashi gaon [2070m]	610m
6	Tashi gaon [2070m]	Kauma [3470m]	1300m
7	Kauma [3470m]	Mumbuk [3570m]	100m
8	Mumbuk [3570m]	Nhe Kharka [3000m]	570m
9	Nhe Kharka [3000m]	Sherson [4615m]	1615m
10	Sherson [4615m]	Makalu Base camp [5000m]	385m
11	REST DAY		
12	Makalu Base camp [5000m]	Nhe Kharka [3000m]	2000m
13	Nhe Kharka [3000m]	Mumbuk [3570m]	570m
14	Mumbuk [3570m]	Kauma [3470m]	100m
15	Kauma [3470m]	Tashi Gaon [2070m]	1300m
16	Tashi Gaon [2070m]	Balung [760m]	1310m
17	Balung [760m]	Pukuwa [550m]	210m
18	Pukuwa [550m]	Bumling [370m]	180m
19	Bumling [370m]	Tumlingtar [460m]	90m
20	Tumlingtar [460m]	Fly to Kathmandu	

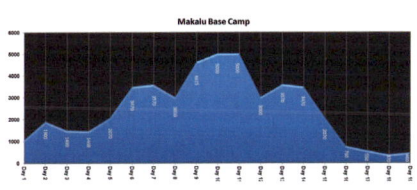

FIGURE 4.14   EXAMPLE ROUTE PLAN FOR TREK SHOWING PROFILE AND ALTITUDE GAIN

where gaining height too quickly can lead to problems such as altitude sickness. Factor these variables into any calculations at the planning stage, and use them to monitor progress while en route. Route itineraries and plans can be produced before the trip to assist with this process *(see Figure 4.14)*.

4.7 Using guide books

Guidebooks are a useful source of additional information, not only at the planning stage, but also while en route. Many travellers' guides (Lonely Planet, Footprint, etc) provide useful information for those venturing into the wilderness. They also make a good companion when trying to navigate around a large town or city. However, in this situation it is worth extracting the most useful information rather than using the whole book since this is less likely to attract attention. Popular routes and itineraries are often covered by a range of literature that include in-depth guidebooks and personal accounts of individual trips.

Specific guidebooks to wilderness areas often provide information about routes, accommodation, weather, hazards and organising logistics. Recently published books, or books written by people who have done a trek and describe topographical features as waymarkers to follow ('5m high boulder' or 'obvious ruined temple'), are likely to offer the most reliable information. It is worth remembering things may change from when the book was printed hence consider obtaining information from a variety of sources.

4.8 Using the Internet

The Internet can provide a good resource for researching and obtaining information and acquiring any relevant maps or guidebooks for a particular area. Many people now publish their trekking and climbing experiences online, which once again can provide a useful source of information. It may also be used to contact any specific embassies and consulates that could also provide information about relevant mapping for a chosen area. Google Earth and other such programs can allow you to explore your chosen destination before you travel. This can provide additional information about the terrain you are planning to travel through, helping you to plan for any alternatives or emergencies.

Using any GPS enabled device in conjunction with the Internet or other applications is likely to provide more and more support to trekkers in years to come as devices become smaller, cheaper and more powerful.

GPS can be particularly useful abroad, providing a host of additional information and features with which to navigate. It is important to spend time initialising and setting up the GPS correctly on arrival in country so that any units, position formats and map datums are set to correspond with those of the maps being used. Part V gives detail on how to do this. Many GPS manufacturers include very simple world-wide base maps as standard. More detailed mapping

FIGURE 4.16 GPS AND MAP IN ACTION ABROAD

FIGURE 4.15 A SELECTION OF GUIDEBOOKS AND MAPS TO VARIOUS REGIONS

can be sought, although at present this is not worldwide and, depending on the manufacturer and the country being visited, it may or may not be possible to purchase large scale digital maps that are compatible with GPS units. If the intention is to use GPS some research beforehand as to the availability of software for the unit would be necessary.

4.9 Use of altimeters

Whether a sophisticated digital type or a classic analogue device, an altimeter is a great light-weight addition to your equipment, and will more than justify its carriage when used properly. Unlike a GPS receiver, an altimeter does not use any external systems for its accuracy. Analogue altimeters need no battery so are almost impervious to cold and incredibly reliable. Digital altimeters are typically very flexible and can support a range of additional features. Some GPS receivers come equipped with an in built barometric altimeter; this can still be used even when the unit is struggling to find its location from satellites.

Altimeters measure altitude by sensing changes in air pressure. The altitude measured can indicate the vertical distance you've covered or your proximity to a particular point on the map. Most altimeters will offer a reading in two formats: Absolute altitude and relative altitude. Absolute altitude is the height above (or below) sea level. Relative altitude is the height above (or below) a reference point. The absolute reading is particularly useful when locating a position on a map using contour lines or spot heights. It is also useful for determining how much further to go to a given landmark. Relative altitude measurement is most useful for targeting an altitude gain, to avoid climbing too high or on a descent to avoid overshooting and having to climb back up.

Fluctuations in air pressure due to changing weather patterns will influence the readings shown by the altimeter. This means it is vital to reset the altitude reading regularly to maintain accuracy. This can be done at a location that has a definite altitude shown on the map, for example spot height or summit. On a similar note most altimeters are temperature sensitive and it is important to keep the temperature as constant as possible so as not to greatly affect the altitude reading.

The accuracy of altimeters will depend on three main factors:
- the length of time since the last setting of the reference altitude;
- the altitude change since the last calibration;
- the air pressure changes due to changing weather and/or location.

FIGURE 4.17 **A** DIGITAL AND **B** ANALOGUE ALTIMETERS

FIGURE 4.18 CALIBRATING THE ALTIMETER AT REGULAR INTERVALS AND KNOWN HEIGHTS WILL HELP INSURE ACCURATE READINGS

Practise using your own altimeter will help you anticipate these changes and mean that you can interpret the readings more accurately.

Digital altimeters combine various memory functions that allow the operator to record time and altitude measurements. This information can be analysed later in conjunction with a map to work out which route was taken and the total ascent or descent. Ascent rate is especially useful when acclimatising to altitude to help ensure a safe rate of ascent. As well as providing information as to whether you are travelling faster or slower than anticipated it can also be used to help pace an ascent or gauge the likely time to reach the next location.

As with a GPS unit, the altimeter should be considered an additional tool and not relied upon solely or used in isolation of other skills. Upper and lower limit alarms are useful for providing an indication that you have arrived at a predetermined altitude. The generally accepted wisdom of 'aiming-off' with an altimeter is to aim low when ascending and aim high when descending which in both cases avoids overshooting the target and having to backtrack.

The biggest advantage offered by an altimeter is the potential for greater accuracy when navigating in angled terrain. Contouring can be very difficult, for example, particularly in poor visibility; the tendency to walk slightly uphill or

downhill in these situations can be removed by simply monitoring the altimeter for any indicated change in altitude. Additional accuracy can be obtained when used in conjunction with a compass to pinpoint a location on contour line and an aspect of slope.

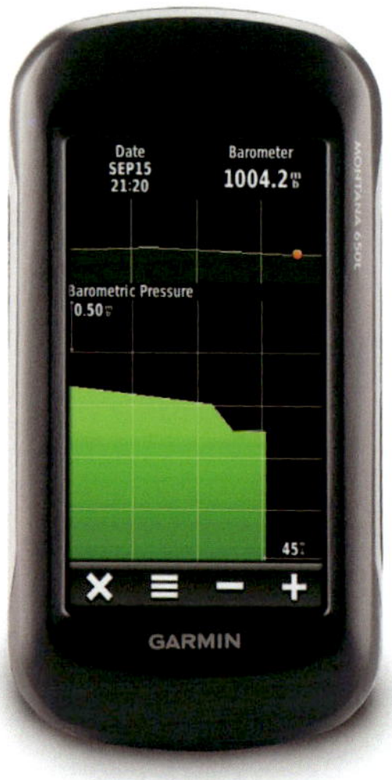

4.10 Alpine navigation

Many of the skills, techniques and strategies described in earlier chapters can also be applied to navigating in Alpine areas. Conditions in Alpine regions can change rapidly and may range from blue skies and sunshine, requiring only a cursory glance at the map from time to time, to storm and white out conditions demanding the use of every navigation skill. It is therefore important to become fully familiar with skills required to navigate in both summer and winter conditions. However, navigating safely in an alpine environment requires more than just familiarity with these skills. Good experience of the terrain and its associated hazards is fundamental. Objective dangers such as loose rock, seracs, crevasses and avalanche potential require a great deal of consideration when planning and travelling in these mountains.

4.10.1 Equipment
Knowledge of alpine equipment and how to use it correctly is beyond the scope of this book. Suffice to say that being practised in the skills of alpinism is important to ensure good decisions are made regarding the techniques used to safeguard travel. In terms of navigational equipment, as in any mountainous region, a compass and good quality map of the area are essential items. A GPS unit and an altimeter provide a wealth of extra information that can be extremely useful when navigation becomes difficult. A guide book will often hint at possible routes, but due to the ever changing nature of the terrain such routes can become affected in some way by crevasses, stone fall or avalanche debris and are no longer passable. Hut guardians and local guides are often a good source of information with regards routes and conditions. Seeking this information at the planning stage is important and can help to assist with planning alternatives and any necessary escape routes.

FIGURE 4.19 PRESSURE TREND GRAPH TAKEN FROM A GPS BAROMETER SHOWING A DROP IN PRESSURE OVER THE PAST 3¼ HOURS, WHICH COULD INDICATE A DETERIORATION IN THE WEATHER

4.10.2 Navigational strategies in Alpine terrain

As already mentioned, in fine weather with good visibility all that may be required in terms of navigation is an occasional glance at the map. Indeed, most of the 'map-reading' will have taken place while planning the route and calculating any timings. Checking the map from time to time in these conditions will help confirm your location and allow you to monitor progress with regards any timing. The odd check with a compass or an altimeter can provide additional information and both can be put to good use when trying to find a way through more complex terrain. In poor weather, navigation becomes a different matter altogether requiring great concentration and the application of a variety of skills. In a mountaineering context many Alpine climbs require a glacier approach, often undertaken in the dark to make best use of time and conditions for climbing. Therefore good preparation and even a reconnaissance of the first part of the journey the previous afternoon can pay dividends.

4.10.3 Navigation on glaciers

Glaciers are moving rivers of ice and are a common feature in Alpine regions, and like rivers flow downhill under the influence of gravity. This constant movement means that the topography of these ice masses is always changing. Different pressures and stresses working through the glacier cause crevasses, icefalls and seracs. As the glacier moves they will over time change in character. However, the underlying terrain can dictate where crevasses and icefalls occur and although they may change in form they will generally be there. A rise in global temperatures is currently contributing to glacial recession in many mountain regions across the world giving rise to changes in a short period of time. Because of this it becomes difficult to rely on the map for accurate information especially if the survey was conducted sometime in the past. While the map does not show the exact location of individual crevasses it may be able to convey an accurate picture of their extent and approximate positions. With knowledge and experience of how a glacier behaves it is possible to predict where these hazards will most likely be found, and how to plan a safe route through this terrain.

When planning a route up or down glaciers use the map and additional information to determine where the greatest hazards lie. Try to avoid

FIGURE 4.20   NAVIGATING IN ALPINE TERRAIN CAN BE EASY WHEN THE WEATHER IS GOOD BUT VERY SERIOUS WHEN THE VISIBILITY IS POOR

Photo: Andy Teasdale

FIGURE 4.21   NAVIGATING THROUGH CREVASSED TERRAIN   Photo: Andy Teasdale

the sides of glaciers where possible as there are likely to be more crevasses and there is greater exposure to the dangers of avalanches and stone fall from the steeper slopes above. On a glacier with no snow cover (dry) crevasses are often easily recognised; however when the glacier is covered with snow (wet) they become far less obvious. Crevasses occur most often where the ice is under tension particularly on bends, where rock ridges run into the glacier or where the glacier falls steeply. In poor visibility attention can become very focused on trying to identify and avoid these hazards and this can often be to the detriment of the navigation. It is worth stressing the seriousness of navigating on a glacier in these conditions and careful consid- eration should be exercised before venturing onto this terrain. When confronted with a crevasse while following a bearing it is important to safely avoid the hazard but also to make sure your course is regained. Boxing round obstacles becomes the best option for this however you should be pre- pared to do this on a number of occasions (*see* ***Section 2.9.7 Boxing***, *page 52*). Plan to use identifiable features as navigation points, for instance rocks, ridges, huts, meeting points with other glaciers or ridges. Occasionally outcrops of rock with-stand the movement of the glacier and protrude through ice. These isolated islands

(nunataks), while they may cause crevasses to occur around their base, can serve as useful landmarks when navigating. More subtle features such as the changes in slope angle also provide identifiable points. Marked changes in slope angle are often clearly shown on the map and a journey up or down a glacier will consist of, and on occasions may rely on, moving from one change in angle to the next.

Careful use of GPS in this terrain can be of great benefit allowing you to pick and choose the most appropriate route while still guiding you toward the ultimate destination. It should be borne in mind that although a GPS can help greatly when navigating in complex glacial terrain it is important to plan routes that avoid the areas of greatest hazard in the first instance. If travelling up and down the same glacier recording the route through terrain on ascent either by anno- tating the map or plotting a series of waypoints in the GPS will greatly help with descent, parti- cularly if the forecast is for deteriorating weather or changing conditions.

An altimeter can be an invaluable tool in this type of terrain, used well the information it provides can help to pinpoint a location (*see* ***Section 4.9 Use of altimeters***, *page 97*). It can often be the best way to prevent ascending or descending too far. This can be particularly

FIGURE 4.22   FOLLOWING A BEARING IN DIFFICULT CONDITIONS   Photo: Andy Teasdale

useful when descending on skis where the rate of descent can be very fast with a greater possibility of overshooting any crucial decision points. Through detailed pre-planning of the route, the altitude of these key points can be identified and the altimeter can be used to navigate the route safely and efficiently.

It is important that all members of the party play a role in navigating, helping to share the responsibility and decision making. This is particularly necessary when the weather is poor and the visibility reduced. In these situations all the group members can combine their knowledge and experience helping to double check any decisions and calculations. As an example, when following a bearing while roped together the people behind the leader can use their compasses to keep on line. In a rope of three the third person can sight their compass bearing through the second and can easily see when any deviation from the line is made.

Part V

Global Positioning System

Since it was launched, devices that make use of Global Positioning System (GPS) technology have become increasingly more sophisticated and affordable year on year, a trend that is most likely to continue. There is now a vast array of receivers to choose from for those venturing into the outdoors, as well as those designed for more general use in cars, boats etc. Apart from providing a position reference, many GPS receivers have extra functions that can provide the operator with a range of useful information to assist with navigation. To gain the best from any GPS device it is important to understand how it works, what the limitations are and most of all how to integrate this tool with map and compass skills.

FIGURE 5.01   USING GPS IN COMBINATION WITH THE MAP

5.1 The Global Positioning System

The original GPS concept was conceived by the USA at the start of the cold war as a way of improving the accuracy of ballistic missiles. Despite its development in the early sixties, the GPS did not become fully operational until 1995. The GPS is made up of three segments, space, ground control and user.

Currently the space segment uses a constellation of at least 24 satellites orbiting 20,000 kilometres above the earth at a speed of 11,000 kilometres per hour. These satellites broadcast radio signals that detail the position of each satellite in the sky and an electronic code. The ground segment is comprised of stations that track, task and monitor the health of these satellites. These stations make the necessary adjustments to keep the system accurate. The GPS unit makes up the user segment; it receives the radio signals from the satellites and calculates its position accord-

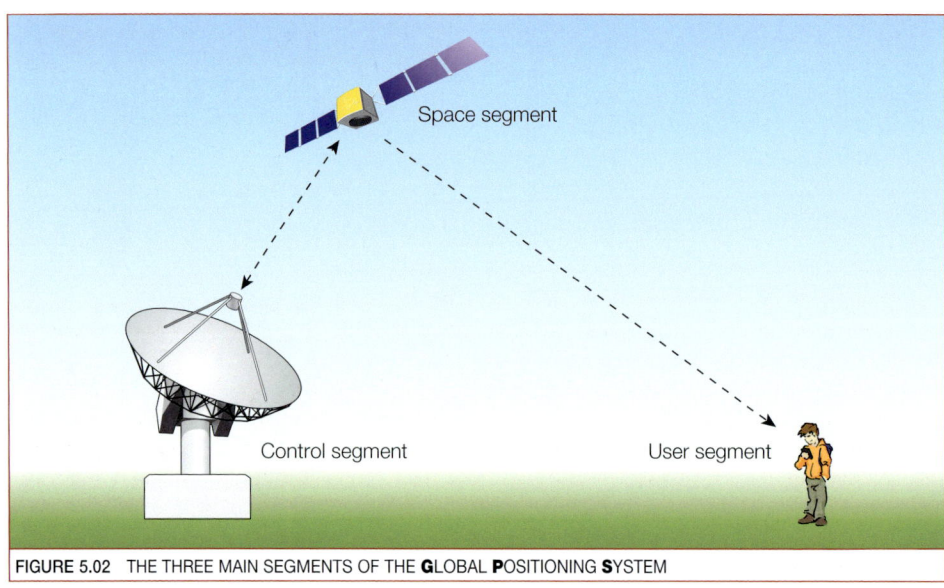

FIGURE 5.02   THE THREE MAIN SEGMENTS OF THE **G**LOBAL **P**OSITIONING **S**YSTEM

ingly. The term 'GPS' has now become synonymous with this segment of the system when in reality 'GPS unit' better describes these devices. Control and maintenance of the GPS is still managed by the US Defence Department.

Further developments in GPS technology have given rise to improvements being developed to enhance the level of accuracy even further. Geostationary satellite systems (satellites that maintain a fixed position overhead) and new ground-based stations are being added to remove actual errors and increase accuracy. Known as *satellite based augmentation systems* (SBAS) they have patchy coverage across the globe with currently only a few countries having developed their own systems (North America, Europe, Russia and Japan). Most new GPS units come enabled to use these satellite based augmentation systems.

When a GPS unit is turned on, it 'listens' to the radio signals and extracts the satellite location information. Each satellite broadcasts the position information for all the satellites. The GPS unit stores this information so that it is able to determine its own position. Known as the *almanac* it takes about 12 minutes to transfer this data to the GPS unit. If the GPS unit has not been used for some time or has been moved a considerable distance (excess of 300 miles) it will need at least this amount of time before it can start to give accurate information.

Each satellite has a highly accurate atomic clock used to send codes containing all this data at exactly the same time from each satellite. Knowing when a signal was sent and when it was received allows the GPS unit to work out its distance from each satellite. Software then triangulates a position in longitude and latitude which can then be converted into a variety of other formats if required, for example the OS grid system. The design of the system ensures there are usually six satellites covering any spot on the globe at any one time. However a GPS unit only needs good signals from four well placed satellites to provide an accurate *3D fix* (location and altitude). If signals from only three satellites are being used the unit may provide a 2D fix; however the location given may be inaccurate and the unit will compensate for the missing satellite by estimating the elevation. Once locked onto satellites the GPS unit will display a continuously updated position.

5.2 Using GPS on the mountain

There are three distinct ways of using a GPS unit to assist with navigating. An additional 'opportunity' also exists that can compliment any of these approaches.

1 **Emergency relocation aid**
   The primary approach to navigation involves using a map and compass. A GPS unit can be used to help relocate precisely when either unsure of a location or to help confirm a location.

2 **Primary navigation aid**
   A map and compass are carried, but stowed and will only be used if all else fails. The GPS unit is on and always to hand, it is loaded with a topographical map of the area, and the route in detail. In addition, it has been pre-programmed with various escape routes and other possibilities. With proficiency it can be used throughout the day whatever the conditions. Due to the sophistication of the information shown it is possible to know exactly where you are, where you have been and where you are going.

3 **A mixture of the above**
   The GPS unit is used as an extra navigational tool to complement the map and compass. This will require it to be close to hand so that it may be referred to when necessary. The GPS unit may have the route pre-loaded, however the map and compass are used as the primary tools and the GPS unit for backup.

Whichever approach is required, a GPS unit can also be used in an additional way for data logging. If the GPS unit is on all the time but stowed in the top of your rucksack, or to hand, and provided it can detect satellite signals it can be setup to record all your movements. In other words, it plots exactly where you have gone (and when, what elevation, and possibly other data as well). This information could then be used to assist with relocation if lost. Once saved it may be used to review the journey or to help navigate the route another time. It can also be used to retrace your steps during your journey if required using the *track-back* function (*see Section 5.10.5 Using track-log function, page 119*).

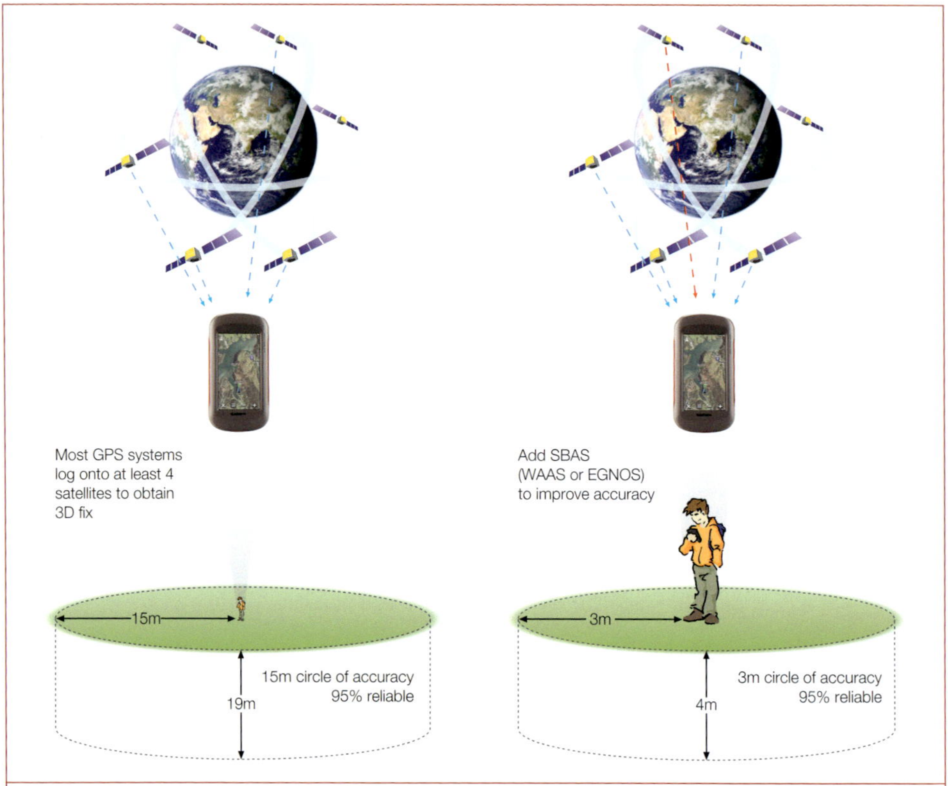

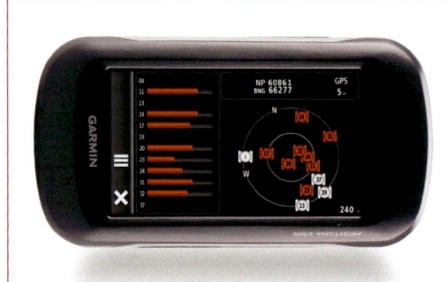

FIGURE 5.03   ILLUSTRATING CIRCLES OF ACCURACY FOR SBAS ENABLED AND NON ENABLED UNITS

Most GPS systems
log onto at least 4
satellites to obtain
3D fix

15m

15m circle of accuracy
95% reliable

19m

Add SBAS
(WAAS or EGNOS)
to improve accuracy

3m

3m circle of accuracy
95% reliable

4m

5.3 Accuracy

Typical accuracy of modern GPS units is to within 15m with 95% reliability. This means that for 5% of the time the information given will be less accurate than 15m. With SBAS and high sensitivity receivers accuracy improves to 3m, 95% of the time.

GPS units are most accurate when they have good line of sight to the satellites and receive adequate signals from four well placed satellites. The stronger the signal they are able to receive the more accurate the position fix. Reception is not significantly affected by cloud cover and poor weather but there are a number of other factors that will influence the accuracy of the positions shown such as deep narrow valleys and forests (*also see **Section 5.3.3 Blocking**, page 107*).

5.3.1 Satellite geometry

Satellite geometry refers to the positioning of the satellites being listened to by the GPS unit and

FIGURE 5.04   THE SATELLITE PAGE GIVES A REPRE-SENTATION OF SATELLITE GEOMETRY. THE BAR GRAPHS SHOW SATELLITES BEING LISTENED TO AND THE STRENGTH OF THE SIGNALS BEING RECEIVED. AN ESTIMATED POSITION ERROR (EPE) IS GIVEN TO INDICATE THE ACCCURACY OF THE POSITION SHOWN. IN THIS EXAMPLE, IT SUGGESTS ± 5 METRES

is of importance when it comes to the accuracy of the information provided. Modern units will display this information along with an Estimated Position Error (EPE) (*see Figure 5.04*).

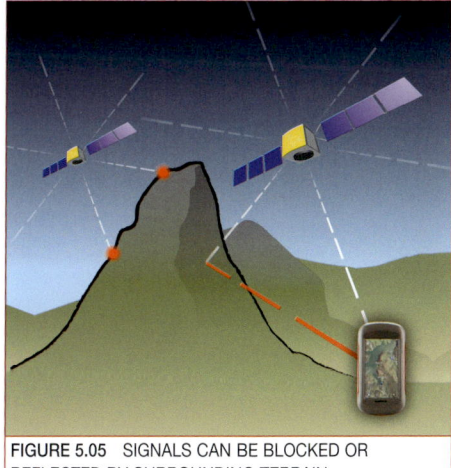

FIGURE 5.05   SIGNALS CAN BE BLOCKED OR
REFLECTED BY SURROUNDING TERRAIN

Using this page it is possible to determine how many satellites the GPS unit is connecting with and where they are in the sky relative to your current location. If they are grouped together or are situated in a line from your position it can affect the accuracy of the location given. The ideal configuration for the grouping of satellites for the greatest accuracy is to have one or two satellites overhead with the rest spread out around the sky. In hilly terrain, moving short distances can often improve reception and help to improve accuracy.

If the GPS unit has a 3D fix (four well placed satellites) and the EPE is low, the position fix will be good. Combined with good satellite geometry this becomes even more reliable. It is worth remembering that the figure shown for the Estimated Position Error (EPE) is based only on satellite geometry and does not take into account the various other sources of error.

5.3.2 Reflected signals

Known as *multipath*, these are signals that have been reflected by something in the surrounding terrain; buildings, cliffs, steep sided gorges. If the signal is reflected, it can have more than one path to the unit's antenna. If the reflected signal is used to calculate the position it will be incorrect. Unfortunately, as an operator it is difficult to determine these errors from the information being shown on the screen. When using a GPS unit, particularly in complex terrain, it is important to be aware of the surroundings especially if there is a potential for multipath errors to occur.

FIGURE 5.06   SHOWING THE BEST METHODS OF CARRYING A GPS SO THAT IT MAINTAINS THE ABILITY TO RECEIVE GOOD SIGNALS. **A** SHOULDER STRAP OF RUCKSACK **B** PLACING GPS UNIT CAREFULLY INSIDE TOP POCKET OF RUCKSACK

Always cross-reference any position information with the map and then the surrounding terrain to confirm the location. A modern unit with a high sensitivity GPS receiver is better able to distinguish between true and multipath signals and as a result will cope better in terrain where this could be a problem.

5.3.3 Blocking

Buildings, dense tree cover, cliffs and high ground, and even your body will affect a GPS unit's reception of satellite signals, as they are either weakened or blocked entirely. For best results make sure the signals are able to reach the unit by avoiding objects that may block their path.

FIGURE 5.07 THERE ARE TWO TYPES OF ANTENNAE:
A QUADRIFILAR HELIX AND **B** PATCH

A common mistake is to carry a GPS unit either in a pocket on your body or buried inside a rucksack. If the intention is to use the device on a regular basis and for it to track your movements it needs to be able to receive satellite signals as you move. Mounting the device on a shoulder strap or inside the top pocket of a rucksack gives the best results (*see Figure 5.06*). Some models allow for the attachment of an external antenna allowing the unit to be carried in a rucksack and the antenna to have an uninterrupted view of the sky.

5.4 Antennae

Handheld GPS units come with one of two types of antenna – quadrifilar helix or patch. The patch antenna is a small, rectangular metal sandwich often mounted within the receiver. Best reception using this type of antenna is achieved when the unit is held or mounted horizontally. The quadrifilar helix antennae are coils of wire beneath a plastic cover and often have to extend beyond the body of the unit (*see Figure 5.07*).

Quadrifilar helix antennae are more sensitive and tend to outperform patch antennae in situations such as tree cover and in terrain where there is potential blocking due to topography, for example valleys. Best reception using this type of unit is achieved when the aerial is held vertically.

5.5 Choosing the right GPS

It is possible to buy a GPS unit to fit almost any budget and the choice on offer from manufacturers can be overwhelming. Not all of these will be suitable for operating in the harsh conditions they may face in the mountains. Many manufacturers produce a range of models to suit all needs from entry level through to advanced. Having said this they will all be able to do the following:

- display time, location and elevation and while moving will show speed and heading;
- determine current position and display this either as co-ordinates or on an electronic map;
- accept a range of different co-ordinate systems and map datums, particularly important if using with different maps;
- store the locations of numerous positions often referred to as **points of interest** (**POI**) or more commonly waypoints;
- calculate the distance and direction from your current location to any stored **waypoint** and navigate you to it;
- link a series of waypoints together to form a **Route** that can be stored and used later;
- guide you to a destination you choose from a map (paper or electronic);
- monitor your movements to create a 'bread crumb' trail or **track-log** that can be stored and used later if required.

Entry-level models often provide more than enough options and functions to assist with navigation. Features on the more advanced units include extra storage capacity for waypoints, routes and tracks, plus it is often easier and quicker to interface with the unit using touch screens or toggle switches to gain access to menus and enter information. Advanced mapping models now have the option to show on-screen topographical mapping allowing the user to identify their location on a digital map in real time. Currently, manufacturers produce mapping that is usually only compatible with their own products, though this may well change. This comes at a premium, so before purchasing a unit, think about how you intend to use GPS both now and in the future. Some units have topographical mapping built-in, or come bundled with mapping and this is sometimes better value than adding mapping at a later date.

FIGURE 5.08   EXAMPLES OF GPS UNITS FROM ENTRY LEVEL TO ADVANCED: **A**, **B** AND **C** ARE ENTRY LEVEL. **D** AND **E** ARE MORE ADVANCED AND OFFER DETAILED MAPPING FUNCTIONALITY. **F** IS AN EXAMPLE OF A SMART PHONE WITH GPS FUNCTION.

When choosing any GPS unit for use in the mountains make sure it is of a good rugged construction and waterproof, it is always worth considering some form of protective case to help secure and protect the unit when in use. The size of the screen and the brightness are particularly important if it is a mapping unit as viewing the maps will be much clearer with a good quality screen. Think carefully about how the unit will perform in a variety of conditions. Is it possible to operate it with gloves on? Can you see the screen clearly in bright daylight or at night? One essential to consider is a high sensitivity receiver as these perform much better in hilly terrain. Other options to include for use in the mountains:

- electronic compass;
- barometric altimeter (*see **Section 7.9 Use of altimeters**, page 97*).

5.6 The compass

All GPS units will display the direction of travel when they are moving; this is normally shown on a compass page. This screen looks very similar to a compass but is better thought of as a heading indicator (*see Figure 5.19 on page 116*). A heading refers to the current direction of travel as opposed to a bearing, which is a straight-line direction from one location to the next. A true heading will only be shown when the unit is moving (usually at a pre-set speed approx. 3kph) as it calculates the direction of movement based on the current location and where it was a few seconds ago. When the unit is being used to navigate to a waypoint, a pointer will appear indicating the direction in which to travel to reach the destination. A GPS unit with an electronic compass has the advantage in that it behaves in a similar way to a magnetic compass. When stationary (but held level) it will orientate itself and show the actual direction to the chosen destination. Modern units often have a 3-axis compass which does not have to be held level and generally performs better than the standard 2-axis electronic compass. Most GPS units will allow the operator to set the North reference for the compass to one of three options: True, Grid or Magnetic North. If carrying a compass it would make sense to set the GPS unit to display Magnetic North bearings as this can then be cross-referenced or transferred to a compass if required. Along with a barometric altimeter, these features tend to be optional extras and not all GPS units have them as standard. For the GPS unit to give accurate information these features will need to be calibrated correctly. Most manufactures give on-screen instruction to help with calibration. In the case of the electronic compass this should be calibrated at the start of every trip and when the batteries have been changed. It is important to remember that electronic compasses are sensitive and easily affected by large metal objects like ice axes. If you use your electronic compass close to an avalanche transceiver or have a mobile telephone in a pocket near the GPS, these may affect the reading as well.

5.7 Power

Battery life is an important consideration with manufacturers quoting anything from 10 to 25 hours. Depending on conditions and use, this could be dramatically reduced, and is especially true when using GPS units in cold conditions.

FIGURE 5.09 SIX MAIN PAGES COMMON TO MOST GPS UNITS: **A** MAIN MENU, **B** SATELLITE PAGE, **C** MAP PAGE, **D** COMPASS PAGE, **E** ALTIMETER PAGE AND **F** TRIP COMPUTER

Disposable lithium batteries which can be used by some GPS units are largely unaffected by cold conditions and as a result out-perform alkaline and rechargeable batteries in these situations. Rechargeable batteries offer a cheaper and more environmentally friendly option but it is important to use the correct types. Low self-discharge Nickel Metal Hydride (NiMH) batteries with a rating greater than 2000mh perform the best, but it is important with rechargeables that they are stored and conditioned properly for use.

Some GPS functions such as backlights and updating the display place a drain on power so unless being used to navigate it is worth switching off these features until needed. Start each day with fully charged batteries to avoid any changes during the journey, and always carry a spare set. Some GPS units have a battery-type setting; it is important to set this correctly in order to obtain an accurate reading from the battery life indicator.

5.8 Setting up a GPS unit

Time spent becoming accustomed with the various button functions, screens and menus will help understand fully how the unit works and make its use in the field much more efficient.

Most GPS units work in a similar way and will display information through a variety of different screens or pages. These screens can often be customised by the operator to display the most useful information (*see Figure 5.09*).

A simple non-mapping unit may only have a few information pages but more advanced models will allow the user to add more pages from a menu if required. Once familiar with the unit it will need to be set up correctly before use. This is of particular importance if the GPS unit is to be integrated with the map and compass. A *Setup Page* is usually accessed from the *Main Menu Page* allowing the user to configure the unit for

FIGURE 5.10   CALIBRATION SEQUENCE OF AN ELECTRONIC COMPASS

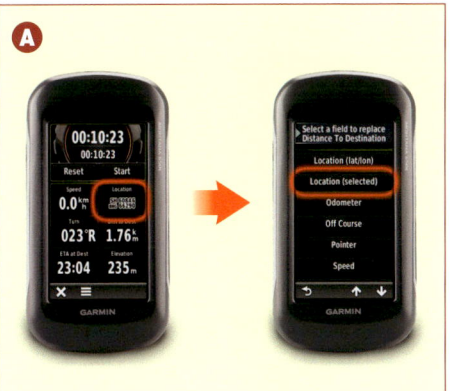

FIGURE 5.11   **A** SETUP OF TRIP COMPUTER PAGE TO SHOW RELEVANT DATA **B** SETTING POSITION FORMAT TO CORRESPOND WITH MAP BEING USED

FIGURE 5.12 CHECKING GPS SETTING BEFORE SETTING OFF

FIGURE 5.13 TRIP COMPUTER PAGE SETUP TO SHOW A RANGE OF USEFUL DATA RELEVANT TO A PARTICULAR NAVIGATION LEG INCLUDING A COMPASS HEADING INDICATOR

·Having set the crucial information, many GPS units will allow this to be displayed in more than one way. A range of options will often allow for the change of screen settings, audible alarms and alter the text sizes on various pages. Many pages and in particular the ***Trip Computer Page*** have small information boxes known as ***Data Fields***. These boxes display a range of navigational statistics and can be changed from an options menu to show the most relevant information (*see Figure 5.11*).

the information they require. It is important to configure the GPS unit before it is first used, when it has not been used for a long time, or when moving from one country to another with a different co-ordinate system.

The setup page will often allow the configuration of any personal preferences, however there are some crucial settings required for the unit to function correctly. The following are ***Essential Settings***; information that should be checked or changed before every trip.

- The time zone and country where you are.
- The co-ordinate system and map datum to be used. This should correspond with the paper map being used.
- All units of measurement. It is best to use the same units as used on the map; for example if the map is metric the GPS unit should be setup to display any units in metric so that distances shown can easily be cross-referenced.
- Calibration of electronic compass and altimeter (*see Figure 5.10 on page 111*).

5.9 Before setting off

Prior to setting off on any route make sure you have a compass plus the relevant map and any other route details required (*see **Section 2.10.3 Route planning**, page 54*). Ensure you have enough battery power for the journey and remember that cold conditions and constant use will reduce battery life.

At the start of a walk:
- Switch on the GPS unit, keep it static with a good sky view, and allow it to obtain a 3D position fix; if possible, leave it switched on for a few minutes after it has first obtained its fix as this will significantly improve its accuracy. If the unit has not been used for sometime or moved a considerable distance since its last use it will require at least 12 minutes to download a new almanac before giving an accurate position fix.
- Check that the ***Essential Settings*** are correct.

Waypoints, routes and tracks

Waypoints

Sometimes referred to as a **Landmark** or **Point of Interest** (**POI**), a waypoint is a reference point or set of coordinates that precisely identify a location. These are locations you may wish to visit or return to later. They may be check points on a route or significant ground features (eg. campsite, footpath junction, summit, or a favourite view point). A waypoint includes position data and may include altitude. Waypoints may be set while a GPS unit is physically positioned at the desired location, or may be defined and stored in the unit manually by taking coordinates from a map or other reference. They can also be set by entering data into mapping software on a personal computer and uploading to a GPS unit for use.

Routes

A **Route** is the name given to a number of waypoints grouped together in the sequence in which they are to be navigated. Creating a route can be done in two ways: either by using waypoints currently saved within the unit's data-base, or more conveniently by using digital mapping software and uploading the information to a GPS unit when complete. A third method involves using a mapping GPS unit with the relevant map to create a route on the screen that can then be followed or saved for future use.

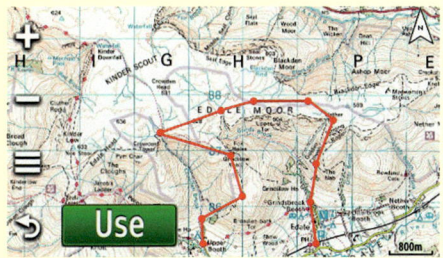

Tracks

As the GPS moves across ground on a specific journey it creates a 'breadcrumb' trail of the path taken known as a **Track**. Tracks are made from numerous track points (similar to waypoints) saved at certain intervals and stored in a **Track log**. Most units can be set up to record these track points at a set distance, a set time or to automatically decide on the most appropriate method depending on speed and movement. Once a track has been created it is possible to navigate back along it using a **track-back** function.

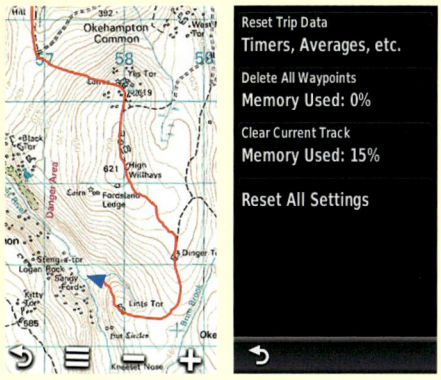

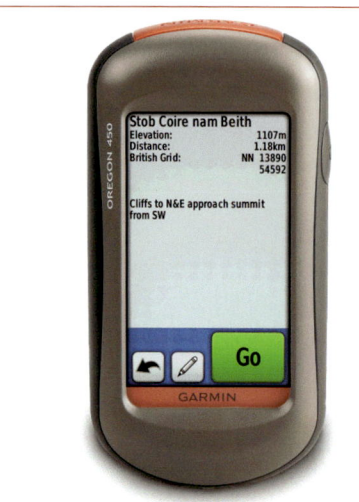

FIGURE 5.14   WAYPOINT INFORMATION PAGE WILL SHOW THE NAME OF THE POINT PLUS A RANGE OF OTHER USEFUL INFORMATION SUCH AS LOCATION, ELEVATION, AND DISTANCE. SOME MODELS ALLOW FOR A BRIEF DESCRIPTION TO BE ADDED

- If the GPS unit has an electronic compass or barometric altimeter, calibrate these functions before setting off.
- Check the battery life indicator to ascertain if you have sufficient battery life for your journey.
- Switch off any functions that may not be required, for example backlights.
- Clear the *Track-Log* and alter any settings if the unit is to build a track of its movements.
- Reset any *Trip Computer* information if recording data from the journey.

Finally, immediately before moving off, check the position given by the GPS unit corresponds exactly with the map to ensure it is working correctly.

5.10 Navigating with GPS in the mountains

For mountain navigation, there are a handful of basic skills required to make the most of a GPS.

These basics are:

- cross-referencing information from the GPS unit to the map and vice versa, especially useful when relocating;
- programming and storing waypoints using co-ordinates taken from a map or your current location, or using the unit's internal mapping;
- navigating to a stored waypoint;
- creating and navigating a *Route* consisting of waypoints linked in succession between a start point and final destination;
- creating a *Track* either to review the journey or to use *Track-Back* to a known location. (*See* ***Waypoints, routes and tracks*** *on page 113*)

5.10.1 Using waypoints

Waypoints are one of the most basic GPS concepts. They are simply the GPS equivalent of an address in the form of co ordinates for a given location.

These pieces of information are stored in the GPS unit for use when required, with a typical device able to store at least 500 waypoints in its database. More advanced models offer the facility to expand this further with the use of additional memory cards. This could be worth consideration if planning a long expedition where using large numbers of waypoints is possible. Most manufacturers supply additional software to allow downloading and storage of waypoints on a PC. There is also a plethora of freeware and shareware available to do the same job.

There are four ways to create and store waypoints:

1 to save the current location, where you are right now;

2 to read the co-ordinates of a location from a paper map and enter these into the unit manually;

3 to use digital mapping software to create a waypoint at a desired location and then upload this to a GPS unit;

4 if using a mapping GPS unit, waypoints can be created from the digital maps shown on the screen.

Every GPS unit will have a slightly different method of creating waypoints using various keys and screens. Most units use the same page for both saving a current position or entering a new location. Being familiar with how a unit marks or

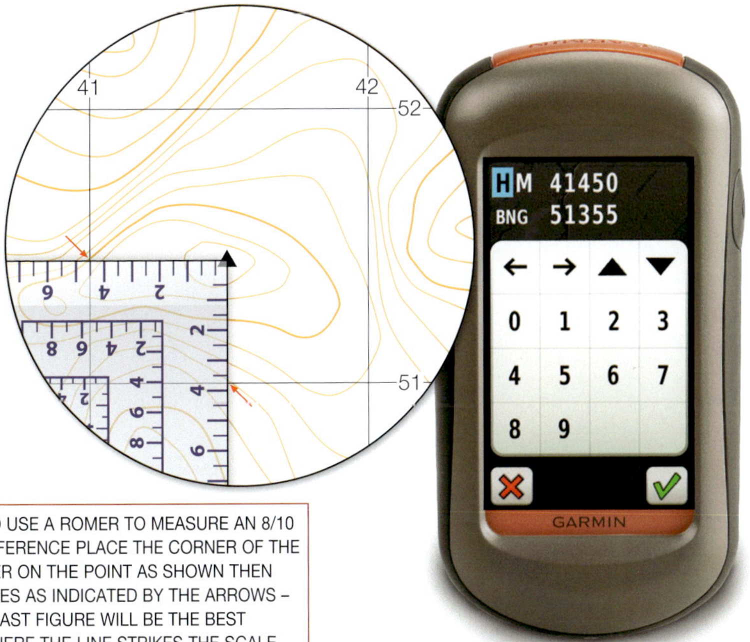

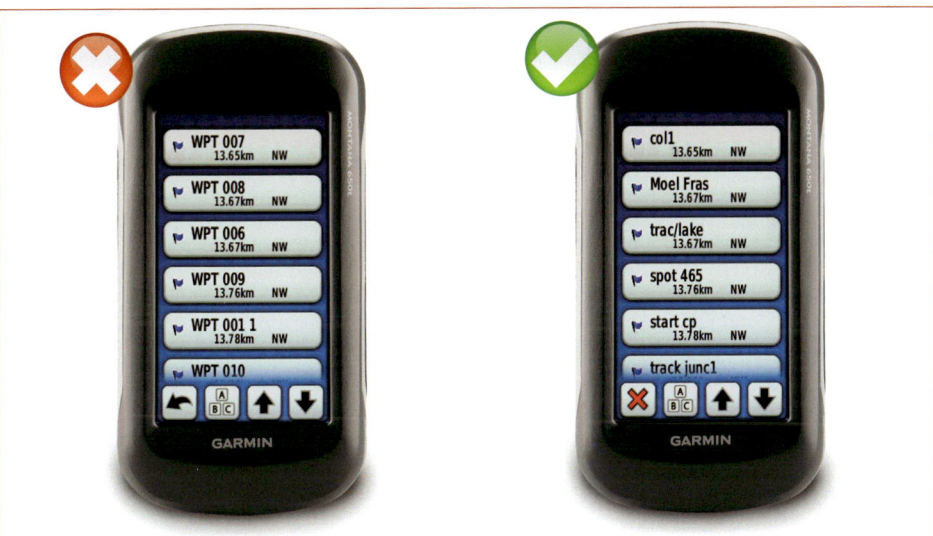

FIGURE 5.15   TO USE A ROMER TO MEASURE AN 8/10 FIGURE GRID REFERENCE PLACE THE CORNER OF THE RELEVANT ROMER ON THE POINT AS SHOWN THEN READ THE FIGURES AS INDICATED BY THE ARROWS – THE FIFTH AND LAST FIGURE WILL BE THE BEST ESTIMATE OF WHERE THE LINE STRIKES THE SCALE. IN THIS EXAMPLE THE GRID REFERENCE IS 41450 51355

FIGURE 5.16   BOTH SCREEN SHOTS SHOW THE SAME WAYPOINTS BUT LABELLED DIFFERENTLY. MORE RECOGNIS-ABLE LABELS MAKE IT EASIER TO IDENTIFY THE REQUIRED WAYPOINT

edits a waypoint will ensure points are saved correctly and retrieved easily when required. Unless marking a present location, creating waypoints can be done anywhere; at home, in a hut or in a tent. In these situations it is not necessary for the GPS unit to be tracking any satellites. This will save having to create waypoints while on route which can be extremely difficult in poor conditions and requires plenty of practice. Planning ahead in this way allows for careful review of the map in order to choose the most appropriate locations to use as waypoints.

FIGURE 5.17 ENTERING WAYPOINTS MANUALLY BEFORE LEAVING

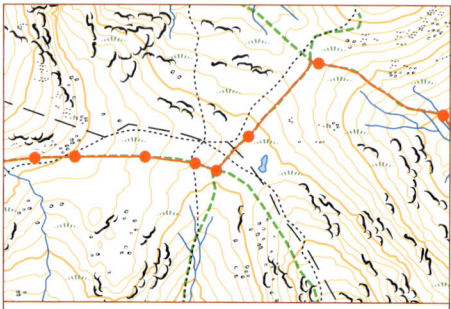
FIGURE 5.18 WAYPOINTS POSITIONED CAREFULLY BEFORE AND AFTER DECISION POINTS ENSURE THE CORRECT DIRECTION IS MAINTAINED

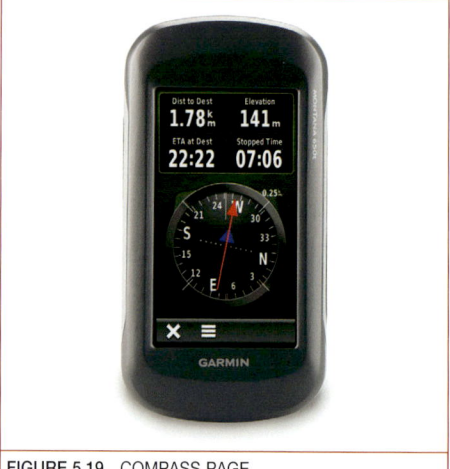
FIGURE 5.19 COMPASS PAGE

When a waypoint is created, the GPS unit will assign it a default name, usually a number 001, 002 and so on. As the database of waypoints increases in size this can make it difficult to find specific waypoints for specific locations. Editing the name of the waypoint to something more recognisable will serve as a reminder of where it was created, and the feature it represents, making retrieval much easier. While this can be done out in the field practically it can be awkward and time consuming, a much quicker option is to use a PC. Changing the co-ordinates will allow waypoints of different locations to be created. It is important to make sure any co-ordinates entered are as accurate as possible to reduce any error in finding the intended location.

5.10.2 Choosing waypoints

Waypoints are essential to GPS navigation and therefore choosing the correct locations requires some careful consideration. The number of way-points and where they are placed will depend on a number of factors, for example the terrain, the weather, the hazards and personal requirements. Use the map to identify appropriate locations to use as waypoints. Review the route carefully, deciding on key navigational features or decision points that may be encountered. Avoid concentrating waypoints within small areas as they can often be difficult to manage and confusing when trying to decide exactly which point is which. As a general principle, avoid placing waypoints closer together than the current level of accuracy (within 15 metres of each other). Make sure they are clearly labelled with an easily identifiable name that corresponds with the location (CAR PARK). Most GPS units will insist that waypoint names are unique so each CAR PARK (and every other waypoint) has to be unique. If hazards are near-by, try to position any waypoints in such a way that even with some error taken into account they are safe places to try and locate.

Some GPS units have the facility to set a *proximity alarm* on certain waypoints warning the operator of a potential hazard at or near that particular location. However, even with these alarms set, it is essential to take note of the terrain at all times and use good judgment as to when to stop. When placing marks at decision points it may require the use of one or more to ensure the correct direction is maintained. Try to place waypoints in these situations so that they lead you onto the next – they help you to decide which path to take.

Once a waypoint has been created, check that it has been stored correctly. Making sure it

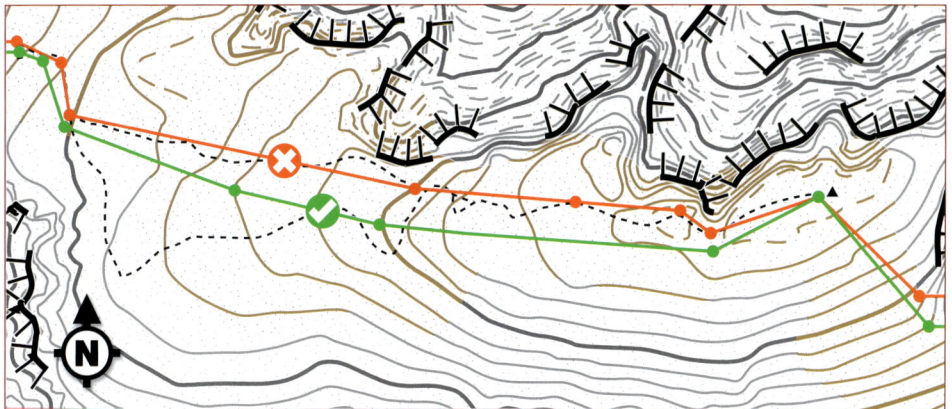

FIGURE 5.20   THE RED ROUTE AND WAYPOINTS FOLLOW THE PATH CLOSELY, HOWEVER THE GREEN ROUTE AND ASSOCIATED WAYPOINTS OFFER A BETTER ALTERNATIVE PARTICULARLY IN POOR WEATHER OR SNOW BY PROVIDING A GREATER DISTANCE BETWEEN THE INTENDED ROUTE AND THE CLIFF HAZARDS TO THE NORTH

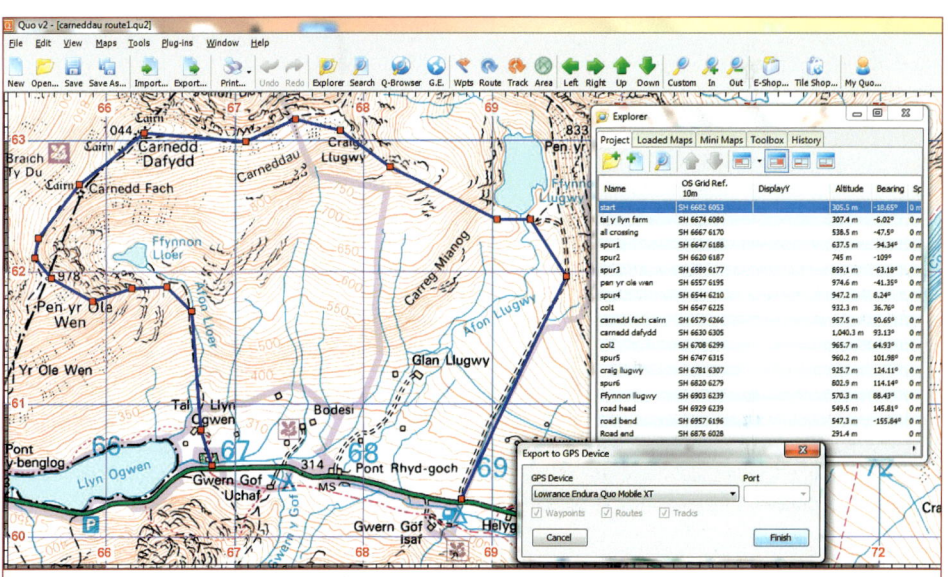

FIGURE 5.21   DIGITAL MAPS CAN BE USED TO CREATE A ROUTE WHICH CAN THEN UPLOADED TO A GPS UNIT

appears in the waypoint menu or on the map page will ensure it has been saved correctly. With a waypoint stored it is possible to travel anywhere and the GPS unit will always show how far away and in what direction that particular point is from its current location. Returning back to that waypoint at any time is a simple matter of setting the GPS unit to navigate to that location.

5.10.3   Navigating to waypoints

All GPS units will have some form of **GOTO** function (sometimes called **Find**). This is one of the most important functions, allowing the operator to choose a waypoint and use the GPS unit to navigate to that particular location. Once a waypoint has been selected and a GOTO activated, the GPS unit will navigate you directly to the chosen destination. It is possible to use a number of different pages to help navigate to the intended location but by far the most useful is the compass page. Remember that the GPS unit makes all its calculations based on a straight line between the current location and the destination, making no allowance for terrain, conditions or hazards. It is therefore important to use the map and the ground ahead to identify the most appropriate and safest route, especially if the terrain is complex.

The advantage of using a GPS device in these situations is there is no need to stick religiously to the straight-line bearing. By choosing the most appropriate route, even if deviating from the original bearing, the GPS unit will be recalculating the distance and direction to the destination every second. In complex terrain it is worth considering the use of intermediate waypoints in order to avoid any hazards or route finding problems en-route to the ultimate destination (*see Figure 5.20*).

The data fields often provide some useful navigational information including estimated time of arrival based on your recent average speed and distance to destination. Because the GPS unit provides so much information it is very easy to ignore the map and compass, particularly when confronted with difficult ground. However, it is at times such as this when it is important to use all three tools. Cross-reference the information from the GPS unit with the map and vice versa on a regular basis. Use the map to look for the safest and most appropriate route to the destination.

Most GPS units will sound an alarm or show a message to indicate arrival at a destination. Audible alarms and flashing messages can often be missed if conditions are poor or you are carrying the unit in a pocket. Therefore it is important when using a GPS unit to navigate to a waypoint to periodically check the information to monitor progress. Once a destination has been reached and you have confirmed the correct position then it is possible to move onto the next point.

5.10.4 Using the route function

A *route* consists of a list of sequentially linked waypoints. Most GPS units will allow for the creation and saving of at least 20 routes although each route may have a maximum number of waypoints available. Those units with expandable memory will have more capacity. Creating a route can be done in two ways, either by using waypoints currently saved within the unit's database or more conveniently by using digital mapping software and uploading the information to a GPS unit when complete. A third method involves using a mapping GPS unit with the relevant map to create a route on the screen that can then be followed or saved for future use.

FIGURE 5.22   PRINTED MAP SHOWING LABELS CAN HELP TO IDENTIFY WAYPOINTS WHEN USING GPS

When using a route, the GPS unit is conducting a series of GOTOs by automatically navigating from one waypoint to the next. Using this method, it automates the navigation process and reduces the time that would be required to navigate to each individual waypoint using the GOTO function. However the point at which the GPS unit switches from one waypoint to the next can vary between units and could be before or after the location of the waypoint. If the route consists of many twists and turns the unit may skip a waypoint in favour of another it feels is closer. This can be more of an issue on circular routes or those that cross back over ground (figure of 8). This can confuse the GPS unit leading to problems. For this reason it is important to consider waypoint placement carefully so as to avoid such issues.

Where routes do criss-cross consider breaking them into several shorter routes rather than having one long one. In situations where it is important to reach a particular waypoint, consider using the GOTO function instead. It is possible to pick up a route from any point even if the GPS unit has been switched off to save power. Navigation from one waypoint to the next while in route mode uses the same pages and techniques used for navigating to individual waypoints. However, it is easy to become ruled by the convenience offered using the route function and ignore the map. Ensure the map is

FIGURE 5.23 MAP PAGE SHOWING A TRACK THROUGH COMPLEX TERRAIN WHERE WAYPOINTS HAVE ALSO BEEN INCLUDED AT TURNS AND HAZARDS

to hand and check at regular intervals to confirm the location. Use the map to identify the best route between one waypoint and the next taking account of any potential hazards. The big advantage of a mapping GPS unit in these situations is that it offers the map to hand on screen. If the route has been created using mapping software it will be possible to print a copy showing the route with the waypoint labels marked on. It is also possible to annotate a standard map with the route and waypoints; this can be used to help keep track of progress and show the next waypoint in the sequence (*see Figure 5.22*).

Placing waypoints to be used in creating a route should also follow the principles outlined previously. When plotting in waypoints to be used, label each point in order, with a number or letter (e.g. wall junction 1, stream 2, gate 3). This makes it easier to remember the sequence of the points when creating the route.

5.10.5 Using track-log function

Most GPS receivers have the capacity to record and store their movements in a *track-log*. As the GPS moves it creates a 'breadcrumb' trail of the path taken known as a *track*. Tracks are made from numerous track points (similar to waypoints) saved at certain intervals. Most units can be set up to record these track points at a set distance, a set time or to automatically decide on the most appropriate method depending on

speed and movement. For walking purposes, where movement and speed is often inconsistent, it is better to set the recording interval to automatic and let the unit deicide on the most appropriate method. Once a track has been created it is possible to navigate back along it using *track-back*. This function allows you to follow the twists and turns of the track back to the start point. It can also be used to navigate the track in either direction. This is useful if saving the track for a future repeat. If the terrain is complex then consider using waypoints at important locations, decision points or where hazards have to be avoided (*see Figure 5.23*).

When using this function the compass page and pointer can be used to show the correct direction. However it is often difficult to determine if any deviation from the track has occurred. Using the map page it is possible to see the recorded track being followed and the new track being laid down over it as your steps are retraced. If the two lines appear as one then the track is being followed however if the lines separate then there may have been a deviation from the original track that can then be corrected.

With digital mapping, it is possible to upload the track-log to a PC and review the journey. If required, the track can be edited and even changed into a route before returning it to the GPS unit or saving for future use.

The track-log should be cleared at the start of every journey if you wish to record your movements during the day for use at a later stage.

5.11 Dealing with problems

There may well be occasions when the GPS might display inaccurate information or cease to function. If its use has been integrated well with map and compass skills, dealing with any problems can be handled in a straightforward manner, by reverting back to using these traditional tools. If time can be spared, there are steps that can be taken to troubleshoot some of these problems.

- Start by cross-referencing any information displayed with the map and the surroundings.
- Make sure the GPS unit has a good 3D fix and is still functioning properly.

Photo: www.pyb.co.uk

Teaching the use of GPS units demands a great deal of knowledge and understanding of the technologies involved. The diverse range of units available can make teaching very difficult, therefore try to ensure students have the same devices when introducing them to GPS for the first time. By using a progressive approach, teaching in small steps, it will allow students to gain practical experience and confidence in using the technology. It is easy to focus attention on the GPS unit during a session and as a result neglect the use of the map and compass. Teaching and exercises should combine tools and help to reinforce how GPS units can be integrated into the navigators 'tool box.'

Any teaching should also provide an understanding of the advantages and disadvantages of this technology. GPS technology can be used in a number of ways to enhance the teaching of many of the basic skills. Combined with digital mapping software it can provide a powerful tool for reviewing performance.

As examples GPS units can be used to:
• Check bearings are being followed correctly.
• Help give an indication of walking speed.
• Check distances (good for helping with pacing).
• Confirm locations.
• Shows routes followed through terrain.

• If you have an electronic compass and you believe the heading shown to be wrong, re-calibrate this feature.
• Check that the batteries are still good. If not, replace them, switch back on, let the unit warm up and get a 3D fix of its position.
• GPS units, like computers, crash from time-to-time. Check that the GPS unit has a good 3D fix, that it still responds to key presses, and the displays update. If any of these are

not the case, switch the unit off, and then wait 5 seconds before turning it back on. If the unit will not switch off, take the batteries out and wait for the display to go completely blank before reinserting them.

If you are unsure of your location and the route ahead it is important to relocate using a map and compass before venturing any further (*refer to* **Section 2.11 Relocation**, *page 59*).

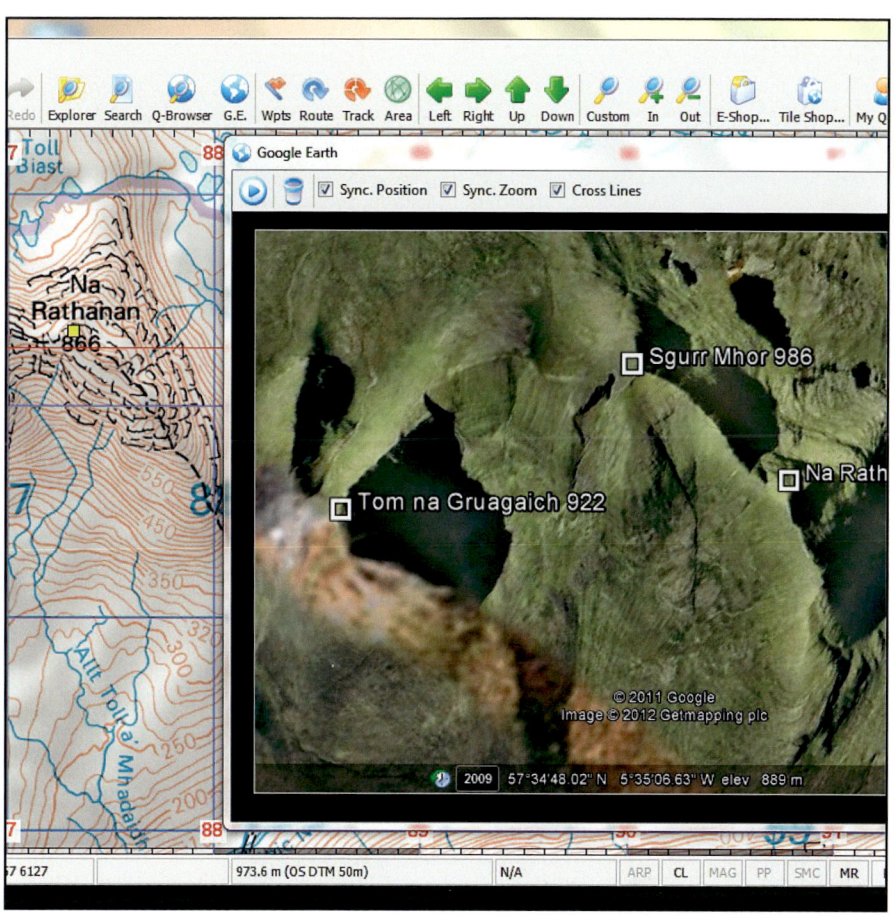

Part **VI**

Digital mapping software

FIGURE 6.01   UPLOADING INFORMATION TO GPS UNIT

Technological advances have lead to the production of sophisticated mapping software that has revolutionised navigation. Digital maps provide the navigator with a wealth of information that can be used at every stage, from planning through to reviewing tracks once the route has been completed. When combined with the use of a GPS receiver they can provide a powerful tool to assist with navigation.

The purpose of any mapping software is to display topographical maps that can then be manipulated in various ways. While there are many products available most perform the following basic functions.

- ***Planning routes***
  Using colour maps on a screen it is possible to overlay information such as waypoints, tracks, areas or routes. This information can then be printed on paper or uploaded to a GPS for use on the journey. Many packages will display the route properties (distance, height gain, journey length and estimated travel time) all of which can be edited to suit. Many products display the routes in 3D allowing you to gain

a greater understanding of the terrain you're hoping to cover. Some packages also interface with online resources such as Google Earth, permitting the display of waypoints and routes on range of other media such as satellite and aerial images. (*See Figures 6.03 and 6.04*)

- ***Printing maps***
  It is normally possible to create and print full colour personalised maps at a scale of your choice. Detail and notes about any route can be added before printing and it is usually possible to print a corresponding route card. Long routes can be printed over several pages with automatic paging. Maps can then be laminated or printed on waterproof paper for use outdoors. (*See Figure 6.08*)

- ***Programming GPS units***
  Mapping software makes the process of creating waypoints, tracks and routes quick and easy and more accurate compared to transferring information from a paper map. Waypoint names can be changed to something more recognisable before sending to the GPS unit allowing them to be easily retrieved from memory when in use. (*See Figure 5.16, page 115*)

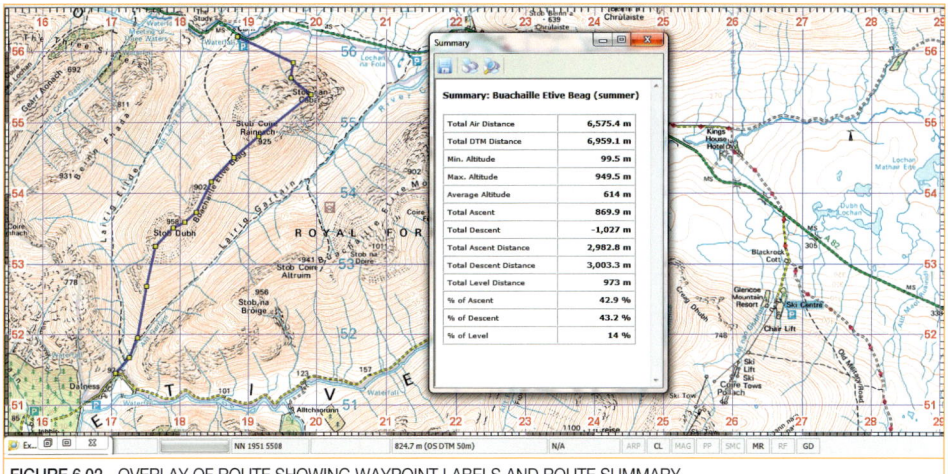

FIGURE 6.02 OVERLAY OF ROUTE SHOWING WAYPOINT LABELS AND ROUTE SUMMARY

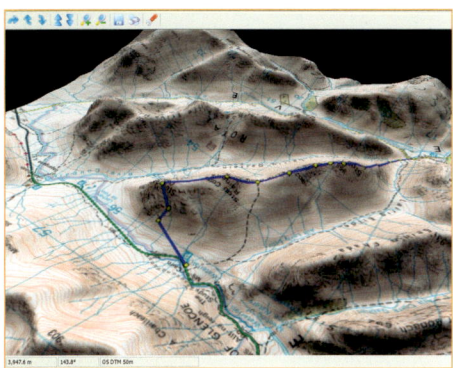

FIGURE 6.03 3D VIEW OF THE TERRAIN AND ROUTE PLANNED IN PREVIOUS FIGURE

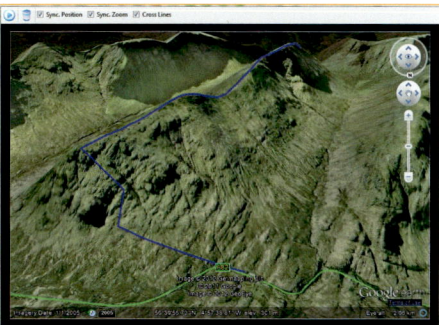

FIGURE 6.04 INTERFACING WITH ONLINE RESOURCES SUCH AS GOOGLE EARTH CAN PROVIDE AN ENHANCED LEVEL OF INFORMATION WHEN PLANNING ROUTES

- *Plotting positions*

  Many systems will connect with a compatible GPS unit and show your position in real time on a moving map display. Taken literally this means you could take your PC with you and watch your movements! However developments in modern technology have lead to the development of GPS tracking devices that transmit their position. Using a receiver back at base it is possible to track the movements of anyone carrying one of these devices on the hill. This technology is becoming particularly useful for search and rescue operations.

- *Performance review*

  Data can also be imported from a GPS unit and used to see exactly where you've been, your speed and distance covered and a range of other statistics.

6.1 Types of products

There are many manufacturers of mapping software but in most cases their products fall into one of three categories.

1 *Standalone software*

  This software is designed for use principally on desktop or laptop personal computers. Specific areas of mapping at a particular scale can be purchased, either on disk or by downloading from the Internet, and stored on a PC. The cost will depend on the size and scale of mapping bought, and within the UK, this is predominantly Ordnance Survey maps under licence. Each manufacturer's software provides slightly different functionality but all deliver similar core functionality in a variety of slightly different ways. All can print maps, plan routes, display tracks and interface with

FIGURE 6.05 ELEVATION PROFILE FOR PLANNED ROUTE

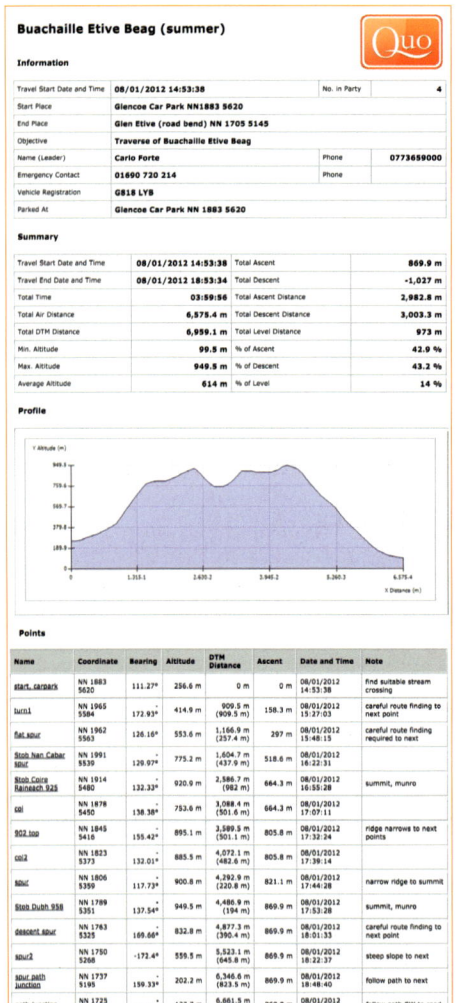

FIGURE 6.06 EXAMPLE OF PRINTED ROUTE CARD GENERATED AUTOMATICALLY FROM A ROUTE PLANNED USING DIGITAL MAPPING SOFTWARE

a variety of GPS units to transfer routes, waypoints and tracks between the PC and the GPS. Most modern GPS units use the standard 'GPS Exchange Format' (GPX), to transfer data between PC and GPS. However some older units do not and may not be compatible with a particular package. In general, digital mapping cannot be transferred from stand-alone software to GPS unit and vice-versa although there are unit available that permit this function, which can provide significant cost savings. The licensing for this type of software usually only permits its use on two devices e.g.: PC and Laptop.

2 Partnered software

Some manufacturers of GPS devices produce their own software designed only to work with specific GPS units. In many respects they appear similar to standalone software, offering a wide range of different mapping with similar or even enhanced functionality. The main difference is that exactly the same mapping bought for the GPS unit can be used with the PC software, and vice versa. It is important to stress that such software is only compatible with specific devices, and may only be licensed for a single device and PC; however, often they offer better integration and functionality compared to standalone software.

3 On-line software

There is an increasing range of on-line software available with maps held on remote computers and accessed via the Internet. Some software is free to use, but will tend to have limited functionality and significant restrictions on the scale, size or detail of mapping. Others are accessed on a subscription basis and, typically, in the UK, these offer Ordnance

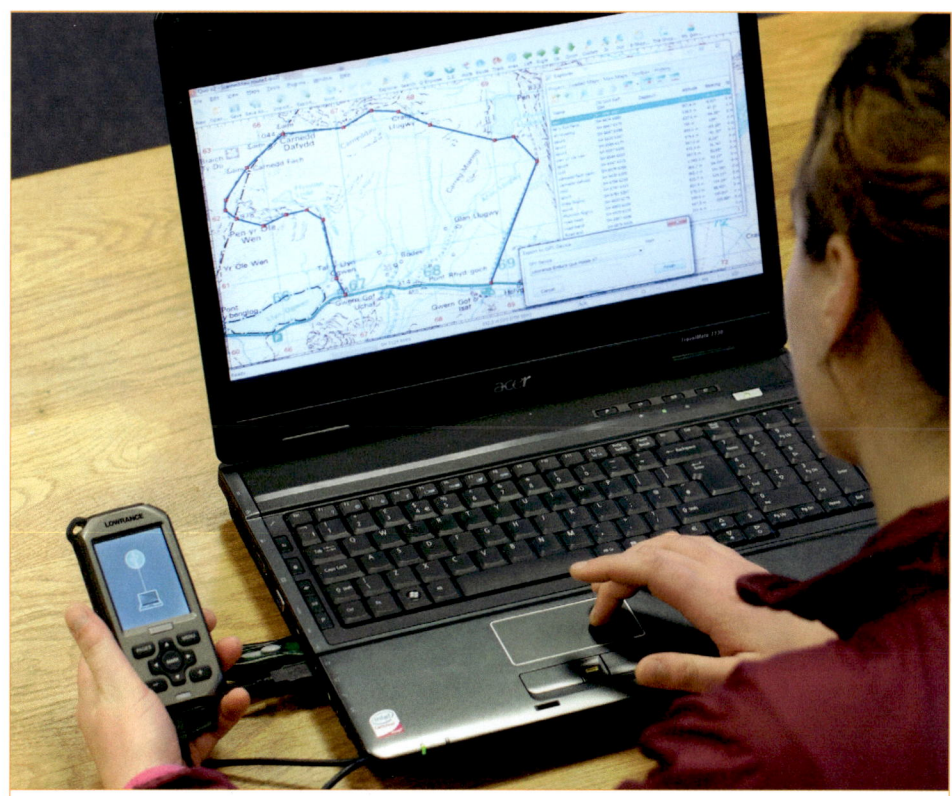

FIGURE 6.07 DOWNLOADING INFORMATION TO A GPS UNIT

Survey mapping of the whole country at 1:25K and 1:50K, as well as road maps and detailed aerial photo mapping. These applications offer reduced functionality compared to standalone software currently, but with the added advantage that a vast selection of mapping is available at a variety of scales without having to purchase or store any of it. For the cost of a subscription you have the maps streamed to your cache where they remain even without an internet connection until the subscription runs out or the cache is overwritten. Mapping cannot usually be uploaded to GPS units, but routes, waypoints and tracks can, although this might be a more involved process. Printing is often limited, but nonetheless possible. Subscriptions are usually very good value compared to other options and, most importantly, you can use on-line software on any computer; however a continuous, reliable, fast internet connection is required for downloading information.

6.2 Using digital mapping software

Most mapping software uses real colour maps, and in the UK, the leading brands all use Ordnance Survey and Harvey's mapping under licence.

6.2.1 Planning
The most useful feature is the ability to overlay these maps with information when planning routes. Waypoints and routes can simply be added by the click of a button and tracks can be drawn freehand if required. Most software is capable of producing a route card showing a range of information.

Parameters can often be set as to the walking speed and rate of ascent and descent making any calculations more accurate for the intended route. The information can be shown in the form of a traditional tabular route card but it is often possible to produce a printed map displaying the overlaid route details.

The use of digital mapping can help enhance any classroom-based session. By projecting images onto a large screen many aspects of planning and navigation can be shown. Projecting onto a white board allowing people to draw and high-light areas of the map can create a large 'interactive map'. The 3D mode and 'fly-through' function can provide a great tool for helping to teach contours and contour interpretation. Using these tools for planning and reviewing of routes can also contribute to learning. A GPS can be used during a day of navigation practice to log routes or points visited and the information downloaded into a computer on return. This can be used to evaluate performance helping to confirm the points visited or provide information with regards any mistakes that may have been made.

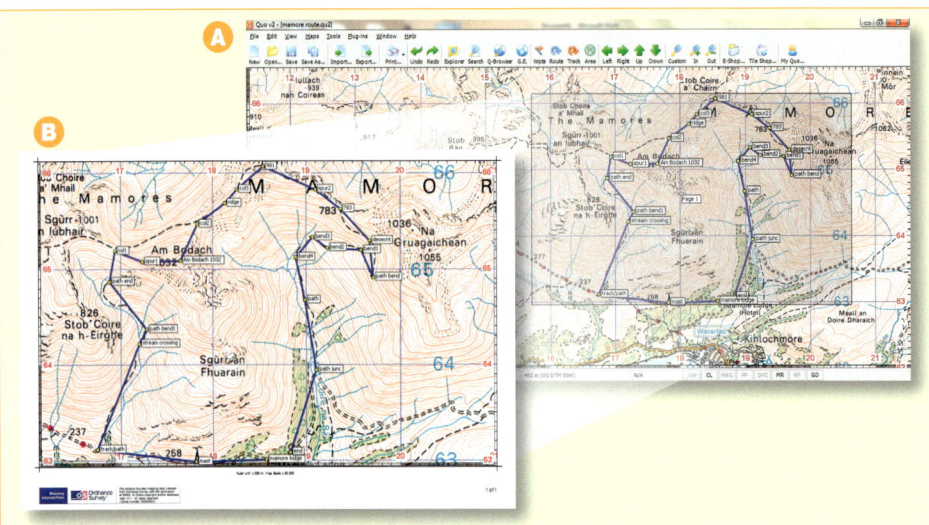

FIGURE 6.08   A ROUTE PRODUCED BY A SOFTWARE PACKAGE: **A** SCREEN SHOT   **B** PRINTED VERSION SHOWING OVERLAID INFORMATION

Many packages offer extra facilities that allow for a more in depth appreciation of terrain or routes planned. Hill profiles can be displayed showing the steepness of any ground encountered en route. Using such a function allows you to view the angles of any slopes and highlights the concavities and convexities; this can be particularly useful in the planning of a winter walk when having to consider the snow and avalanche risks. The 3D function on most software shows a topographical view of the route and the surrounding terrain and when combined with an aerial photography image this can provide a very realistic view of the ground. The 'fly-through' function on some products provides an animated view of the terrain allowing for closer inspection of the route.

Printing and copying maps

There are various legalities to consider before copying or printing maps. Photocopying maps is illegal unless it is performed under licence. Printing from software based sources in situations that involve financial gain, requires a commercial licence. However, printing for personal use from these sources is permitted. An enlarged map of a small area can occasionally be useful for training exercises in order to provide a clearer view of the map information. Remember, however, it will be a copy of an existing map and thus subject to copyright issues. Information regarding licences and permissions for UK maps can be obtained from OS and Harvey. Also check the terms and conditions provided with any software package before printing. Many local authorities have a blanket licence for copying OS maps and maps based on OS mapping such as orienteering maps and school grounds maps. If maps have been obtained through a visitor centre or orienteering club then royalties should have been paid by the club. Buying a single map to photocopy is simply illegal and would breech any copyright agreement.

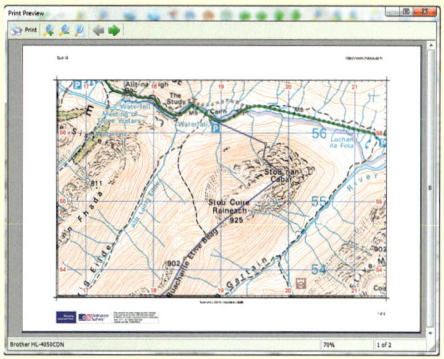

6.2.2 Programming and reviewing

Any information created using the software can be saved and stored for future reference. This information can also be uploaded to a GPS unit and used to assist with navigating the route. Data collected when using a GPS unit can be downloaded providing the opportunity to review the route and save this information for the future. Some software will allow for access to Internet sites making it possible to share route information created by other people and overlay this onto the map. These routes, waypoints or tracks can then be uploaded to a GPS unit or printed as a route card or map for use. In many cases this information can also be shared with others via email and other social media such as Twitter and Facebook. Depending on how this information is stored it can be used by others to upload to their GPS units. Some software also allows for interfacing with Geocaching websites.

6.2.3 Printing

Some products offer the ability to create your own digital maps that can then be used for planning trips. By using a scanned image of a section of map it is possible to use certain mapping software to calibrate and create an overlaid grid. Once this has been achieved it is possible to then use this map to plan routes in the same way. The information can then be printed or uploaded to a GPS unit as before and used for navigation in the field. Google Earth and certain other websites can provide latitude and longitude positions for anywhere in the world. This information can then be used to help calibrate maps or it may be loaded manually into a GPS unit and used on the trip. These tools are particularly useful when planning journeys abroad, especially when travelling to destinations where the mapping is limited.

Advancing technology means the nature of these tools are constantly changing; it therefore becomes important to research the market before purchasing any products to ensure compatibility with your computer, GPS and the areas of ground you wish to use.

Photo: BMC

Part VII

Teaching navigation

Having the ability to navigate is a fundamental requirement of most outdoor activities and of everyday life. Walkers, skiers, climbers and canoeists all need to know some navigation techniques. At some point in their career, leaders of outdoor activities will find themselves teaching navigation skills, whether introducing novices to map reading or training other potential leaders at a more advanced level. Teaching navigation to others can be fun and rewarding, often generating interest and enthusiasm amongst the individuals while providing them with an essential skill to help keep them safe in the hills.

It is also an excellent way to sharpen your own navigation skills. Due to the complex nature of navigation it becomes important to apply considerable thought and planning into training sessions. A structured approach to these sessions will allow people to develop their confidence and skill level in a progressive manner. Breaking techniques down into component parts and constructing a logical framework for how they might be delivered. Progression requires the teacher to have a high degree of personal skill and a good awareness of the processes involved. Above all sessions should be fun and engaging for those involved as this often helps to set the group at ease providing them with a comfortable and interesting learning atmosphere. When planning any navigation training it is worth considering the following points.

7.1 The learning environment

It is said that navigation is fifty per cent skill and experience and fifty per cent confidence, therefore it is important to consider how to build confidence in individuals. Ultimately, people learning to navigate will want to have the ability to operate independently and a key factor in achieving this goal is a supportive learning environment.

Leaders should give attention to the way in which they connect with their groups. Good interpersonal skills contribute greatly towards building an environment in which an individual feels able to engage and connect with the learning. Learning names and individualising any input will help to build positive relationships. Building the confidence to learn is the first step towards ensuring a successful session and is especially important when people are being introduced to skills for the first time.

The terrain and conditions influence how well the aims and objectives can be achieved. Therefore the environment should be appropriate for the age, size and ability of the group and as competence increases the terrain and conditions can be varied to suit. As an example when working with novices it is important to use ground that is safe and non-threatening with plenty of easily identifiable features and handrails. Having obvious features to work with makes teaching the fundamentals easier and ensures people achieve success and belief in their ability to use these skills. Working with people at a more

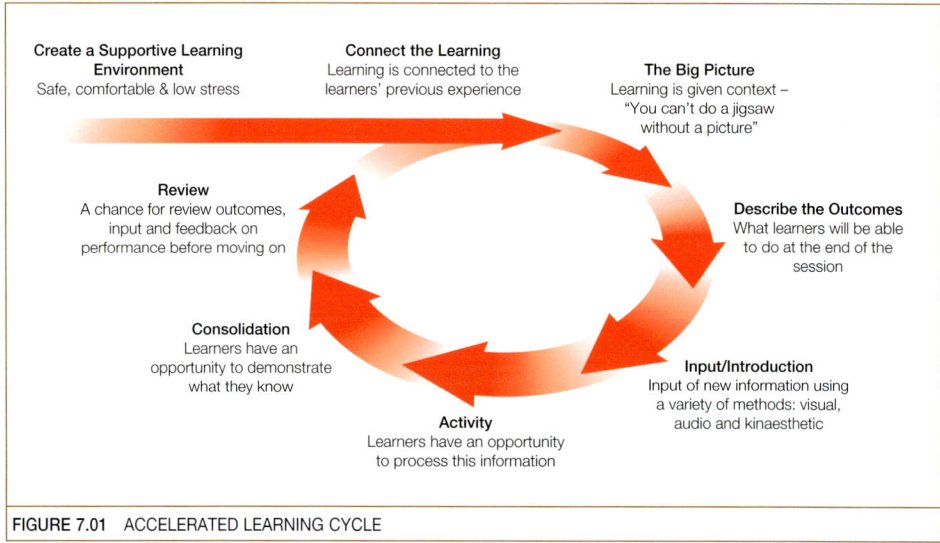

Create a Supportive Learning Environment
Safe, comfortable & low stress

Connect the Learning
Learning is connected to the learners' previous experience

The Big Picture
Learning is given context – "You can't do a jigsaw without a picture"

Review
A chance for review outcomes, input and feedback on performance before moving on

Describe the Outcomes
What learners will be able to do at the end of the session

Consolidation
Learners have an opportunity to demonstrate what they know

Input/Introduction
Input of new information using a variety of methods: visual, audio and kinaesthetic

Activity
Learners have an opportunity to process this information

FIGURE 7.01   ACCELERATED LEARNING CYCLE

advanced level may require the use of more complex terrain and possibly different conditions, such as darkness, winter or both! Safety while teaching is a primary concern and in all cases leaders need to be satisfied they can manage risk carefully while still allowing people the freedom to practise and, in certain situations, experiment. It is important that individuals have the necessary technical skills and experience required for the demands of a new environment. Only once they are ready to operate in more demanding terrain and conditions will they benefit most from the experience. It is always preferable to teach navigation in context so that individuals can see the relevance of the skills being shown, although there are times when this may be difficult to achieve. On a clear sunny day where we can see our route and destination we may have no need to use a compass bearing. However there is good reason for showing and allowing novices to practise these skills under these conditions in order for them to build experience and confidence before they actually require them. In these situations when teaching skills out of context, give people clear guidance on where and when they may be used. Having examples that may relate to their previous experiences can help them connect with the learning and see the relevance of the teaching.

7.2 Personal experience

Having clear aims and objectives at the planning stage means sessions will have a purpose and information can be delivered in the best order. Understanding the experience and needs of both the group and individuals is fundamental to this process. To do this effectively time should be set aside to talk with the individuals to learn about their knowledge and experience. While questions and answers may provide some information, practical activities that test this information will provide an opportunity to gain a better insight into an individual's level of knowledge and ability.

FIGURE 7.03   LEARNING NAVIGATION SKILLS CAN BE A GREAT WAY TO ENAGAGE YOUNG PEOPLE IN THE MOUNTAINS AND PROVIDE THEM WITH SKILLS FOR THE FUTURE   Photo: Karl Midlane

FIGURE 7.02   WHEN CONDITIONS ARE DIFFICULT GATHER THE GROUP AROUND TO SHELTER THE MAP TO ENSURE EVERYONE CAN SEE AND HEAR

15 **Assessing navigation skills**

Many of the exercises highlighted in the teaching inserts throughout this book can be used to assess a person's navigation ability. Setting these exercises will allow the leader to see a person's level of experience in using a particular skill. As an example, choose a simple navigation leg at first and use the map memory exercise highlighted on page 53. Over a series of navigation legs which could increase in difficultly it will be possible to see how much experience group members have of using this particular skill in a variety of situations. These situations will often provide opportunities for leaders to provide further coaching to help develop their group's skills further. The prospect of being assessed can conjure feelings of apprehension and sometimes fear in some people. It is important for leaders to create a relaxed atmosphere in order to allow a person to perform to their best ability. Choosing the right environment and providing support throughout any given task will allow leaders to assess skills and group members to feel comfortable about the process.

Structuring a plan that builds on this and their previous experience will allow them to connect more easily with any new information.

7.3 Communicating with learners

There is much written about the subject of good teaching practice, with a wealth of information available that reaches beyond the capacity of this book. It is in a leader's interest to research these practices to help develop a range of teaching strategies and styles that will meet the many differing needs of individuals. However, there are a number of simple guidelines that leaders can take to help improve their teaching and enhance the person's learning.

7.3.1 Structure and progression

Having chosen the correct environment for everyone and established their prior experience and skill level, the next step to successful development of individuals is progression. Achieving this requires new skills or techniques to be introduced so that they naturally follow on from previous ones and therefore build on existing

knowledge and experience. Being able to break the techniques down into their component parts (building blocks) can help with both planning and teaching, allowing a session to be delivered in a logical order. As a basic example, the progression for learning to use linear features such as tracks or streams as handrails may work as follows:

- introduction of linear feature symbols and terminology; handrails;
- orientating the map using handrails;
- following obvious handrails – tracks, foot paths, rivers or streams;
- following more subtle handrails – ridges, re-entrants or individual contour lines (contouring).

Similar building blocks and progressions can be constructed for all aspects of navigation. However, it is worth remembering that skills and techniques are interconnected, and aspects of one skill cannot easily be taught without introducing aspects from another. In the above example the progression of handrails leads to the use of more complex terrain requiring knowledge of contour lines and contour interpretation. When planning progressions leaders should sequence the input of knowledge carefully so people can make the next step with ease.

With a suitable plan in place the next challenge is delivering this to the group. Adopting a structured approach to the delivery of any information will greatly enhance anyone's ability to learn from this input. Having an understanding of how people receive information can allow for any input to be individualised. People receive information in a variety of ways using a range of senses. Simplistically this is a combination of:

- **V**isual via observation
- **A**uditory via listening
- **K**inaesthetically via physical activity

While we all receive information via these three means we often have a preference for one we respond to best. The **IDEAS** model (*see Figure 7.04*) of delivery works well to ensure that all preferences are catered for.

- **D**emonstration for **V**isual input
- **E**xplanation for **A**udio input
- **A**ctivity for **K**inaesthetic input

Introduction	Introduce the skill highlighting how this builds on previous knowledge and experience. Give an overview of when, where and why it may be used. Keep it clear and brief.
Demonstration	Give a clear demonstration.
Explanation	Give a clear and concise explanation to highlight the key points and some of the finer detail.
Activity	Allow the students to have a go. This could be facilitated with exercises to help practise.
Summary	This should include a review of the activity.

FIGURE 7.04 A SIMPLE MODEL TO FOLLOW WHEN INTRODUCING NEW SKILLS IS **IDEAS**

Keep in mind people tend to teach in a manner that is in line with their preferred learning style, for exmple those who prefer listening to instructions will tend to use a larger amount of verbal input in their delivery.

7.3.2 Verbal input

Some aspects of navigation can be complex to teach, and while creative use of demonstration and activity will help, to be truly effective there will need to be verbal input. The following points should help to make any verbal instruction more productive.

- Plan carefully what you are going to say and how you are going say it as this will often result in much clearer instruction.

- Only give instruction when the individual is ready. Wait until they have finished the previous task or when they have recovered from walking uphill!
- Limit the amount of information. Less is often more!
- Breaking down the instruction of complex skills into component parts will allow for some practical interludes. This allows the information to be digested more easily in bite-sized chunks. (*Figure 2.26, page 44 and 45 show how to take a compass bearing* in four stages.) These stages could be used as building blocks when teaching this particular skill. A practical interlude can be included at the end of each stage before moving onto the next. A final task will be required to show how all the stages fit together.
- Using verbal instruction to conjure visual images is often a good way to help link new skills to prior knowledge and experience and even everyday life. (*See Notes for Instructors on **Contours**, page 34*)
- Questions and on-going dialogue with people can help to reinforce their understanding of the instruction.

7.3.3 Using language

Consider carefully the use of any technical jargon as this can often confuse people; however it is important to be consistent with use of language and terminology when giving explanations. This will make building blocks easier to link together and with careful planning can help when teaching more complex skills. (*See Notes for Instructors on **Slope aspect**, page 50*)

A slightly different way of using language might involve mnemonics, acronyms and phrases. These can be useful learning aids, and when used sparingly are often a good way of highlighting and remembering key pieces of information.

7.3.4 Demonstration

Demonstrations are an important way of communicating practical skills to the learner. A good initial demonstration will provide a blueprint for everyone and will be of particular importance to some learners providing them with a very clear image of how to implement the techniques being shown. There are some steps that can be taken to ensure any demonstrations are well received.

FIGURE 7.05 GROUP UNDER INSTRUCTION IN WINTER USING A HUDDLE TO SHELTER THE MAP
AND WATCH THE DEMONSTRATION

Photo: Keith Ball

- *Make sure everyone can see*
  Choose the environment carefully and make sure all group members can see the demonstration and any related land features. As an example, when showing novices how to set a map it is important they can see the map and also all the land features being used. Facing into the wind, rain or sun can be off putting for people observing and in these situations it is good practice to seek more sheltered areas for demonstrations. As an alternative if the group have their backs to the prevailing conditions they can focus on the instructions while providing the leader with some shelter. This is particularly useful when the weather is poor.

- *Make sure the demonstration
  is clear (visual)*
  Plan demonstrations carefully and even consider a rehearsal beforehand. An unconfident or incorrect demonstration can set the wrong picture for the learner meaning they are likely to be confused or have a negative experience when they try to copy.

- *Consider when you give
  the demonstration*
  Make sure the demonstration illustrates the techniques being taught and that it is delivered at the appropriate stage of the learning.

- *Consider carefully the amount of verbal
  input (auditory)*

Used wisely, verbal input can enhance a demonstration helping to highlight important points that may need to be remembered. However too much verbal input during a demonstration will often confuse the individuals.

- *Ask questions (auditory)*
  Asking questions is a good way to engage the learners and check for understanding.

- *Experiment (kinaesthetic)*
  Where and when appropriate allow students the opportunity to experiment with skills and strategies to develop their understanding.

- *Consider carefully the use of
  a negative demonstration*
  While this can be a powerful tool in the correct situation allowing students to compare good and bad performances may cause them to retain the wrong image. Plan and time the use of these demonstrations carefully.

7.3.5 Activity

There are two main approaches to support the teaching of navigation.

1 Setting navigation legs from one point to another. This relates the learning to a realistic context. To build confidence in your learners it is important that each navigation leg is carefully planned so that it tests the skill being practised and is at an appropriate level of difficulty. When teaching novices it is important to choose points that are actually there and easily visible. In practice this means

FIGURE 7.06 GROUP WORKING IN PAIRS CAN SUPPORT AND LEARN FROM EACH OTHER

that the teacher should be familiar with the map and the area. (*See **Section 7.8.7 Choosing a navigation point** on page 142*)

2 Practical exercises and games. Throughout this book highlighted text boxes have been used to give some examples of practical exercises and games that can be used to practise skills. Any exercise or game should be engaging, non-threatening and can help with motivation. They can also help to facilitate learning and consolidation of skills. Once again a little preparation will help to ensure these exercises are appropriate for the group and that they will work in the chosen environment. Extension exercises can provide further learning opportunities and can also be used effectively to occupy the faster learners within a mixed ability group. As an example, page 48 describes how a star burst exercise can be used to practise walking on a bearing. For those people who master this skill quickly, the extended star burst task could be used as an extension exercise to help improve their skills further.

7.3.6 Practice

Whether using navigation legs, games or exercises, practice is an essential part of the learning process providing the opportunity for the learner to implement techniques, experiment and gain vital experience. However, poor practice will only serve to make a poor performance permanent. The use of any activity when practicing needs to be considered carefully so that it may enhance the learning and increase the

FIGURE 7.07 WORKING SOLO CAN IMPROVE SKILLS AND CONFIDENCE

performance. Different types of practice will produce different results:

- **Blocked practice** is where a particular technique is practised time and time again. As an example, using a compass to take bearings from a map in a classroom can be done numerous times. The advantage of such practice is that it allows the learner to gain lots of experience in a short space of time; however the lack of variety and context may mean they are unable to replicate their performance when confronted with different situations out on the hill.

- **Random practice** is where techniques are practised in a variety of different situations sometimes integrating other skills alongside. To use the example above random practice of this skill would include taking bearings outside on the hill in a variety of situations: rain, wind, snow or darkness.

Both types of practice have their place. Blocked practice will quickly improve performance although this may only be short term, so is particularly useful for novices learning techniques for the first time. Random practice may produce less immediate results, that is it takes people longer to pick up the skills, but in the long term they are more able to retain the knowledge and use it in a more transferable way in wider range of situations.

Refer to *Section 7.8 Improving your navigation through practice* on page 139 for more information on how to structure activity in a progressive manner in order to build confidence and competence.

7.4 Consolidation

When the person has a good understanding of the skills it is important they are allowed to navigate realistic legs that require them to formulate their own strategies. This is fundamental to developing understanding and confidence. Learning from mistakes can be a valuable experience, and will often also provide the opportunity to teach skills such as relocation. When teaching at a more advanced level mistakes can potentially have more serious consequences. As a result intervention from a leader may be required to influence the outcome compared to working in a safer environment where the leader may feel happier to let the mistakes run their course.

7.5 Review

Continually reviewing a person's progress will highlight areas that require further tuition or when it is necessary to move onto the next stage. Reviewing can be a powerful learning tool and people can benefit a great deal from evaluating their own performance. Good use of questions and dialogue on a regular basis, such as after each exercise and at the end of the session, will help them connect to their learning and allow them to create their own action plans for future development. It can also provide a time when the skills and techniques can be linked to the 'bigger picture', that is the real situations in which these may be used.

As a leader it is important to reflect on your own performance and evaluate the success of your session. Critical analysis of your teaching methods will lead to even more effective and imaginative teaching in the future.

7.6 Resources

When introducing skills to a group for the first time teaching is more effective if everyone has the same equipment, for example same scale map and same type of compass. With a more advanced group it is important to check that the equipment they bring is serviceable and appropriate for the session. It is always worth carrying spares to ensure people can continue in the event of a breakage or a loss. The following list has some suggestions for extra resources that can help facilitate a session outdoors none of which take up too much room in a rucksack.

- Overhead projector (OHP) markers or chinagraph pencils for marking laminated maps.
- A laminated blank sheet of paper or card with a grid marked on one side can be used as a portable white board with an OHP marker.
- Paper, pens and pencils for drawing sketch maps.
- Enlarged maps of an area (photocopies or prints), particularly useful for contour work.
- Different scale maps to compare and contrast detail.
- Different types of maps, OS, Harvey or orienteering maps.
- Large magnifying glass.
- Briefing sheets for any tasks or exercises.
- Markers that can be used for any exercises such as glow in the dark tent pegs for marking

FIGURE 7.08   A SELECTION OF TEACHING RESOURCES

16 NOTES FOR INSTRUCTORS **Planning checklist**

- Have the aims and objectives been considered?
- Does the chosen environment match these needs?
- Is the chosen environment safe and non threatening?
- How will the weather affect the environment and session?
- Does the environment allow for teaching to take place in a progressive manner?
- Should the area be visited before the session?
- Does the environment allow for slower progression or extension exercises depending on the group's ability?
- Does the environment allow people to work independently if necessary?
- Does the group have appropriate navigation equipment such as maps, compasses, stopwatches?

- Does the group have appropriate personal equipment?
- Do you have appropriate safety equipment?
- Is there a need for additional resources such as different maps, paper, pens, spares, GPS?

points when conducting compass exercises in the dark (*see Notes for Instructors **Darkness**, page 21 for additional information*).
- GPS for tracking and confirming.

7.7 Classroom teaching

It is always preferable to introduce skills in a realistic environment. However, certain aspects of navigation can be introduced and practised initially in very simple situations. For example, walking on bearing can be introduced and practised in any large open space: a field or playground for instance. Some skills can be introduced or the learning enhanced through classroom sessions.

Teaching indoors requires a great deal of thought and planning if students are to gain maximum benefit. It is important that sessions complement input given outdoors. Teaching navigation outdoors should involve as much

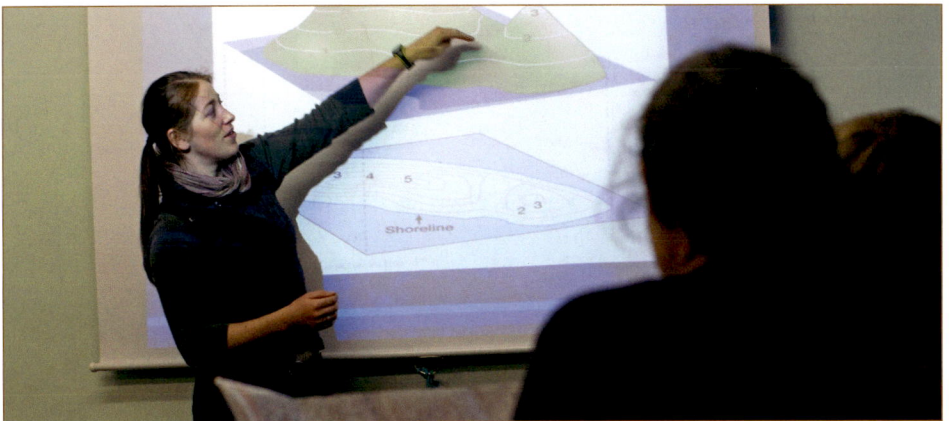

FIGURE 7.09 TEACHING SESSION USING A DIGITAL PRESENTATION

17 **Digital presentations**

All too often digital presentations have too much text, too many slides and an array of different sounds and animations. A good presentation will be short, simple and compliment the teaching:

- Keep the text VERY simple.
- Avoid sentences or slides full of text; use bullet points instead. A picture paints a thousand words – use a photograph or diagram instead of text.
- Use a simple contrasting background; if light use dark text if dark use light text. Use simple text animations.

- The best options include 'Appear', 'Wipe' (from top or left, very fast), Fade (only if very fast). Make sure fonts, text size, colours and animations are consistent throughout the presentation. NEVER just read a slide – YOU are giving the presentation. The purpose of the slides is to help you and the audience follow your presentation not to BE the presentation.
- Avoid using unnecessary sound and elaborate animations as they often detract from the focus of the presentation.

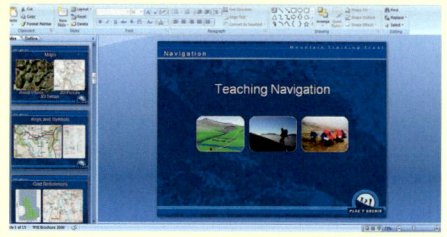

FIGURE 7.10   CLASSROOM SESSION

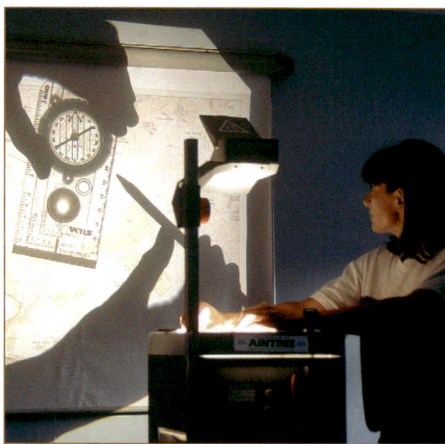

FIGURE 7.11   OVERHEAD PROJECTOR AND COMPASS

activity as is possible to give students the opportunity to develop their skills and confidence. This principle should be reflected in any classrooms sessions, as it can be easy to talk for long periods without any activity. Good use of indoor practical exercises can help to reinforce concepts before they are put into use outside. Exercises that allow students to work together and build on current knowledge will have a positive impact on the learning process allowing them to learn from each other as well as the instructor.

Careful consideration should also be given to the use of any visual aids. The old saying 'a picture paints a thousand words' can be very true, reducing the need for talking and increasing the opportunity for practical activity. When used with careful consideration OHP, slides and digital presentation software such as PowerPoint can greatly enhance any classroom session. However a word of caution, it can be very easy to allow this media to dominate delivery and as a result it becomes the focus of a session rather than a supporting tool. This is particularly true when using PowerPoint. A few good slides used sparingly will often compliment the teaching and could be designed to promote involvement or provoke discussion.

Other digital media such as mapping software can also provide a powerful support tool to indoor sessions. The ability to plan routes, project maps in different ways and fly through terrain using 3-dimensional views can greatly enhance the teaching of certain subjects. In particular, digital mapping can be a useful review tool. When combined with the use of GPS it is possible to see where you have travelled and so allow for a more in depth review of the day.

If this type of technology is to be employed it is important to know how it operates and how to solve any potential problems so that they do not impact on the session. It is always worth having a backup plan just in case the media doesn't behave itself!

7.8 Improving your navigation through practice

For those who aspire to leading others in the hills or visiting the more remote, wilder mountain areas time needs to be spent practising your navigation. There are three obvious ways of practising navigation, you could go on a course, go orienteering and or plan your own navigation training. This section is written with the last group of people in mind, those who are going out on the hill with the main aim of improving their navigation.

7.8.1 Level of difficulty
When practising your own skills or teaching someone else to navigate it is important to get the level of difficulty just right so that you can continue to build confidence and competence. How difficult it is to navigate a given leg will depend on a number of obvious factors as well as some more subtle ones and in addition there are a number of techniques that can be used to help ensure that your navigation legs are planned at an appropriate level *(See Figure 7.12 for more details on level of difficulty)*. Many of these ideas

are drawn from orienteering and for ease of description the orienteering term 'control' will be used to describe the feature you are aiming for. In the diagrams the start of a leg will be shown by a red triangle centred on the feature you are starting at and the 'control' will be shown by a red circle centred on the feature you are aiming for *(see Figure 7.17, page 143 as an example)*.

7.8.2 Choosing the right area and map
Figure 7.13 make some suggestions for the types of area that are suitable for different ability levels but sometimes we have to work with what is easily accessible. Using mapping software or tracing paper it is possible to remove footpaths or water features or produce contour only maps which can alter the level of difficulty of an area. It is also possible to add spurious features to simple maps of non-mountainous areas such as local parks and produce a worth-while navigation exercise where the challenge becomes spotting the extra features on the map!

The type of map you use will also alter the suitability of an area for practising a different set of skills. See *Section 1.3.1 Choosing the right map*, *page 8* and *Map scales*, *page 6* shows four different maps of the same area and just by comparing them it is easy to see that they each have their strengths. The orienteering map would be great for detailed micro navigation, contour appreciation and in particular for night navigation but the mapped area is limited. The Harveys map would be good for introducing contours (contour interval of 15m means that only the larger landforms are mapped and the grey contours mean that steep rocky ground is easy to identify) and for inexper-ienced navigators planning longer walks as the paths are usually mapped accurately and very clear. The latest Harvey mountain maps add a further level of detail by including colour shading which helps the topography 'jump out' at you in 3D. The Ordnance Survey 1:25,000 map is more universally available and is great for developing the 'art' of navigation as well as for micro navigation work. The latest editions of the 1:25,000 are clearer because many of the repre-sentational black markings have been changed to grey allowing the contour detail to be read more clearly. The Ordnance Survey 1:50,000 lends itself best to route planning and timing exercises but is also good for introducing contours because the slopes tend to be much more obvious.

LEVEL	AREA AND MAP	TYPE OF NAVIGATION LEG	CONTEXT	SKILLS AND KNOWLEDGE
1 **EASY** Starting off	• Well defined • Lots of line features • Big contour shapes • Accurate map • Terrain easy to move over	• Short legs (less than 500m) • Distinctive control features • Line features close by (handrails) • Clear tick-off features • Simple distance judgement • Clear catching features	• Day time • Good visibility • Summer • Supportive 'instructor' navigating with you • Calm weather	**Knowledge:** Conventional symbols, National Grid, map scales, parts of a compass, contours and slopes, measuring distance and height differences. **Skills to practise:** Orientating the map using compass and/or terrain, measuring distance on the map and estimating distance in terrain, navigating using handrails; developing ground to map and map to ground awareness by methodically matching features; simple relocation using paths and line features; identifying large contour shapes in the terrain.
2 **MEDIUM** Moving toward independence	• Large area clear escape routes • Complex terrain with line features • Small contour detail • Clear map ~possible inaccuracies • Practise on different scales • Contour only maps	• Medium legs • Attack points • Catching features • Simple route choice • Micro nav/ compass • Reinforcement at feature (a control kite/feedback • Choice of technique • Several decision points	• Day poor visiblity • Night clear visiblity • Summer conditions • Solo with a remote 'coach' • Windy/wet	**Knowledge:** Different types of map, different map scales, grid references, Naismith's Rule, route planning and recoding. **Skills to practise:** Navigating off paths, taking and walking on a bearings, estimating distance travelled using pacing and timing, navigating using larger contour features, attack points and aiming off. Relocating using smaller and smaller features. Identifying smaller contour features such as small hills and reentrants. Navigating at night or in poor visibility during the day.
3 **HARD** Equivalent to navigation required for Mountain Leadership Award	• Remote or challenging terrain • Any map, any scale • Magnetic rocks etc. • Terrain makes it difficult to maintain course • Switch between scales on same day	• Long legs • Complex route choice • Ambiguous start • Small features • Multiple techniques required on same leg • Multiple decision points	• Day poor visiblity • Night good visiblity • Solo • Leading others • Own evaluation • Wild weather	**Knowledge:** The use of GPS and altimeters in navigation, different types of compass, how maps are made, remote supervision of groups. **Skills to practise:** Accurate compass work and distance judgment in poor visibility, navigating fluently using techniques such as simplification and map memory. Using contours as the prime method of navigation, micro-navigation, navigating with distractions, using back bearings and aspect bearings, navigating with the map alone, teaching navigation. Navigation in white outs, dead reckoning, using the group as an aid to navigation.
4 **VERY HARD** Equivalent to navigation required for Mountaineering Instructor Award or Certificate	• Specially produced maps with features missing or added, designed to confuse! • All types of terrain including steep rocky ground and exposed ridges	• All of the above • Good mountain experience and judgement required to choose the best route for the situation	• Night/poor visibility • All weather conditions summer and winter • Leading and coaching others in challenging mountaineering terrain	**Knowledge:** How to structure teaching and coaching sessions, and assess others' ability to navigate. **Skills to practise:** Speed and efficiency of navigation, terrain and map visualisation, navigating under pressure, relocating in extreme conditions, coaching navigation.

FIGURE 7.12   TABLE SHOWING LEVELS FOR NAVIGATION DIFFICULTY

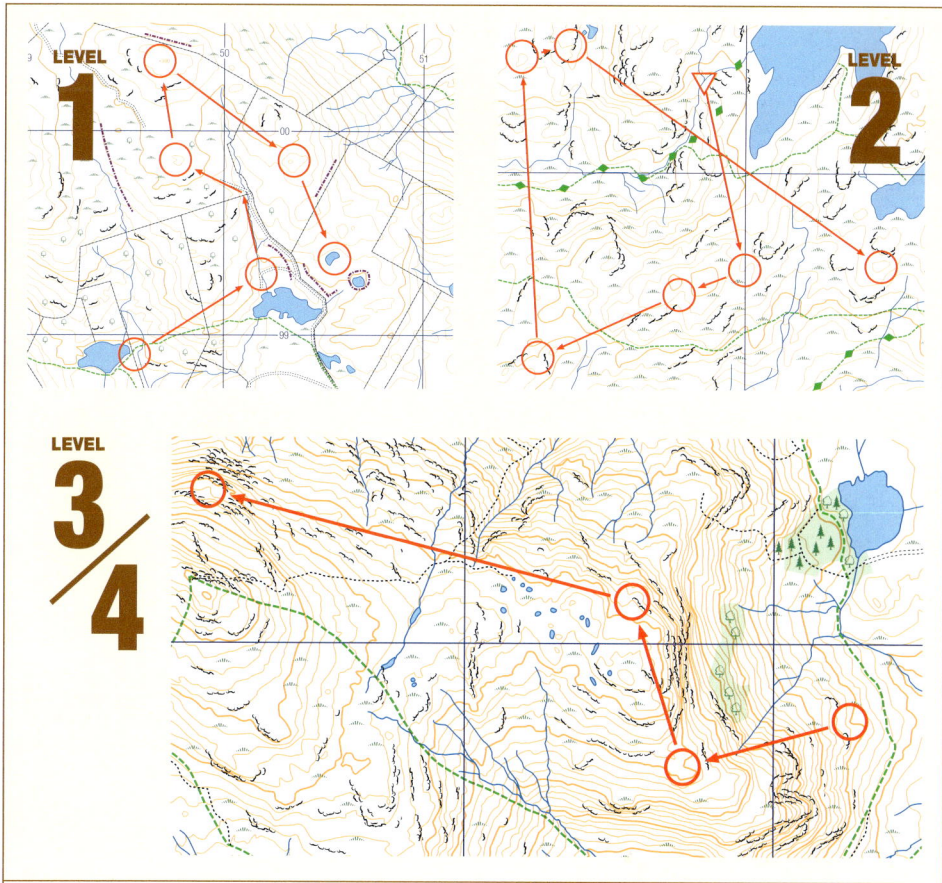

FIGURE 7.13 MAP SAMPLES SHOWING EXAMPLES OF THE TYPE OF NAVIGATION TASKS THAT COULD BE USED AT EACH LEVEL

7.8.3 Deciding which skills to practise

There are no hard and fast rules about what order to introduce the various skills and often the sequence of learning will be determined by the area available for practise. Many skills such as using a compass and route planning can be practised indoors. However most rapid improvements in skill level will occur through application in real situations.

As well as planning to provide a progression from skill to skill it is important to plan a progression within each skill. *Figure 7.14* shows an example of a progression for the use of line features: Level 1 (easy) might use line features such as circled in orange; large features easy to follow intersected by other line features. Level 2 (medium) might use a line feature such as the stream circled in pink as a way of leading you to a different feature, in this case the tarn.

Level 3 (hard) and 4 (very hard) might consider the use of more subtle line features such as following a contour line or a line of crags (as indicated by blue arrows) or even using the straight line joining two control circles as a line feature to follow!

7.8.4 How often to practise

Legs should be planned so that each skill is practised repeatedly. This will not only ensure that the skill has been learnt but will also encourage development of a methodical system for navigation. Embedding good habits early on, such as using ticking off features and finding three close points of proof to confirm a destination, is vital if we are to navigate effectively.

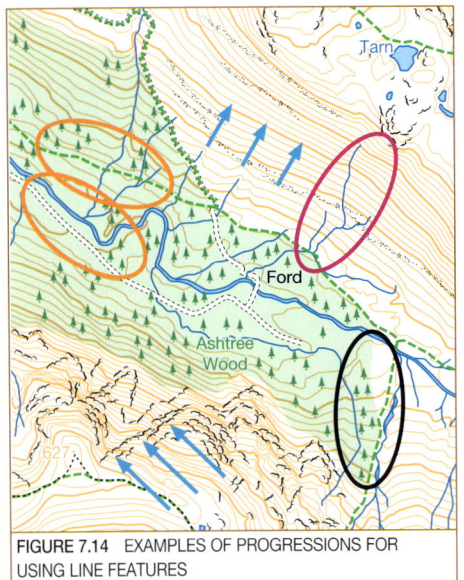

FIGURE 7.14   EXAMPLES OF PROGRESSIONS FOR USING LINE FEATURES

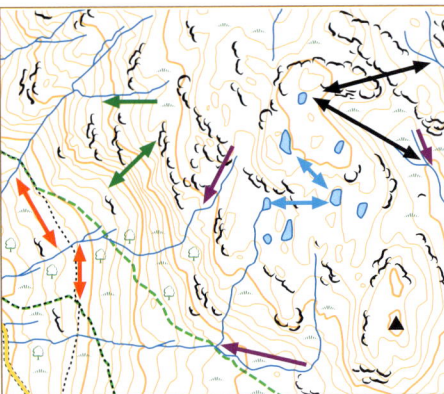

FIGURE 7.15   AN EXAMPLE OF HOW THESE FACTORS OF PROGRESSION, REPETITION AND CONTEXT MIGHT BE COMBINED WHEN PLANNING A SESSION TO DEVELOP SKILLS IN DISTANCE JUDGEMENT USING PACING. **BLUE:** FLAT GROUND, DEFINITE POINT TO DEFINITE POINT.   **RED:** VAGUE START TO DEFINITE FINISH. **PURPLE:** DEFINITE START AND FINISH, COMPLEX UNDULATING TERRAIN.   **GREEN:** UPHILL, DOWNHILL. **BLACK:** CHANGING GRADIENT (REQUIRING PACING ADJUSTMENTS EN ROUTE).

7.8.5 Context

Each navigation skill should be practised in a range of different places and conditions. For example on steep ground; on flat ground; in wild windy conditions and calm days with good visibility, at night, with or without immediate feedback, with or without distractions, alone, leading a group, etc.

Carefully structured practice and feedback will help you develop skills to such a level that it is possible to execute them automatically. This in turn will help build awareness and confidence in your ability to navigate under pressure.

7.8.6 Optimising use of the terrain available

When planning a navigation leg it is important to think about the challenges on the actual navigation leg itself rather than just selecting a particular feature to use as a destination.

Figure 7.16 also shows an example of detailed planning choices; here the planner has identified three possible control sites, all re-entrants and all of a similar size. The route to the purple one is most obvious because there is a line of crags and then a stream to follow to a straightforward attack point very close to the control. This is stress free 'hands in your pocket' navigation! The route to the green control is also fairly straightforward although the navigator will have to do some work to find the correct col to go over. They should be able to tick off the small tarn and once over the col it is just a matter of

following down the valley to stream. The sting in the tail in this leg comes with the decision of when to leave the stream to find the re-entrant. The route to the red control is much more challenging to navigate to fluently. The rounded

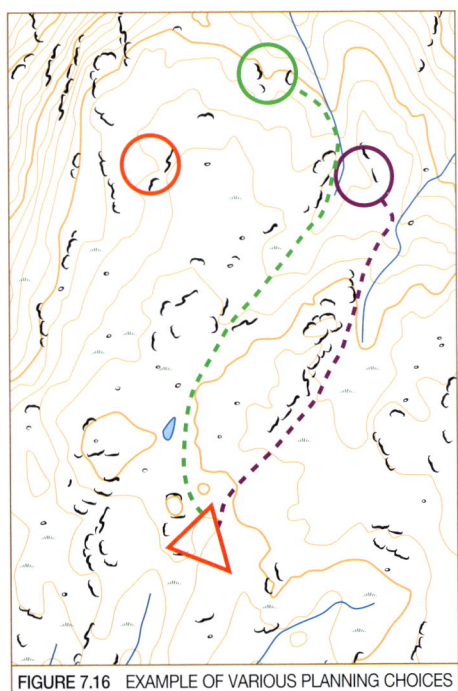

FIGURE 7.16   EXAMPLE OF VARIOUS PLANNING CHOICES

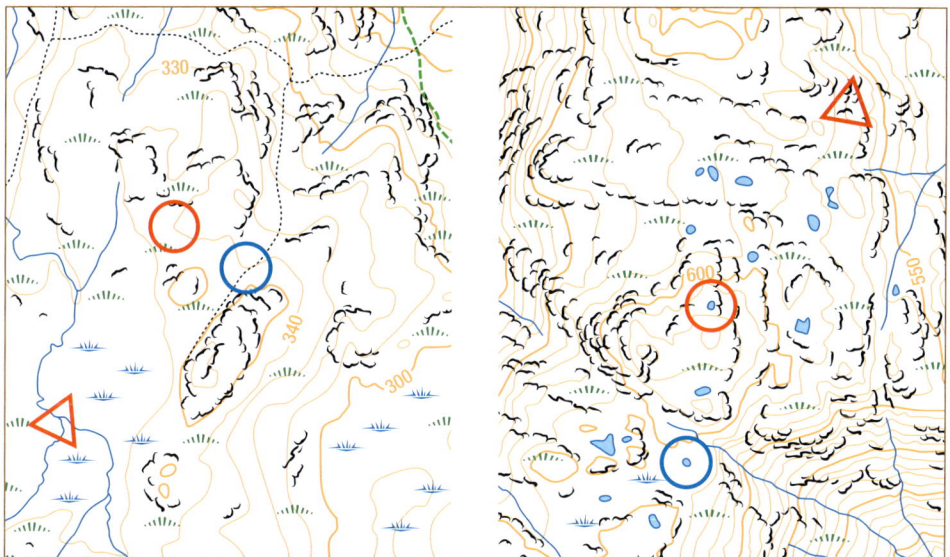

FIGURE 7.17 INDICATES HOW THE POSITIONING OF A CONTROL FEATURE RELATIVE TO LINE FEATURES CAN DRAMATICALLY CHANGE THE DIFFICULTY OF A NAVIGATION LEG (IN BOTH CASES THE RED CONTROL IS HARDER THAN THE BLUE ONE!).

spur and steep slope to the west will help stop you going too far off route but the navigator will have to make several decisions along the leg and use a variety of techniques to find the control efficiently – a good test of navigation skills and confidence, especially in low visibility!

7.8.7 Choosing a navigation point

Ordnance Survey maps of mountain areas are not an accurate picture of what is actually on the ground; the outcrop symbol for example is representational and often small contour features

such as re-entrants are not mapped. Learning to navigate with these inconsistencies is part of the art of navigation but too subtle a skill for the beginner. Night navigation in particular can be intimidating and often involves short legs using compass and pacing. To develop confidence as a novice or while navigating at night, the feature needs to exist on the ground and be easy to identify. When teaching navigation the easiest way to ensure this is to use local knowledge and only visit familiar features that you know are well mapped. An alternative is to visit the area

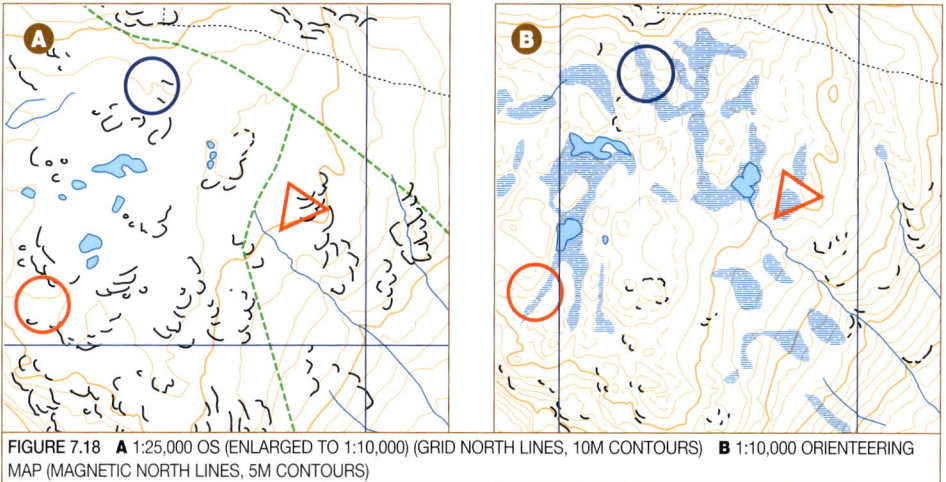

FIGURE 7.18 **A** 1:25,000 OS (ENLARGED TO 1:10,000) (GRID NORTH LINES, 10M CONTOURS) **B** 1:10,000 ORIENTEERING MAP (MAGNETIC NORTH LINES, 5M CONTOURS)

FIGURE 7.19 MARKING A MAP CAREFULLY USING A PERMANENT PEN

FIGURE 7.20 ADDITIONAL MARKING CIRCLES USING COMPASS TEMPLATE

and check features or use a more accurate, reliable, map such as an orienteering map to check their existence on the ground. Orienteering maps may also have inaccuracies but because they are based on specialist photogram metric plotting and have been ground surveyed at a larger scale they will be more accurate than the OS map.

The leg to the 'red' re-entrant is similar on both maps. The distance is within 15m and the direction within a few degrees. The orienteering map suggests more height gain and 'ups and downs' than are shown on the OS map and also shows a cairn on the high point which is not shown on the OS map. Both maps show the small tarns to the NE of the control, which could be useful as an attack point. This leg would be a reasonable leg, at about Level 3, both in the daytime and at night.

In contrast the leg to the 'blue' re entrant would be quite confusing even for an experienced navigator. The re-entrant clearly shown on the OS map is not clear on the orienteering map which means that the control feature will not look like a re-entrant on the ground. The OS map suggests that there is an outcrop and three little tarns about half way to the control but although the orienteering map shows these as a hill and some marshy ground there is no indication of rocks and the most significant feature is a fence running at right angles to the direct route. Legs like this are great as discussion points and certainly keep you on your toes but at night or in misty conditions they can all too quickly destroy your confidence.

The control circle needs to be drawn accurately on the map and centred on the correct feature (*see Figures 7.19 and 7.20*). Many compasses have a small hole for hand drawing accurate circles; however it is more accurate to use a specific circle template. Use a fine tip pen to ensure that any lines do not obscure vital map detail.

Appendices

GOOD NAVIGATION SKILLS CAN ALLOW ANYONE TO ENJOY BEAUTIFUL PLACES SAFELY   Photo: www.pyb.co.uk

A.1 Mountain Training Awards

The awards administered by Mountain Training are valid throughout the United Kingdom and Ireland. All have the same stages and begin with the assumption that candidates are already committed climbers who wish to lead and/or instruct others. With sufficient personal experience candidates can register on the appropriate scheme and receive a logbook in which to record their relevant experience. The next stages would be attendance on a training course, completion of a consolidation period then attendance on an assessment course. For extremely experienced candidates there is the possibility of receiving exemption from the training part of the scheme. All candidates at assessment must hold a valid First Aid Certificate and after gaining the award must continue to log relevant personal and leadership experience.

A1.1 Walking Group Leader (WGL)

This award is for leaders of walking groups in non-mountainous hilly terrain, known variously as upland, moor, hill, fell or down. Navigation skills, group management, environmental responsibilities and the overnight experience are covered during the 30 hours of training and 30 hours assessment courses.

To attend a training course, candidates must have a minimum of one year's hill walking with at least 20 days logged. For assessment a minimum of 40 hill walks is required in at least 3 defined areas of the UK and Ireland.

A1.2 Mountain Leader Award (ML)

This award is for those who wish to lead groups in the mountains and hills of the UK and Ireland under summer conditions. Navigation skills, group management, mountain hazards, environmental responsibilities, expedition skills, river crossing and emergency rope work are covered during the 6 day training and 5 day assessment courses.

To attend a training course, candidates must have a minimum of one year's mountain walking with at least 20 quality mountain days. For assessment a minimum of 40 quality mountain days are required in at least 3 defined mountain areas of the UK and Ireland.

A1.3 Winter Mountain Leader Award [ML(W)]

This scheme trains and assesses people in the skills required for the leadership of hill walking groups in winter conditions. The award is administered by *Mountain Training Scotland (MTS)* and is valid throughout the UK and Ireland.

Prior to registration, candidates must hold the *Mountain Leader (ML)* and have a minimum of 20 quality winter mountain days in at least 3 defined mountain areas of the UK. Snow and avalanche awareness, snow holes, emergency procedures, ice axe and crampon skills, security on steep ground, navigation, winter weather and expedition skills are all covered during the 6 day training and 5 day assessment courses.

A1.4 Mountaineering Instructor Award (MIA)

This scheme trains and assesses people in the skills required for instruction of mountaineering, including all aspects of rock climbing. Prior to registration candidates must hold the Mountain Leader Award. Registration requirements include extensive multi-pitch rock climbing experience at VS 4c or above and substantial group leading experience since passing the ML award. Candidates attend nine days of training and five days of assessment. Personal climbing skills, teaching of leading, improvised rescue, the mountain environment and mountain scrambling are covered at both training and assessment. For further details contact MTUK.

A1.5 Mountaineering Instructor Certificate (MIC)

This scheme trains and assesses people in the skills required for instruction of mountaineering, both summer and winter, including snow, ice and rock climbing. Registration requirements for MIC are MIA and Winter ML, winter climbing experience at Grade III and group leadership experience in winter. Candidates attend 5 days of training and 4 days of assessment. Personal winter climbing skills, teaching of all aspects of winter mountaineering and general mountaineering skills are covered and candidates should hold a current First Aid certificate. For further details contact MTUK.

A1.6 International Mountain Leader

The International Mountain Leader Award (IML) provides comprehensive training and assessment for individuals who aspire to work as leaders in Europe and further afield. It integrates training, experience and assessment in a variety of realistic situations.

It is designed for leading and educating groups worldwide in summer conditions and also on easy snow covered, rolling, Nordic type terrain in the "middle mountains" in winter conditions. The scheme does not involve the techniques and equipment of alpinism or glacial travel. The scheme consists of the following stages: Gain Mountain Leader Award, Log twenty quality international summer mountain days and twenty quality UK or international winter mountain days, Register for IML scheme with MTUK and receive logbook and IML Handbook. Attend IML Summer Training course which includes the IML Speed Navigation Test, successfully complete Summer Assessment, attend IML Winter Training course and completed at least thirty quality winter mountain days in total, of which a minimum of ten should be overseas and finally successfully complete Winter Assessment.

A.2 National Navigation Awards Scheme

About the Scheme

The National Navigation Awards Scheme was instigated in 1994. It is administered by a Board of highly experienced navigators and outdoor industry representatives. Its aim is to encourage people of all ages to enjoy and explore the countryside responsibly through the ability to navigate competently and independently. NNAS has around 300 registered course providers who offer training and assessment courses.

The structure of the Scheme
The scheme offers two award sets. While each set of awards serves a different purpose, there is a small overlap in technical content.

Outdoor Discovery Awards
These awards encourage the exploration of local areas using simple maps such as orienteering maps, street maps and pictorial park maps. They are aimed at all age groups and are beneficial for anyone needing to learn at a slower pace.

The awards are available at three levels with navigation content as follows. Other topics are included in the syllabus.

One Star
Map orientation within a room progressing to a journey around a building with map orientation against the building and simple features.

Two Star
Use large school grounds or small park to orientate the map, follow easy handrails and recognise prominent collecting features.

Three Star
Use a large park with clear footpath networks to orientate the map, follow routes with decision making, recognise prominent collecting features and identify catching features.

Navigator Awards
The Navigator Awards offer the skills needed for exploration of open countryside. There are three levels with a logical progression from one to the next. The skills and techniques are unrelated to altitude. Award holders use their own discretion on where to use their award depending on previous experience.

An outline of the awards is given below. Related topics are included in the syllabus.

Bronze Navigator Award
Map orientation, handrail navigation and recognition of major relief features. The compass is only used for map orientation.

Silver Navigator Award
Navigation by major relief features and recognition of smaller relief features. Compass techniques in relatively small open areas.

Gold Navigator Award
Navigation in complex terrain using any kind of relief including micro navigation. Additional compass techniques are included. Award holders should be able to navigate confidently in any terrain and in any weather conditions.

Course Provider Qualifications

To deliver any of the levels within the NNAS, providers have to meet the following minimum requirements:

Outdoor Discovery Awards – Qualified teacher, youth leader or orienteering coach.

Bronze – SLUK Day Walk Leader or BEL.

Silver/Gold – WGL or ML.

See NNAS website for precise details.

Course providers must register with NNAS and pay an annual fee. An Application Form can be downloaded from their website.

How to get the Awards

NNAS Course Providers and contact details are listed on the NNAS website.

Contacting NNAS

www.nnas.org.uk
Email: **info@nnas.org.uk**

A.3 Orienteering

A3.1 The sport

Orienteering is a competitive sport and Great Britain is successful on the world stage in both male and female events from junior to veteran categories. Like most sports it has a large recreational following where local rivalries replace fierce competition, it is also a great family activity.

Orienteering is currently diversifying and developing other events such as sprint, urban, night and relay orienteering, which are more spectator and media friendly. Trail Orienteering is also available to those with limited mobility or in wheelchairs. Electronic systems provide proof that the competitor has visited a control, the time taken on each leg and the overall results are instantly downloaded and published on the web. There's even a web based tool called RouteGadget where you can mark on the map the route you took and compare it with other competitors. Some of the big events such as the Scottish 6-day event (a festival week of events) attract more than 3000 competitors of all ages from 9 to 90.

There are clubs all over the UK organising regular events on weekends and often mid week training evenings as well. Anyone can enter club level events so long as they pay for the map; it is cheaper to be a member though. British Orienteering has a calendar of events covering all of the UK on its website. There are permanent orienteering courses in forests around the UK, with maps usually purchased at the local tourist office, further information is on the website.

A3.2 How coaching and competition combine

The sport is carefully coached, all the navigation skills and strategies from map setting to relocation skills are divided into five levels of technical difficulty (TD). This provides an excellent system of progressions for teaching navigation to any group of novices whether the aim is orienteering or hill walking.

Orienteering courses use a colour code system to indicate course difficulty which is linked to the 5 TD levels. Courses are laid out to strict guidelines which help the participant make a sensible choice of course to compete on. Colours go from light through to dark as they increase in length and difficulty, similar to ski runs and mountain bike trails.

White	TD 1	1 – 1.9km
Yellow	TD 2	2 – 2.9km
Orange	TD 3	2.5 – 3.5km
Light Green	TD 4	3 – 4km
Green	TD 5	3.5 – 5km
Blue	TD 5	5.5 – 7.5km
Brown	TD 5	8 – 12km
Black*	TD 5	10 – 14km

*rarely provided at local level

At big competitions which course a competitor runs is set by their age and gender.

The course planner must follow strict guidelines to ensure the difficulty and length of each leg on a course is appropriate to the colour and TD level. For example how close the best attack point or catching feature is at Orange is defined as within 50 metres and at Green around 200 metres. Essentially a Green course in Sussex should be a similar challenge to a Green course in the Highlands.

A3.3 Orienteering and Mountain Navigation

Orienteering can provide a useful benchmark to all those participating in the mountain leader schemes. A mountain leader approaching assessment should be able to walk and navigate around TD 5 courses consistently and accurately. The sport provides practice in navigation skills which in turn develops confidence and understanding. Getting lost enables practise of relocation skills in a less threatening environment and as orienteering is a solo event it allows the participant to resolve problems without additional pressure or interference. Navigation on the move also improves efficiency and speed. Understanding the criteria around what makes a leg easy or difficult also provides an insight as to how trainers and assessors might be able to ensure suitable and equitable legs for candidates.

Orienteering is a valuable complement to gaining quality mountain days as well as other outdoor activities where navigation plays a part. It is a very effective way to practise the full range of navigation skills under a little pressure. Confidence plays a big part in navigation and you cannot be confident in something you do not practise.

A3.4 Reference books

Carol McNeill *Orienteering Skills, Techniques, and Training* ISBN 978-1-84797-206-4

Gareth Bryan-Jones *Orienteering Techniques* (available from Scottish Orienteering)

Martin Bagness *Mountain Navigation for Runners* ISBN 0-9521005-0-9

Carol McNeill, Jean Cory-Wright and Tom Renfrew *Teaching Orienteering* ISBN 978-0-88011-804-0

www.britishorienteering.org.uk
www.scottish-orineteering.org
www.catchingfeatures.com

A.4 Access legislation

A.5.1 Current legislation on access

	Recent legislation	Code	Access	Natural Heritage
Scotland	Land Reform (Scotland) Act 2003	Scottish Outdoor Access Code	Scottish Natural Heritage	Scottish Natural Heritage
Northern Ireland	The Access to the Countryside (Northern Ireland) Order 1983	Northern Ireland Country Code	Northern Ireland Countryside Access and Activities Network (CAAN)	Environment and Heritage Service
Wales	Wales Countryside and Rights of Way Act 2000	Country Code	Countryside Council for Wales*	Countryside Council for Wales*
England	Countryside and Rights of Way Act 2000 Marine and Coastal Access Act 2009	Country Code	Natural England	Natural England
Republic of Ireland	Occupiers Liability Act 1995 *This is not a specific act regarding access, but includes access issues*	Mountaineering Council of Ireland 'Good Practice Guide for Walkers and Climbers'	Mountaineering Council of Ireland	The Heritage Council

* In 2013 a Single Environment Body will be formed in Wales combining the work of the *Countryside Council for Wales*, the *Environment Agency* and the *Forestry Commission for Wales*.

You can find out more by visiting the following websites:

Scotland
Scottish Natural Heritage
www.snh.gov.uk

Scottish Outdoor Access Code
www.outdooraccess-scotland.com

Legislation for Scotland
www.scotland-legislation.hmso.gov.uk/
legislation/scotland/acts2003/20030002.htm

England
Natural England
www.naturalengland.org.uk

Legislation for England and Wales
www.legislation.hmso.gov.uk/acts/
acts2000/20000037.htm

Wales
Countryside Council for Wales[4]
www.ccw.gov.uk

Legislation for England and Wales
www.legislation.hmso.gov.uk/acts/
acts2000/20000037.htm

Northern Ireland
Environment Agency
www.ni-environment.gov.uk

Countryside Access and Activities Network
www.countrysiderecreation.com

Republic of Ireland
The Heritage Council
www.heritagecouncil.ie

Legislation for the Republic of Ireland
www.oireachtas.ie/parliament

UK
Dept of Environment, Food and Rural Affairs
www.defra.gov.uk/wildlife-countryside

Joint Nature Conservation Committee
www.jncc.gov.uk

Her Majesty's Stationery Office
www.opsi.gov.uk

---

4   In 2013 there will be a new 'Single Environment Body' in Wales, which will combine CCW, Forestry Commission and Environment Agency

A.5 Bibliography

Books

BMC (2010) *Safety on the Mountains*

Cliff P. (1993) *Mountain Navigation*

Fyffe A and Cunningham A. (2007) *Winter Skills* MLTUK

Gooley T. (2010) *The Natural Navigator* Virgin books

Langmuir E. (1995) *Mountaincraft and Leadership* MLTE/Sport Scotland

Letham L and Letham A. (2003) *GPS Made Easy* Cordee

Long S. (2003) *Hill Walking* MLTUK

Mee P and B. (2010) *Outdoor Navigation handbook for tutors* Harvey

Tippett J. (2009) *Navigation for Walkers* Cordee

Websites

Maps
 Harvey Maps
 www.harveymaps.co.uk
 Ordnance Survey
 www.ordnancesurvey.co.uk
 Cordee
 www.cordee.co.uk
 Standfords Ltd
 www.stanfords.co.uk

Digital Mapping
 MAPYX Quo
 www.mapyx.com

Organisations
 National Navigation Award Scheme
 www.nnas.org.uk
 British Orienteering
 www.britishorienteering.org.uk
 Royal Institute of Navigation
 www.rin.org.uk

A.6 Useful contacts

A6.1 Weather sites

www.met-office.gov.uk
www.mwis.org.uk
www.bbc.co.uk/weather
www.wetterzentrale.de

A6.2 Rescue

**Mountain Rescue Committee
of England and Wales**
www.mountain.rescue.org.uk

Irish Mountain Rescue Association
www.imra.ie.eu.org

Mountain Rescue Committee of Scotland
www.mrc-scotland.org.uk

**National Search and Rescue Dogs
Association**
www.nsarda.org.uk

A6.3 Mountain Training

Mountain Training England
MTE, Siabod Cottage, Capel Curig,
Conwy LL24 0ET
Tel: 01690 – 720 314
Fax: 01690 – 720 248
www.mountain-training.org/england

Mountain Training Northern Ireland
MTNI, Tollymore MC, Bryansford,
Newcastle, Co Down BT33 0PT
Tel: 02843 – 722 158
Fax: 02843 – 726 155
www.mountain-training.org/northern-ireland

Mountain Training Scotland
MTS, Glenmore, Aviemore,
Inverness-shire PH22 1QU
Tel: 01479 – 861 248
Fax: 01479 – 861 249
www.mountain-training.org/scotland

**Mountain Training Cymru
Hyfforddi Arweinwyr Mynydd Cymru**
MTC, Siabod Cottage, Capel Curig,
Conwy LL24 0ET
Tel: 01690 – 720 361
Fax: 01690 – 720 248
www.mountain-training.org/cymru

Mountain Training UK
MTUK, Siabod Cottage, Capel Curig,
Conwy LL24 0ET
Tel: 01690 – 720 272
Fax: 01690 – 720 248
www.mountain-training.org/uk

A6.4 Mountaineering councils

Association of British Climbing Walls
www.abcclimbingwalls.co.uk

British Mountaineering Council
BMC, 177–179 Burton Road,
Manchester M20 2BB
Tel: 0870 – 010 4878
Fax: 0161 – 445 4500
E-mail: **office@thebmc.co.uk**
www.thebmc.co.uk

Mountaineering Ireland
Sport HQ, 13 Joyce Way, Park West Business
Park, Dublin 12, Ireland
Tel: 00 3531 – 625 1115
Fax: 00 3531 – 625 1116
E-mail: **info@mountaineering.ie**
www.mountaineering.ie

Mountaineering Council of Scotland
MC of S, The Old Granary, West Mill Street,
Perth PH1 5QP
Tel: 01738 – 638 227
Fax: 01738 – 442 095
E-mail: **info@mcofs.org.uk**
www.mcofs.org.uk

A.6 Index

W

Notes

Notes

Notes

Notes